**WITHDRAWN**
UTSA LIBRARIES

# NIGERIA
A CRITIQUE OF BRITISH
COLONIAL ADMINISTRATION

WALTER R. CROCKER

# NIGERIA

A CRITIQUE
OF
BRITISH
COLONIAL ADMINISTRATION

 BOOKS FOR LIBRARIES PRESS
FREEPORT, NEW YORK

First Published 1936
Reprinted 1971

INTERNATIONAL STANDARD BOOK NUMBER:
0-8369-5832-2

LIBRARY OF CONGRESS CATALOG CARD NUMBER:
76-160964

PRINTED IN THE UNITED STATES OF AMERICA

# PREFACE

THE question of colonial revision, be it a political pretext or be it based on genuine economic needs, is rapidly becoming of firstrate importance in international affairs so that it is probable that England will soon have to justify her possession of so great a portion of the colonial world when other countries as highly organized and with as big a population have no colonies. Foreign scrutiny and criticism of the Empire must therefore be expected; it behoves us to leave no loophole for their shafts. There will be little difficulty in meeting the economic arguments about raw materials and outlets for population, and little difficulty in accounting for our trusteeship of the natives. But this is not to say that there are no defects in our Colonial Administration. There are defects, and some of them are grave. The purpose of this book is to show what they are and how they may be remedied.

When serving in the Administrative Service of Nigeria the author kept a journal, from which extracts covering the full circle of the twelve months between June 1933 and June 1934 have been published herein. These touch on the sights and sounds of Africa and on the ways of the African, but their selection has been made primarily with the end of showing the Administrative Service in action day by day and how the English official spends his life.

In the second half of the book a tract is offered on Colonial Administration, which points the moral of the journal. The first part of the tract attempts to define the defects of our Administration in one Colony and to outline a reconstruction which, in the author's opinion, would eliminate or mitigate them; in the second part he traverses the administration of the Colonial Empire as a whole; and in the third part he ends with a general discussion of the vital question of public administration.

For though the present book is concerned with Colonial Administration and more particularly with the administration of one Colony, the great issue of public administration in the modern State—the dual issue of the efficiency of modern bureaucracies and of the growing inability of the modern State to control them—forces itself to the front again and again. In the author's judgment it is an issue of quite fundamental importance to an understanding of the malaise of society to-day, and, to cite an example, the economic rehabilitation of England is subordinate to a re-ordering of the governance of England.

In fairness to Nigeria it should be emphasized that the criticisms made of its administration could be made, *mutatis mutandis*, of other Colonies. Nigeria is singled out because it happened to supply the author with first-hand information. Nor is the whole of Nigeria in this book. Much more could be said of cheerful and decent and disinterested colleagues, and much more of the attractiveness of the African, and much more of the lighter side and the pleasures of life out there; but the book is intentionally provocative and singles out those defects and those qualities which the author believes to be the root of the trouble.

It is probable that some readers will object that to attack careerism as an evil, as the author has done, is to tilt at windmills and to fly in the face of human nature. The history of man's progress (in so far as he has made any progress) is a history of flying in the face of human nature; and the point about careerism is that while it may possibly be true that it can never be entirely eliminated, modern society cannot afford a system which encourages blatant careerism and hands over the control of her complicated institutions to men who do not necessarily have either disinterestedness or intelligence, but merely the requisite cunning for somehow getting to the top.

The author believes that no such book as this has been published before. It could only be written by someone with experience inside the Service. He therefore feels that although from a junior official the facts and the point of view put forward may be of interest to students of Colonial Administration no less than to those (especially members of Chatham House and the *Round Table* group) concerned with the fulfilment of England's colonial obligations.

For fear of associating them with any of the responsibility of what is perhaps an unorthodox book the author hesitates to acknowledge by name the friends both in and outside the Service who have helped him with information and criticism, but he cannot refrain from admitting his debt to Mrs. Patrick Seery and Mr. Kenneth Bell. He is also under obligations to Miss Margery Perham, whose knowledge of and insight into British Colonial Administration are without a rival. Dr. W. P. Morrell, too, read the manuscript and made many helpful comments. The author alone, however, is responsible for the book and it must not be assumed that any of these friends are necessarily in agreement with what has been written. The author regrets that the Colonial Office could not see its way to grant him permission to use circulars that were addressed to him when in the Service. The permission sought would have revealed no official secrets and would have abused no confidences. On the contrary it would have been a public service to illustrate defects in our Colonial Administration by quoting chapter and verse, the more so as documents issued to the Service from a Lieutenant-Governor's secretariat are not always known to the Governor, let alone to the Colonial Office. Here and there in the text the author has quoted the reference to a document which has not been published so that in case anyone with official power wishes to follow the matter up he will be able to do so.

W. R. CROCKER

GENEVA
*January 1936*

CONTENTS

|  | PAGE |
|---|---|
| *Preface* | 5 |
| *Introductory Note on Nigeria* | 11 |

PART ONE
Journal of an
Administrative Officer     13

PART TWO
A Tract on
Colonial Administration

I. ADMINISTRATION IN NIGERIA     193
  1. The *Milieu*     193
  2. The Personnel     199
  3. The African     202
  4. Indirect Rule     213
  5. Missions and Missionaries     223
  6. English Law: Legalism and Lawyers     228
  7. Inferiorities in the Quality of Administration     235
  8. Demoralizing a Service     239
  9. Our Task in Africa: The Essentials     248
  10. Our Failure     250
  11. We Can Do the Job     251
  12. Reconstruction     252

II. ADMINISTRATION OF THE COLONIAL EMPIRE     262

III. THE PROBLEM OF PUBLIC ADMINISTRATION IN THE MODERN STATE     271

# AN INTRODUCTORY NOTE ON NIGERIA

NIGERIA, the most important of our Crown Colonies (excepting, perhaps, Ceylon), is as large as three United Kingdoms and has a population of over twenty millions. For purposes of administration it is divided into twenty-three Provinces—eleven forming the Southern Provinces, under a Chief Commissioner (until recently Lieutenant-Governor) and a Secretariat at Enugu, and twelve forming the Northern Provinces, also under a Chief Commissioner (until recently Lieutenant-Governor) and a Secretariat at Kaduna. Both of these officials and their Secretariats are responsible to the Governor and the Central Secretariat in Lagos. British rule has obtained in the Southern Provinces, though with varying degrees of effectiveness and regularity, for more than half a century. In the North it dates from Lord Lugard's campaigns of 1900–3. Until 1914 the Southern and the Northern Provinces were two separate Crown Colonies: in that year they were amalgamated. The two groups have distinct traditions. Northern Nigeria (excepting the mandated territory) contains more than half the population and more than two-thirds the land.

The Administrative Service now numbers about three hundred and fifty; before the retrenchments of 1931–2 it numbered four hundred and thirty. (There are, of course, a still larger number of technical and various departmental officials—medical, agricultural, educational, forestry, and the like.) Entrance to it is gained not by a competitive examination but by the nomination of the Secretary of State for the Colonies.

On receiving nomination the recruit is, like all Colonial Administrative Service recruits, required to spend a year at Oxford or Cambridge studying subjects relevant to his future work. He is then sent to Nigeria as a Cadet. Three years later he becomes an Assistant District Officer; and eight years after that a District Officer. Thenceforward the peak of his ambition is to attain to a Residency, a promotion depending on merit, not on seniority.

Officials do tours of service lasting eighteen months, on the conclusion of which they have eighteen weeks' leave of absence in England.

The machinery of government, owing to the system of Indirect Rule, is dual. That is to say the functions of government are shared between the Suzerain (generally referred to as Government) and the Native Administrations (or "N.A.s"—the Emirate or tribe or other native group forming a Native Administration). Thus there are Government Police and N.A. Police, a Government Treasury and N.A. Treasuries, Government Courts and N.A. Courts, and so on. Though the functions are shared, ultimate control is not: it belongs to the Suzerain alone. Government revenue (i.e. excluding N.A. revenue) now amounts to about £5 millions a year.

Exports before the Depression amounted to about £16 millions a year, the bulk being in the form of oil or oil nuts or oil seeds or oil kernels. Tin, cocoa, and skins are also important. Gold has become important since the great rise in gold prices.

Natives are spoken of as Christian, Moslems, and Pagans, the last being a comprehensive term covering all who do not come within one or other of the former groups. In general the Pagans are the most primitive.

# Part One

## Journal of an Administrative Officer

June 1933—June 1934

*1933. June 29th*
    Tap-tap at my cabin door. "Your tea is getting cold, sir. All passengers must go into the lounge with their passports." This is the third assault on my slumbers by the steward within the last twenty minutes or so, and once again I ignore him. I know from past experience what the day just dawning is going to be—a long day of damp heat, spurts of hurry, spells of waiting, and reams and reams of red tape, beginning when the boat berths a half-hour hence and ending at 9.30 in the night when the train leaves for the North. And after that two or three or more wearing days in travelling to one's Station.
    Glancing out through the port-hole I see, in the light of the early day, that we have just entered the lagoon, a pleasant sight of smooth water and green trees and bold colours in the sky.
    Half an hour or so later the *Appam* comes to anchor. Instead of joining in the usual rush to the lounge for mail I dress and pack, and that with leisure. Also I have mislaid or left at home my passport, and I judge that the Immigration Officer will be better able to cope unexcitedly with the ensuing problem after he (and I) have breakfasted. So down to breakfast, and then, when the shouting and tumult has almost died, up to the lounge. Much struck with the pasty, anaemic, drawn faces, and with the air of utter exhaustion of the shore visitors to the boat—husbands meeting wives, friends coming over to greet friends, and just the ordinary visitor coming aboard to diversify the monotony of local life. How ill they looked. When one is living amongst them and is in the same plight oneself one does not notice it; but coming from home, and after five months of living amongst healthy people, the contrast forces itself a little violently upon one's consciousness. And this is Lagos, where they have all the amenities and can get continuous supplies of good European food from the boats and where, too, the climate (despite the general belief to the contrary) is much easier than throughout the country as a whole.
    After an agitated period with the Immigration Officer, concluding with my giving an undertaking to produce the passport, I got my mail. Three telegrams. An official telegram instructing me to proceed via Makurdi and the River Benue to Adamawa Province (instead of to Kano whither I had been instructed to proceed before going on leave—a mere difference of about one

thousand miles and, at this time of the year, of two to three weeks' travelling); one from a colleague in Adamawa asking me to bring him a case of apples from the boat; and another from a friend who has been looking after my dog saying that on account of the heavy rains he would be unable to get him to the railway (at Zungeru) in time to meet the train.

Then on to shore. First to the Post Office to send off the usual telegram to my senior officer, the Resident of Adamawa, reporting my arrival. Then to Government House to make the usual call. Then to the Treasury for an advance in preparation for the long canoe trip up the Benue. Then to the Lagos shops for various provisions omitted from the stock brought out with me. Then back to the boat just in time for lunch, which from heat and enervation I could scarcely touch.

After lunch I left the boat, joined the launch, and crossed over with various colleagues (Lagos is on an island) to Apapa, whence the Northern train leaves and where my luggage and provisions were lying waiting at the Customs shed. At length I got my things through the Customs, paying the 15 per cent to 20 per cent duty on the foodstuffs which Europeans are obliged to import. (A supply of carbolic tooth-paste powder was charged for as perfumery!) My total charges were considerable; I saw a colleague pay out over £20. Then there was the getting of my things on to the train. Then the drawing and signing of warrants for the ticket. And, then, the worst being over, tea at the local buffet.

While I was sipping the tea a Post Office messenger came up calling out my name. He handed me an official telegram which cancelled the previous official telegram and informed me that I was posted to Benue Province now and not Adamawa. As I was to have proceeded to Makurdi in any case the change did not involve pulling my things off the train, but it did involve setting about making another set of mental adjustments. . . . And Heaven knows where my servants and camp equipment are after all these changes.

It was now after five and I set off for a walk along the waterfront. Again a pleasant view, especially looking west into the sun setting across the water. Coming back I fell in with a senior officer who is as modest as he is interesting and able. He has remarkable eyes and something of the gait of a scholar (he was a mathematician at Oxford and is now an Arabic scholar of some weight). He is going up to Bornu to take over the Province. We went back to the buffet and had a drink, but soon had to give up attempts at conversation because of the singing and holloaing of a party consisting of a couple of N.C.O.s and a couple of railway foremen who were celebrating their return to Empire building. Cocoa is not yet the popular beverage here. England is behind and West Africa is now our terrain. The holloaing increased and a railwayman (whom I knew personally, a good fellow), with lungs like a lion, kept roaring out a ditty with surprising perseverance. He never slackened throughout dinner. The young wife (an Oxford girl) of a colleague who had come out with us for the first time, and who still kept a healthy English complexion, every now and then threw a puzzled glance at the chanter. The glance will be less puzzled when she leaves for home.

But all things come to an end. It is now after ten and nearly an hour since the train left. Lagos and Apapa are behind and the worst day of the whole eighteen months' tour of service is over.

## June 30th

A quiet day in the train, playing Patience, or just sitting, for most of the time. The train is too bumpy to allow reading. At Minna, where we arrived after ten in the evening, I saw most of the people with whom I spent a part of last tour (I was stationed in Niger Province for a while—Minna is the H.Q. of the Province): the ——s of the Railway, the ——s of the Niger Company, —— of the Police, and also ——, who is acting as Resident during the substantive Resident's absence on leave. This is the first time he has acted as head of a Province and I hear bitter complaints from old colleagues as to his new vice-regal manner. Mrs. B., who was very well when I last saw her six months ago, just after her arrival from home, now looks ill.

## July 1st

Our part of the train separated from the Kano train at Kaduna this morning, eight o'clock. At midday at Kafanchan, on the Plateau, I had to get out and join a "local" *en route* for Makurdi. I did not know that the train would be a "local" and would therefore have no restaurant car attached. As a consequence I have had nothing to eat since breakfast this morning, and can get nothing now until to-morrow morning in Makurdi. Also there is no water in the train although there is a filter, but it is empty. For a part of the way I had a fellow traveller, an Irish doctor in the Medical Service, who got off about half-way down the line. He had a bottle of beer and a bottle of mineral water, which he insisted on my sharing, but no food. Further, the coach is pre-war and neither the light nor the fan will work, so that after sunset I have had some hours to spend in the dark, uninterrupted in my broodings on the quality of the staff-work.

It is now nearly midnight. The train is due at Makurdi at midnight. Where my kit and servants will be I do not like to imagine. Nor have I any idea as to what Makurdi is like, where the European Station is, and where I proceed after that. Fortunately I have got a new and powerful Hellisen electric battery lamp and so can lighten the darkness a little on arrival, and, for the rest, I hope for the best.

*July 2nd (Sunday)*

The train arrived at Makurdi a little after midnight. O—— of the Provincial Office very decently stayed up in order to meet me in his car, and to take me to the rest-house I was to occupy for the time being, and had even prepared a meal for me. None of my kit was at the rest-house but my D.O. had made up a bed for me. I thus could go to bed though I could not bath nor wash nor eat *chez moi*. Also two of my four boys have turned up, after an odyssey of their own keeping up pace with the changes in posting. It was good to see their cheerful welcoming faces even though much of the cheerfulness is no doubt due to expectations of gifts from England.

About nine this morning a note arrived from J——, my D.O., inviting me to have all my meals with him to-day and to come over for breakfast forthwith. I did so. J—— was in Niger Province while I was there last tour and had been in charge of Abuja Division prior to my going there, but we had never met. He has a good reputation, which the first appearances seem to confirm. He looks remarkably young for his seniority (he came out very young straight from the war), and very good-looking. There was a dinner-party to-night, but as I was feeling tired I excused myself early and went to bed—the first proper rest for four nights.

## July 3rd

The D.O. excused me from office to-day as some of my loads have arrived, but by no means all. During my five months' absence the white ants attacked some of the cases left in the Niger Provincial store so that their bottoms have fallen out in whole or in part. Two boxes arrived with nothing in them, and a fair amount of crockery is missing or broken.

## July 4th

I began work to-day at the Divisional Office. Reading files and recent reports most of the time so as to get an idea of the Division. J—— says I should spend the next few days doing nothing but this.

In the afternoon I walked about the Station. Makurdi is not only the H.Q. of the Division, but also the H.Q. of the Benue Province and therefore the seat of the Residency. It is comparatively new —post-war; in fact, I think, not more than ten years old. There was no Benue Province until a certain official, on his promotion to the Lieutenant-Governorship of the Northern Provinces, set about on what is known in the Service as the "Great Disorganization," when many of the old Provincial boundaries throughout the country were ruled out and new ones were drawn, various old Provinces being suppressed and new ones created. It is said openly in the Service, this officer now having left the country, that no substantial purpose was served by at least some of these expensive and disturbing changes. Anyhow Makurdi as Provincial H.Q. dates from then, and it became H.Q. of the historic Abinsi Division still later.

Since the building of the railway line between Jos (the tin-mining centre on the plateau) and Port Harcourt, it has rail communication, and last year the great bridge over the Benue here was completed. (Hitherto the trains were ferried across the river.)

The Station is laid out admirably, occupying a hill and commanding fine views of the river on two sides. The Government bungalows, of which there are a dozen or more, are well built and placed far enough away from one another and in grounds of a good size. The native town is rather more than a mile away, always a matter of importance not only for hygienic reasons but because the nervous strain felt by most Europeans from native drumming and similar noises (which can and usually do go on all night without ceasing) is thus eliminated—and anything eliminating nervous strain in a *milieu* where all but the small minority become neurasthenic is of quite first-rate importance. Great credit is due to whoever was responsible for the lay-out, which is a surprising departure from what is usual, in Northern Nigeria at least. It is difficult to credit the lack of forethought, of imagination, and of attention to the elementary amenities of life, in the planning of many of the Stations. Had the usual form been followed Makurdi would have been dumped down at the foot of the hill on the water's edge and adjacent to the native town, and the Government houses would have been built in rows close to one another as in a London suburb.

But, as though to prevent any illusions as to its not being in Nigeria, there is no Station garden! River, water, pumps, soil, cheap labour—all these are here, but nothing is done to grow the greens and vegetables so much needed. Thus, too, in Kaduna eighteen months ago I could not get milk, and large numbers of people were using tinned milk when a Government dairy farm would have more than paid for itself. To such a degree do we tend to lose out here one of the deepest instincts of the English race—knowing how to live.

There is a club, generally a very mixed blessing. It has a 9-hole golf links, two tennis courts, and a fine view from the club house.

The Europeans in the Station consist of the Resident, the D.O., two other Administrative Officers, the M.O., a Sanitary Department foreman, the P.W.D. Engineer, the Railway Engineer, the Commissioner of Police, several railway foremen or artisans, and three or four Trading Company men. Most of them are married. There is an unusually large number of women, which, if they are to be here at all, is a good thing; for in numbers is safety, or at least less likelihood of tension.

I notice on the river side of the hill a number of empty cement houses belonging to the Railway. I wonder how many dozens of empty, expensively-built houses belonging to the Railway Department there are in Nigeria.

*July 5th*

The house I have been put into has a verandah on three sides, and to the west commands a magnificent view of the river where it is wide and lies round an island. The sunset across the broad smooth steel-grey water this evening was something to remember. Sunsets during the rains are usually worth watching, and they have been very good here.

The River Benue is half a mile wide at the bridge, which lies over the narrowest width, and is, I should estimate, about a mile wide further up; that is, at this time of the year. Both the width and the depth vary with the rainy and dry seasons. The river is said to rise thirty feet between the two seasons. The bridge, which cost rather less than a million pounds, makes a fine impression.

After an absence from the country one becomes conscious of certain things that escape attention as soon as one makes the usual adaptations. Thus ever since my return I have been struck with the din of a tropical night—bats, frogs, cicadas, mosquitoes, and myriad other insects. All around, too, the night sparkles with fireflies. And one sits sweating profusely in the damp heat. A tornado will blow up within an hour or so. As is usual at this time of year, there has been a tornado every day since my arrival.

*July 7th*

The rest of my loads (except two cases) arrived to-day. As my chairs and tables are among them their arrival will make life brighter. Hitherto I have had one borrowed chair and various packing-cases to sit on.

Spent the afternoon leaving cards on the married households in the Station.

It is now a perfect African moonlit night, unbelievably lovely.

*July 8th*

The Resident, who has been absent on tour of the Province for about a week, returned with his wife yesterday afternoon. The D.O. took me to the Residency at mid-day to make the usual call. The Resident is said to be the youngest of his rank in the N.P.S, and has a good reputation throughout the Service (nearly always a good sign), qualified only by a passion for detail—for crossing t's and dotting i's. He was pleasant and kind, and quite free of the pompousness which characterizes too many of the Residents. Unfortunately he is a sick man and appears to be subsisting at the present on nothing but air, medicinal beverages, and large glasses of a diluted quinine solution. The marvel is that he manages to keep going.

## July 11th

Had dinner with the Railway Engineer to-night. His wife is Russian and has succeeded in making a home that is a model of taste and comfort. She keeps poultry and has a garden, and is a doughty tennis player; she gets the best out of life here.

About ten we watched the moon—a couple of days after the full—rise over the Benue, which was dappled with a honey-coloured light, later turning white. This is the Africa that is worth all the travail and that we shall never forget.

## July 13th

An old acquaintance turned up at the Divisional Office this morning, a Mr. Peter,* an Ibo Mission School graduate, who engaged a good deal of my attention when Political Officer on the Railway Construction between Minna and Kaduna last year. He incarnates the vanity and trickery and litigiousness of so many of the Southern Nigerian literates or semi-literates. He was a contractor on the Construction, i.e. he contracted to dig a cutting or make a bank of such and such dimensions and was thereby the employer of fifty or so native (illiterate) labourers. Either through attempting to falsify his work or to underpay his labourers, he was always in trouble. The Railway Engineer got to the stage of almost foaming at the mention of his name; but it was I upon whom most of the pother fell. On one occasion he engineered a robbery wherein his brother and partner held him up when returning from the pay-train with the monthly wages and decamped!— but unsuccessfully. On another occasion he laid a charge against a native policeman of assaulting his wife, when investigation showed that Mr. Peter and relations and friends had beaten off the policeman when he attempted to deliver a court warrant on Mr. Peter. The incident which I best remember, however, is the petition of forty odd pages, written in Southern Nigerian pidgin English, scarcely legible, on thin paper with the lines close together, and full of the usual irrelevancies and rhetoric. He charged the Alkali of Kuta—i.e. the Moslem judge who presided over the local court— of partiality, etc., etc. Those were the days when the policy of the then Governor towards the Moslem and other Native Courts was not fully understood, but the worst was feared and it was currently believed that in any case of this sort, no matter how trivial, he,

* Not the true name.

the Governor, would intervene to the advantage of the Southern literate. It was thus vital always to settle such matters so as to prevent the petitions from going out of the Province or at least beyond Kaduna. This particular petition was referred to me for report and investigation. The mere deciphering and extracting definite meaning out of it was a labour of two days. Both the D.O. and I, independently of each other, found the charges false. . . .

To-day Mr. Peter presented himself to lay a complaint against the Alkali of Makurdi. He has now left the Railway Construction and is trading here in ground-nuts (he is the sort that will always be trading in something: he will never grow or make anything). A fellow Ibo and he have been in partnership, quarrelled in the usual way, took their case to the Native Court, and the Alkali decided against Mr. Peter. Hence the complaint. I am required in such matters to investigate and record my findings. The whole day has been taken up with it. I called for the Alkali and his books and summoned witnesses and the other party, and finally found that Mr. Peter was up to his old game. The Alkali, a gentle old Moslem, said that he had spent several days over the case.

On hearing my decision Mr. Peter muttered something about getting a lawyer, the final threat of the Wog litigant and a threat that sometimes intimidates D.O.s under the present régime.

*July 16th (Sunday)*

Sunday though it was, I went down and made the weekly inspection of the Divisional Prison this morning—which, on account of so much other work, is here always reserved for Sunday. About fifty prisoners, a happy lot, as African prisoners usually are.

This Division (Abinsi Division) has an area of about ten thousand square miles and a population of nearly half a million, and a D.O. and two A.D.O.s to administer it! The natives along the Benue are Jukons, a riverine people once the rulers of an extensive "Empire," but now numbering less than 30,000 and scattered in small fishing villages. In Makurdi, and along the Railway, are the usual colonies of Southerners, mostly Ibos. But the vast bulk of the population is Munchi (or, as they call themselves, Tiv). Abinsi Division is the Munchi Division *par excellence*, where, in fact, nine-tenths of the tribe live. They are Pagans; their social and political organization is based on families and kindreds, they having achieved no tribal centralization; and their religion is an obscure animism, very difficult to fathom. They are good farmers, strong in physique, short and stocky, and with a character and disposition as pleasant as that of any natives in Nigeria. A very attractive people; there is not an officer who has served amongst them who does not like them.

News has come through that Northern Nigeria is no longer to have a Lieutenant-Governor. Only a Chief Commissioner. Emoluments, however, will remain as before and the C.C. will still be addressed as "His Honour."

*July 17th*

Now that all my loads have arrived and also my servants and that I have got some idea of the Division, the D.O. has sent me out to Abinsi. The Division is marked off into two sub-Divisions or "Touring Areas," each being under the direct supervision of an A.D.O. living on the spot, the headquarters of my "Area" being at Abinsi and the headquarters of the other "Area" at Gboko, about forty miles away. The D.O. himself lives in Makurdi, occasionally touring the Division, but the work of running the Divisional Office these days keeps him pretty well tied to Makurdi.

I came out to Abinsi on a motor-lorry. My house is raised off the ground and consists of two big rooms and one small, with a wide verandah on all four sides (which with the use of screens can be made into four or more rooms). The rooms have glass windows in them, the floors are concrete, and the roof is galvanized iron covered over with thatch; altogether an admirable *ensemble*. The grounds are big and it will be possible to make a good garden. Though built at the foot of a hill (not high) the house has a fair view across the river, where it bends and widens into a fine sheet of water, and beyond which, in the distance, is a range of hills. There is an office of sorts in the grounds about thirty yards from the house. I shall be spending about a quarter of my time here, my headquarters, and the rest will be spent on trek in the bush. There are no other Europeans in the Station. I am very pleased with Abinsi and look forward to the eighteen months during which it is to be my home.

On arrival here this morning I was met by the local chief and his men. He is a Jukon; Abinsi is a Jukon town. He had a villainous face, and as soon as the formalities were over started on a complaint against a neighbouring Jukon chief. I asked him to postpone it until to-morrow, when I shall have more time to go into it. My staff was also waiting for me: it consists of a clerk (but because he is an N.A. clerk his official designation is scribe), his assistant, two cycle Messengers, and a Dogari, all good Munchi lads, and a Messenger, a cheery Hausa. There is also a caretaker who fetches wood and water and looks after the bungalow.

Abinsi used at one time to be an important administrative H.Q., with a posse of European officials; but, as has so often happened in Nigeria, the H.Q. was removed. Now ruined houses and buildings are to be seen in all directions, rapidly crumbling; and the gardens are overgrown with weeds and bush. My bungalow and the native dispensary are all that remain of the past.

There is a herd of Cob here (I have counted over forty) living in and around the Station, tame or nearly tame.

*July 20th*

Instructions have come from the Secretariat that a series of new investigations are to be made throughout the country in order to ascertain what proportion of the tax-payer's income is being absorbed in paying his annual tax now that the depression has reduced so severely the prices of his produce. I am therefore to assess one of the Districts (Mbachor) in my Area. As I have cleared up what was waiting to be done at Abinsi and have got things more or less in order I set off for Mbachor this morning.

The local chief concerned, a Munchi—all are Munchi away from the river—lives in a hamlet about seventeen miles from Abinsi. On account of the tsetse in this country it is impossible to keep horses, so that trekking is done on bicycle where the paths permit it, or on foot where they do not. There is a good road to Wannune, the H.Q. of Mbachor, but on account of its sodden state after the recent heavy rains I had to walk most of the way, and, being out of training for such pre-breakfast spurts, I felt the three and a half hours.

The rest-house here is built on the top of a flat-topped hill, at the bottom of which is the Chief's hamlet (there are no Munchi *towns* or *hamlets* really—only *households*, though generally patriarchal households and therefore containing several related families). It was formerly the house of the Education Officer working among the Munchis. In fact I think one such built the place before the war, when it must have been a very lonely and isolated Station.

Chunk, my dog, who recently arrived, is unwell. In spite of daily treatment with the mixture of tobacco and grease used out here as a prophylactic, a tick has penetrated one of his ears. It is a ceaseless fight to keep an animal healthy out here, and in the long run one loses the fight. These ticks are particularly predatory. There are others further North which drive horses mad by getting under their tails, a place from which the victim cannot dislodge them unaided.

*July 23rd (Sunday)*

Yesterday a party arrived in the hamlet early in the evening, and as a little later I heard good strong Munchi voices singing some well-known hymns I concluded that the party must be one of missionaries. I was right. They are the Rev. and Mrs. Brink and two assistants from the Dutch Reformed Church (of S.A.) Mission. I called on them this morning (they are camping in native huts) and they asked me to have dinner with them. I went, and spent an agreeable evening. Mr. and Mrs. Brink have been here over twenty years. When they first came the country was not opened up, and they were genuine pioneers. Their Mission is still the only Mission working amongst the Munchis (although I believe the R.C. fathers in Makurdi have a few Munchi converts), and whatever one's opinion may be of Mission effort in general, or of many particular manifestations of it, one cannot but admire the disinterestedness and devotion of such people as these. The stories told, and the knowledge of the native gained, by people who have had such long and close association with the Munchis could not fail to be interesting.

*July 24th*

On account of a number of matters requiring attention there I have trekked across to the neighbouring District (Mbatierev) and will leave the local assessment work for a couple of days. The old Chief and his Elders met me on the road and accompanied me to the rest-house. The Chief is unwell, and asked if I could give him some medicine for his eyes, which were clearly in a bad state. He said that he and the Elders were alarmed at the number of recent deaths among the young people and he hinted that witchcraft was the cause. The Munchis believe strongly in divination and witchcraft. For example they do not believe that an unelderly person dies from natural causes: witchcraft must be responsible. Hence when an unelderly person dies they seek out (illegally, of course) a diviner who by arranging stones, or by some other method, discovers that x of y has compassed the death in question. The extraordinary thing is that x of y when informed of the diviner's findings admits the charge. He will even name his confederates and give a detailed account of the whole business, specifying, e.g., how they ate portions of the body and where they buried this or that bone. When the body is actually exhumed it is found to be intact. Murder confessions, no matter how explicit and specific, are thus of little or no value by themselves. It can be assumed that despite the law the old Chief here and his Elders are spending many hours in investigating occultly the deaths of the young.*

Fortunately I have no murder case to deal with here and need not wrestle with the dark and eerie world of Munchi witchcraft yet. But I have to investigate the working of the local Native Court, against which are many complaints.

It is curious, but a fact, that it is not possible to say definitely whether the African population in Nigeria has increased since our taking over the country thirty-three years ago. There has probably been little change, perhaps a tiny increase, in the size of the total population. On the other hand there have been contrary movements in local groups: e.g. the Munchi appears to have increased his numbers fairly perceptibly, while the Gwari has, if anything, declined. In most areas, however, population seems to be nearly stationary with perhaps a very slight upward trend.

## July 25th

The local Native Court consists of the Chief (as President) and four Elders (paid 10s. per month). It appears to be working creakily. There are twenty-one litigants whose cases are still outstanding, some of whom have been waiting for a decision for months, and others who appeal against its decisions. As is usual amongst the

* Cf. leading article in *Manchester Guardian Weekly*, January 25, 1935, on witchcraft and divining cases in N. Rhodesia and Kenya. A striking case was provided in the Emirate of Bida in Nigeria in 1932. How to deal with the African's attitude to witchcraft is a very difficult problem in African Administration, for there is no escaping the fact that millions of Africans believe in it and fear it without qualification.

Munchis all the cases concern women—either the right to possess or dispose of a woman or of the money which has been or should be paid for her. (The money is not our legal currency, but brass rods which, despite their cumbersomeness and though they are not legal tender, are still used.) Broadly speaking women are chattels, the main item in Munchi commerce.

It emerges that the Court is slack and very probably venal. A big handicap is the health of the Chief. He is not only almost blind but deaf as well, so that he hears little of the evidence; and during his frequent absences through ill-health the other members of the Court decline to sit, or if they do anything it is to adjudicate out of court in the old pre-British personal way.

*July 28th*

I returned to Wannune yesterday morning and have spent the last two days in collecting in the field more data for the assessment. I have now finished and will return to Abinsi to-morrow and work out the results there.

One fact has struck me during the work and that is the disparity between the numbers of the sexes in this area. There are more men than women. Now it is a fact of human biology that more male children are born than female, but that Nature more than corrects this initial disparity by maintaining a high death-rate at all ages for the male. For any year of age more males die than females—at age 1 or age 9 or age 19 or age 52 or at any other age. Thus in countries which do not receive large doses of immigration (as, e.g., U.S.A. until recent years) it is normal to have a surplus of women over men. The position in England is about 46 men to 54 women, in Germany 47 men to 53 women, in Norway 48 men to 52 women, and so on. In some countries, e.g. India, where, as is well known, girls in general are neglected while special care is given to boys, the position is reversed (in India the ratio is 51 men to 49 women). Not only is such a factor not at work here (if anything the contrary factor is at work as females are valuable and easily marketable goods, fetching in bride-price, and also contributing as much as males to the common family income before their marriage), but the disparity is still more pronounced. According to the figures I have collected from house to house in Mbachor District there are about 54 men to 46 women. It is not probable that my figures are absolutely accurate, but I believe they are sufficiently accurate to establish that there is here a pronounced reversal of the usual disparity in sex composition. I notice, too, that according to the Census taken in 1931 (*Census of Nigeria*, vol. ii, pp. 95–6) this reversal was found throughout the Tiv tribe as a whole. The explanation offered in Volume I of the Census that the death-rate for the female is very high is a guess based upon no knowledge of death-rates of the Tiv as the rates have never been ascertained.

It is a question of considerable demographic interest. It is also of immediate administrative interest because it is probably a main cause of the extraordinary amount of litigation over women. All but a slight percentage of both criminal and civil cases here arise over women. Given a community where the more powerful (in their case generally the older) men are polygamous and where no attempt is ever made to stabilize life on a basis of celibacy, and where, too, there is a shortage of women to begin with, the competition for women, both licit and illicit, is bound to be intense.

*July 29th*

As it rained all last night and again this morning I had to walk a good part of the seventeen miles between Wannune and Abinsi. When I arrived I found the D.O., on his way to Makurdi from Gboko, waiting for me. He had called in to see how I was getting on. He also took the occasion to meet the local Head of Abinsi and to soothe his savage breast concerning the feud between him and his fellow Jukon chief, Sarkin Ankwe.

One of my boys, Umoru, told me this evening that he never speaks to his mother except to make a formal salutation. According to Hausa conventions it would be shameless for a mother and her eldest or next-to-eldest-son to engage in anything but strictly formal relationships. Likewise between a man and his mother-in-law: if the mother-in-law visits a man's wife (i.e. her daughter) he leaves the compound. So, too, between a man and his son's wife.

Another Hausa (or Moslem?) custom is that no barbering is done on Thursdays.

*August 1st*

Chunk recovers; also from effects of journey. After a week of lorries and trains and delays in getting here from Kontagora he was a little dazed; but he flattered me with the instantaneousness of his recognition. It makes an enormous difference having him about.

*August 3rd*

I have now finished working out the assessment data and sent in the report. My conclusion was that the tax of 4s. per annum paid by each adult male amounts to about 3 per cent of his income. Any such figures are bound to be very approximate (indeed, even the full-dress assessments, involving a couple of months' work for one Officer, are empirical and approximate to a degree, and to this day no satisfactory technique of estimating income has been worked out in Nigeria;* but I am convinced that despite the fall in the price of produce these people are very lightly taxed and suffer no hardship).

The facts brought to light by the assessment are interesting as showing how some Africans are still living to-day. Here the settlements are in scattered hamlets or, more accurately, households, of one family group, consisting of the household head and his wives, his sons and their wives, his own and his sons' children, excepting the adult daughters who would all be married and would be living with their husbands. This is the general rule, although prolonged returns and sojourns in the father's house are common, and, so elastic is their form of marriage, that very often the returning daughter contracts a new alliance and refuses to return to her previous husband: whence arises a court case, the previous husband demanding either the return of his wife or the restitution of the price he paid for her. A common complication arises when the father has already received this money from the new husband and has laid it out on a new wife for himself so that he has nothing with which to pay the ex-husband! Over a period of years the woman may have changed her husband several times and money passed hands in confused and roundabout fashion, leaving a trail

* It is remarkable that so loose a method of making assessment reports—inevitable as it was in the early days—has been retained, and that without criticism. An assessment report is a medley of perfunctory anthropological odds and ends, a local "history," and a haphazard attempt to estimate wealth. Thus in an assessment report of a District in Hadejia, which was regarded so favourably as to be printed and sent home for the use of Colonial Office Probationers, there was no adequate estimate of income, but it included laborious calculations as to the gestatory period of goats, camels, etc., in that District—as though it would vary there from what it is in the several other hundreds of Districts in Nigeria.

of claims and counterclaims so intricate and, through African lying and trickery, so confused, that it is almost beyond the wit of man to establish the facts, let alone give justice.

In general each woman has a separate hut to herself. The economic structure of the society is that of a self-subsistent husbandry. A household supplies practically all its needs. On the other hand it does not consume all that it produces: it grows one important exchange-crop—benniseed—and it grows that in order to come by the money necessary for its tax bill. Practically all the legal tender currency (shillings, pence, halfpence, and tenths) circulating amongst them is derived from selling their benniseed to the traders' canteens on the river, and most of this money is paid out again to the tax collector. Trading in the local markets—and there is little such market trading in comparison with what is done throughout the Moslem parts of the country—is, saving a few cheap trinkets and cloths hawked by Hausa peddlers, a matter of one household exchanging its surplusses (e.g. tomatoes) for those of another (e.g. pawpaws), and with the exception of pennies and tenths legal tender currency is little (if ever) used. The normal exchange media are brass rods. In bigger transactions they often resort to barter. Thus the payments made by bridegrooms to the parents of their brides are normally made in animals, produce, cloths (a wrap about the size of a hand towel), and brass rods.

The chief crops are yams, millet, guinea corn, and benniseed. They also grow a variety of vegetables, cotton, nuts, and such luxuries as tobacco, pepper, ginger. Most of the farm work, but not all, is done by the women. The livestock is dwarf cattle, goats, sheep, pigs, and poultry. In most households one or more native crafts is carried out, such as spinning and weaving, stool-making, basket plaiting, and blacksmithing. There is very little wild game left, owing to wasteful methods of hunting. There is no land shortage—a wide margin between population and economic resources exists.

Given their needs I should say that they are a well-off people to whom poverty is unknown. They are certainly a happy people, far happier than European urban groups. It is a pity that all this is doomed and that soon we shall have taught them or their children new needs and wants, and all the curses that come with them.

*August 5th*

I am not going to spend my tour here after all. Word has arrived that I am to go to Katsina Ala in Wukari Division (in this Province), a fortnight hence. Had I known it before I could have spared many hours put in at reading files and books to make myself acquainted with the details of this Division.

*August 6th (Sunday)*

X——, who is waiting in Makurdi for a river boat to take him up to Yola, motored out with four others towards the end of the afternoon and spent the evening here. The main item of news was the case of the Benue Bridge clerk. Tolls are charged for all vehicles (which naturally are few and mostly officials' cars) and droves of animals (which are not few) that cross the bridge. A Southern clerk (or may be two Southern clerks) is stationed at the Bridge to collect the dues. For some time a steep drop in the earnings was observed for which no reason could be thought of and it was suspected that the clerk was succumbing to the temptation that few of his kind can resist. A watch was set and he was caught red-handed helping himself to the tolls. The case came before the District Officer in the usual way and the clerk was convicted of the offence and sent up to Kaduna prison to serve his sentence. He appealed against the sentence. The Secretariat ordered an enquiry, called for details, and finally quashed the case and ordered not only the release but also the re-instatement of the clerk. Reason, not that the clerk had not stolen the money; the evidence for that was not questioned; but that the charge had been laid under one section or sub-section of the Criminal Code (which is agreed to leave something to be desired in its draughtsmanship) when it should have been laid under another. It also appears that when the Resident was recently up at Kafanchan he mentioned this case and the acting Lieutenant-Governor agreed, or was understood by the Resident to agree, to the clerk's conviction. The acting Lieutenant-Governor now repudiates this. For once, my visitors say, the Resident fought against the Secretariat.

But what a business. Here is a man who is caught stealing Government money; his case is reviewed and the fact that he did steal Government money is not questioned; it is agreed that the evidence showed as much; but because of a mere legal technicality not only is he not punished but he is hoisted over the heads of the men who are responsible for running the Government on the spot, and put back into his old job. It is not surprising that the average Administrative Officer has no enthusiasm for the Law.*

*August 7th*

*Dies Irae!* As I have to go off and trek over another part of my Area I sent off my trekking kit and all my servants, except one, at 4.30 this morning, my intention being to follow on bicycle as soon as the sun rose. But an hour after they left it began to rain. When, about 6.15, I set out the track was a brook and the first waterway to be crossed, a couple of miles from here, was deep in flood. All ways were tried of getting over it but without success. So back we turned. The rain kept coming down and did not cease until two or so in the afternoon. I then made another start, but once again was held up at the first stream. Leaving a man there to watch it and to let me know when the water slackened enough for crossing I returned to the house. Something after 5.30 word at last arrived that the stream could now be crossed. So off once more. At length, between 8.30 and 9.0, I reached the place where I arranged yesterday for my tent to be set up, after walking in pitch darkness (and not unmindful of the possibility of stepping on snakes) and along water-sogged paths for a couple of hours. My first meal for the day was ready at 9.30 p.m.—my cook and utensils having gone on ahead this morning.

*August 10th*

I arrived here (Igbor) this morning, the seat of the District Chief and Native Court and of a school and a dispensary and a market. It is therefore much bigger than the usual villages that grow up around chiefs' houses. There is a rest-house in the village which is significant of a type of mind and imagination that has been too much in the ascendent out here. It is built at the foot of one of the rare hills in the Area and right against the village. Not only does it thus get the noise and smells and other unhygienic effects of the village (and these are of a kind unknown in England), but it misses the chance of getting on to high ground where you can catch what breeze may be going and, still more important, where

* I leave this entry from my Journal as it stands as, though I never confirmed the statements of my guests—all officials—by consulting the relevant files in Makurdi, I have no doubt that the substantial facts were as above. Other similar cases have happened. It is a fair example of the contrast between Law and Justice.

you can get something of a view. When one's life is spent on swampy lowland and where the bush is so thick, the grass so tall, and the country so flat, one has to fight against a sense of stifling, suffocation, and imprisonment. It is remarkable, therefore, that when the rare opportunity of getting out and above the prison walls does present itself it is not taken. The average junior Political Officer spends most of his time living in rest-houses, and did so even more in the past; yet again and again one will find a rest-house built on the edge of swamp or in a hollow when by going a little further off, sometimes a few hundred yards or so, a hill or hillock could be used. I have noticed this in the Provinces of Kano, Bornu, Zaria (South), and the Benue. The only Division to my knowledge where rest-houses have been built with imagination is the Kuta Division of Niger Province, and there they are very good, a monument to some unknown builder of imagination.

The Native Court here also working creakily. The same delay in settling cases. Twenty-nine litigants found to be waiting for decisions, some of whom have been waiting as long as two years. As at Mbachor and at Mbatierev, the President of the Court and his four assessors seemed nonplussed when confronted with a man who refused to pay what was found against him or to carry out a decision. These Courts are foreign introductions and not indigenous to the Tiv, and although in many cases they do accomplish much valuable work and in general are getting better they still need much help and supervision. There is not enough touring by Political Officers (partly due to the ever-mounting rise of office work and partly due to the political staff being too small for what it has to do to-day), and the Courts are not provided with the physical force necessary for insisting on the carrying out of their decisions. More Dogarai\* are needed.

Among the complaints I had to deal with were those of two girls, one of whom had been seized and the other voluntarily surrendered as a debtor's pawn. The girl who had been seized had been seized by one of the four Native Court members! This of course is a statutory crime. Yet despite the Criminal Ordinance, and an Official Report to the effect that it has stopped, the seizing of persons or accepting of persons, always girls in my experience, as a pawn for debt is not yet stamped out. A friend of mine found

\* Dogari is a policeman of the Native Administration as distinct from Government Police.

numerous cases in the Emirate of Bida last year, and when acting as Political Officer attached to the Minna-Kaduna Railway Construction I found and released several dozen Yoruba girls who were working as common labourers at the command of (and turning over their earnings to) the men who held them as pawns. Given the attitude to debt and to women that prevails throughout most of Nigeria it is bound to be a slow business to stop the practice.

*August 12th*

On my way back to Abinsi I am staying a day in the household of Gnor, one of the four Native Court members. It is an arcadian sort of household: thirty or so huts hidden away from the world in a pleasant peaceful valley, which provides them with all the abundance that their needs can require. Gnor himself, in early middle age, is a handsome, intelligent-looking, and attractive Munchi. And no conservative: he wants to get a bicycle, as bold a step as a European buying a private aeroplane. He says that he has had an excellent benniseed crop this year and notwithstanding the new "low" in prices he will have more cash from it than the tax bill of his household will amount to.

The insects, always numerous and to the fore in this part of Nigeria and at this time of the year, have been prodigiously active. That there were flies, fleas, and mosquitoes goes without saying; but I also noticed some tsetse, and in the late afternoon was so harassed by a small black fly that I had to go inside the tent. I would have soon been driven in in any case as the immediate neighbourhood appeared to be the rendezvous of swarms of biting ants—but as they also came inside the tent I had a hurried meal and went to bed, sheltering myself from them under the mosquito net, the *sine qua non* of life in Nigeria.

*August 16th*

X——, a Wadham man, who is to take over the Area from me and who has just returned from leave in England, arrived to-day. He has served here before and in addition is one of the few Political Officers who can speak Munchi, so there will be no need to help him find his way about; rather he can help me.

Another piece of news has arrived as to the doings of our masters. A Cadet in the Service,* and now serving in this Province, was

* He is no longer in the Service. He later resigned.

informed on his departure for leave that he would be posted to a certain Province on his return from leave. A few days before sailing from England this instruction was countermanded and he was told that he would be sent to another Province. As he had done only one tour of service and was therefore unfamiliar with what course under these circumstances he should himself take for ensuring that his servants and kit met him on arrival, and as it was too late then for him to get a mail to Nigeria before his own sailing, he wrote to the Crown Agents and asked whether he should send a cable to Nigeria. The Crown Agents advised him to have a cable sent through them, which he did. Shortly after his return to Nigeria he received the following document:

*Confidential*
No. 264/3,

To ——, Esquire.                      Makurdi

    Mr. ——, *Cadet.*

I attach for your information and return copies of correspondence received from the Crown Agents for the Colonies.

(2) I am to say that His Honour, the acting Lieutenant-Governor, is surprised that an officer with previous experience of the country should doubt that the Secretary would make all possible arrangements with regard to your transfer and should display such apprehension and lack of confidence in your own capacity to deal with situations as they arise.

(3) I am to point out that much unnecessary trouble to all concerned has been caused and to inform you that His Honour has ruled that the cost of the cable (19s. 6d.) shall be borne by you. I am to instruct you to pay this amount into the Treasury forthwith and to inform me of the number and date of the Treasury receipt.

Resident, Benue Province.

This document, being considered confidential and urgent, was sent out to the Officer concerned, who was in the bush at the time, by a special messenger.

He sent the following reply:

*Confidential*

To

The Resident, Benue Province.

Mr. ——, Cadet.

I have the honour to acknowledge the receipt of your Confidential Memorandum No. 264/3 of the 29th July, 1933.

(2) I regret that any action of mine should be a cause of surprise to His Honour the Acting Chief Commissioner. It was precisely my previous experience of the country, to which His Honour refers, that led me to ask for the advice of the Crown Agents. Last tour I saw the case of an officer who on account of a sudden change in posting arrived at his Station without either loads or servants and who was obliged to remain in that condition for over a week; and listening to the remarks of the Station at the time a first-tour Cadet would have understood that this officer's predicament was not entirely unprecedented.

(3) Under the circumstances, and solely with the motive of obviating any such inconvenience as was caused to others by that officer's condition, on receiving notification as to my transfer to Adamawa from the Crown Agents, five months after I had left the Colony and six days before being due to return to it, I asked them when acknowledging their letter whether communication should be made with Nigeria regarding my loads. I should have thought that it was not a particularly unreasonable procedure for a Cadet who had not previously had experience of returning from a leave to have sought the advice of the official representatives of the Nigerian Government in England. On their replying with an implication that such communication was desirable I wrote saying that such and such are the facts regarding my loads and servants and that I leave it to your superior experience to judge whether the cable under the circumstances should or should not be sent.

(4) I am afraid I am at a loss to discover how His Honour sees in such action a display on my part of a lack of confidence in my capacity to deal with situations as they arise.

(5) In accordance with your instructions I have paid 19s. 6d.

into the Treasury and on receiving the Treasury Receipt will inform you of the date and number.

Cadet.

This straightforward reply to His Honour's censure led to a pained and rapid private response from the Resident:

"Dear ——,
   May I advise you to tear up the attached memo. and to let the matter pass into oblivion. Kicking against the pricks never serves any useful purpose and such a memo. as this ... will only mean an unpleasant comment on your sense of discipline. ...."

and so on for two more paragraphs.

The incident is illustrative of the irresponsibility and extravagance with which seniors, like Lieutenant-Governors, who cannot be touched and against whose bullying there is no redress, pass censures. The effect of such an episode on a junior officer, as also on the spirit of the Service as a whole, needs no emphasis.

*August 18th*

I left Abinsi this morning for Katsina Ala, about sixty miles South-East, in the Wukari Division, whither I have been transferred, after spending two agreeable and informative days with my successor here. I left in a motor lorry about eight and was due to arrive at Katsina Ala about 1 p.m. But there have been heavy rains yesterday and the road was in a dreadful state. The first mishap occurred about twenty miles from Abinsi when the Southerner (an Ibo) who was driving let the heavily laden lorry stall just before reaching the top of an incline. As soon as the engine stopped the lorry began to coast backwards, and, as the driver brought the lorry out with the brakes not working, he had no means of stopping it except by putting it into reverse. But as it gathered speed he lost his head and did nothing—he let it go over the bank. Fortunately the bank was so sodden that it prevented the lorry from turning right over. But most of my loads and my dog and servants and their wives and myself were all thrown out into the bushes. Chunk, my dog, hurt his paw when falling and one of the women broke her leg. I rated the driver, who was speechless with fear. I then had to send out my boys, none of whom can speak Munchi, to find men to dig the lorry out and push it up on to the road. After an hour or so we collected about twenty men and at last got ourselves on the way.

There were several minor mishaps, and then, not far beyond the Agricultural Station at Yandev, without any warning, the lorry went down to the axle in the treacherous earth. Once again we had to go out and call for men to unload and dig us out. By the time that was finished it was five o'clock. As there was no hope of going on to Katsina Ala I had the lorry turned round and driven into Yandev. The Agricultural Superintendent was away, but one of his men showed me into the second (and unoccupied) house there. The foreman (a Munchi) at the Station tells me that six inches of rain fell here yesterday.

*August 19th*

The road was still impassable so that I had no alternative but to sit down here and practice patience. I spent the morning in looking over the Agricultural Station, a pleasant place with a good view looking towards Gboko Hill, a landmark for many miles round here. Surprised to see that among other things growing here are some vines, which are bearing heavy crops.

About midday a messenger arrived from X——, the A.D.O. in charge of the Southern Touring Area, and therefore my ex-opposite-number, with an invitation to come and have tea with him and his wife. The road to his place is good and is only three miles or so away. In addition to his work as the local Political Officer he has also to supervise the building of the new headquarters—Prison, Divisional Office, Native Administration Treasury, the D.O.'s house, and about four other houses, etc. Although it is only a few years since the Divisional H.Q. was removed from Abinsi into Makurdi it is now going to be moved again. Makurdi is a bad place for the H.Q., but then it should never have been put there in the first place. The amount of money that has been wasted in Nigeria through building a H.Q. Station and then abandoning it and moving on to another and then abandoning that and re-building it elsewhere would tot up to a pretty figure. The game has gone on for years, and still goes on. I have just heard that Kuta, the old H.Q. of the Division bearing its name in Niger Province, is being abandoned and the Divisional H.Q. removed into Minna, the Provincial capital, and that, too, only a year after new buildings were erected there in order to provide for the transference of Zungeru Division to Kuta. As Minna is entirely unsuitable as the H.Q. of the Gwari tribe we can look forward confidently to its being shifted back again a few years hence. These moves are generally brought about by some ambitious man who draws up a scheme for re-organizing the Division to which he has just been posted. The game is to proffer the scheme with an imputation that the Division is in a shocking state and has been neglected and that before it can be run as it should be run it must be "re-organized." If the Resident can get any credit out of the "re-organization," or if the "re-organizer" is a man of force and the Resident stands to lose nothing by it, he will recommend the "re-organization" to the Secretariat. (Of course there are Residents, just as there are D.O.s, who do not play this game.) Lieutenant-Governors themselves have played the game in a larger Lieutenant-Gubernatorial way, as in the celebrated re-organizations within this decade. As for moving the Divisional H.Q. from Makurdi, that was sound; but whether to put it here or not is another matter. It is not clear either from reading the files bearing on the subject or from a study of the Munchi terrain why precisely it should have been put here. Excepting for the view of Gboko Hill (which admittedly is something) a more desolate outlook could hardly be found; all around lies the bush and tall grass rising and falling in monotonous undulations with never an island and never a line to break the sea-like everlastingness, receding dismally into infinity. The A.D.O. says that some days you can see a range, the name of which I have forgotten, but it was not visible to-day when the visibility, as is usual after a rain, was good. If not visible to-day it will certainly not be visible during the dry season; which is nearly half the year. It could also be claimed that it is nearly in the centre of the Munchi map; but that is of no importance whatever.

The X——s are living in a hut which used to be one of the foreman's huts when the Makurdi Bridge was being built. They complained about it and clearly not without reason. What a life to ask a woman to lead! She looked jaded and ill and very tired, so tired that, as one often notices out here (but with women more often than with men), to use her voice seemed an effort.

*August 21st*

The road having on the previous night been reported as passable up to the Ipav River, rather less than half-way to my destination, whence I should have to walk and use porters for my loads, and the lorry having been loaded, and arrangements made for a posse of men to be waiting at the river to carry my loads, I set off at 5.30, in the dark. We had not gone many miles, and the sun had not yet risen, when the lorry bogged. Over an hour was spent in hunting up villagers from the bush, unloading and digging out the lorry, and in finding and inducing enough men to carry the loads to the river. It took another couple of hours to march to the river and nearly as long to get the things over it. A bridgeway had to be improvised with what was left of the old bridge and some felled trees, and the men arranged chainwise across the crazy structure to pass the loads from hand to hand. It was difficult in the extreme and, as the flood was deep and strong, even dangerous, to get men and goods across; but by going slowly it was at last finished without mishap. Then began the trek to Katsina Ala. I was already far from fresh with the four hours' work of unbogging the lorry, getting the loads to Ipav and then getting them across the river; I was also hungry and thirsty (my water-bottle was dropped in the river); and now the sun had come out in all its fury. For mile after mile we marched in the heat, until I got to the stage of having to stop and rest for a few minutes every now and then; then the Munchis themselves began to straggle, then to drop their loads and run into the hamlets near the road, and some even abandoned their loads so that other men had to be persuaded to take their places. For the last three hours I had to keep the laggards together and drive them on, though I was so exhausted that speech itself became a task. I had already sent Mohammadu, my boy, on ahead to Katsina Ala, on the bicycle, from Ipav with instructions to tell the Chief to send out a relief of labourers together with my staff and a bicycle; but no sign was forthcoming. About 1.30, from the top of a rise, someone pointed out the river, lying like a silver thread in the desert of grey-green bush and grass, and indicated the position of Katsina Ala (nothing could be seen of it—nothing but the wilderness of grey-green) perhaps five miles away. I got up again and pushed on.

We had gone only about half a mile when forty or fifty men from Katsina arrived and relieved the laggards; but no bicycle for me and I was too fatigued to waste energy in asking the Dogari who came with the relief why there was none. The last two or three miles to the water's edge (Katsina Ala lies across the river) seemed without end, and I managed to keep going only mechanically and without full consciousness. When at length I got there I lay down on my back for perhaps twenty minutes before being ferried across the half mile stretch. On getting out of the boat I found my own staff, with not less than half a dozen bicycles between them (I found later, too, that they had been waiting there since the morning!), and the Chief with his usual entourage and drummers tapping out a lusty beat. I somehow went through the welcoming formalities and asked that any further discussions might be postponed until to-morrow morning, making excuses for going straight to my house. This was nearly two miles away. I got a couple of Munchis to push the bicycle on which I sat in a semi-coma. As soon as I reached the house—it was four o'clock—I lay on the floor and sipped brandy and water.

By sunset, having recovered somewhat, I had a bath and then opened a letter which had been handed to me on my arrival. It turned out to be a bright note from the lady in the Station asking me to come round and make up a tennis four.

That was yesterday. To-day I have spent in bed.

All my boys and their families are exhausted. Mohammadu's wife in such a state that she has drunk some charm-water, Mohammadu informs me. Charm-water is produced by writing out on paper a text taken from the Qur'an and washing it in water. The water is then drunk, normally with good results, the force of faith-healing being what it is. The African has a medicine for every trouble, either of the body or the heart. An interesting study would be that of all the medicines of, e.g., the Hausa, on the one hand, and a Pagan tribesman on the other.

*August 22nd*

Felt less near death to-day. I went through the current files, Court books, District books, and other records here in order to see how things lie. I also had a longish interview with the Sarkin Katsina Ala, the Alkali (the judge of the Moslem Court), a pleasant old man, as these alkalai generally are, but now nearly blind, and I inspected the dispensary, the market, and the town. Katsina Ala is an enclave of foreigners, most of them Hausas but also many

Berri Berri, Fulani, and other groups, living in Munchi country. The settlement was founded before our arrival in Northern Nigeria and probably a majority of the present townsmen were born here. My boys are contemptuous of the accent of the Hausa spoken here and are very snobbish in their attitude to these Hausa Colonials. Katsina Ala is a Hausa town with most of the characteristics and (to the Hausas) amenities of a Hausa town, but it is soiled and wears a bedraggled look. It has seen vicissitudes. It was once an important Divisional H.Q. and there was a European settlement here, but nothing remains of this now but ruined buildings. Apart from the A.D.O. (myself), there is no other European but the Superintendent of Education—the Education H.Q. for the whole Province is here—and, for a couple of months of the year during the benniseed harvest, a representative of the Niger Company and of Holts. Both these representatives happen to be in the Station now, the latter having his wife with him. My house is set in spacious grounds and is close to what was once a very good garden, but the situation is too near the river and the house is in much disrepair; white ants are all over it. The Education H.Q. is well chosen and well arranged on the top of a hill about a mile away and with a far-reaching view.

There are two European graves here—one man, an A.D.O., died in 1917. The other was a soldier and died before the war.

*August 23rd*

B——, the D.O. in charge of the Division in which the Katsina Ala Area is situated, arrived to-day from his H.Q. at Wukari to meet me and to give me general and specific instructions. He is a pleasant fellow, free from pompousness and the heavy man-of-state manner, and a mighty tennis player. His instructions, however, will involve a considerable amount of overtime on my part. I shall have to shelve some of them. Amongst other things I have to arrange for the repair of various roads and bridges; to mark out a site and to make arrangements for the building of a new dispensary in Katsina Ala (the present one is to be abandoned); expedite tax collection, which began ten days or so ago; to send in returns as to the condition of the crops at the end of each month; fill in the District note books; to write up the Native Court books at the end of each month and to send in the Court statistics to Divisional H.Q.; to study and write a report on the question of agricultural indebtedness among the local peasantry; to watch and report on any touting done by canteen employees for benniseed; to keep a Confidential Political Diary (in addition to the ordinary routine diary); to do as much touring as possible and clear up various outstanding matters in the Districts; and finally to go out to the scene of an alleged ritual murder to prepare a case against the suspect and to report fully thereon. The sting is in this last. Not only is the place miles away, the journey thither involving trekking through swamps and water-sogged bush, but as it is several months since the death of the alleged sacrifice took place I shall have to wring out of primitive people evidence which must necessarily be concerned with minute details differentiating hours, when they, the primitive witnesses, will not be able to recall even the larger differentiae of days.

*August 25th*

I set out on my trek up to the scene of the alleged ritual murder this morning. It rained all the way and I had to walk at least fifteen miles in a heavy rain and through paths that were rivulets.

In the evening various surrounding chiefs came to the camp to greet me and to report on the progress they were making in collecting their tax. They all complained that on account of the slump in the price of benniseed they were finding it heavy going. The Munchis in this District have to pay 4s. per adult male. The Jukons, however, have to pay 9s. I think the discrepancy is too great: it is almost certain that the per caput income of the Jukons is not more than twice as high as that of their Munchi neighbours and probably less. I promised them to bring the matter to the attention of the D.O.

*August 26th*

Another water-logged trek this morning. The made pathway is washed out and nearly every culvert or bridge-way is washed out, so that at times one had to wade through streams. I am camping in a Munchi hut: there is no rest-house in the vicinity.

The evening was again devoted to interviewing the local chief about the progress of his tax collection. He has not begun yet: the requisite exhortation was given and a meeting arranged for the near future when his collection to date is to be shown me. The tax here is not 4s., but 4s. 6d. per adult male, though the neighbours in the next District pay 4s. The discrepancies in tax assessment amongst the Districts of the Munchi tribe throw a sidelight on certain aspects of our Administration. Tax assessment varies from District to District, from 3s. 6d. (I think even from 3s.) to 4s. 6d.: men living on contiguous areas and under the same culture and with the same farming technique may thus enjoy a lesser assessment by as much as 33 per cent. No justification can be made for these discrepancies. No doubt there are Munchi Districts where some, or where a special temporary, discrepancy might be justified, but they are not these. This, in fact, has been pointed out by the local Administrative Staff. I have seen correspondence wherein the A.D.O. in charge of a certain area has written to his D.O. pointing out such a discrepancy in assessment, and also the absence of a reason for the discrepancy, and therefore proposing abolishing it. The D.O., after examination, has then written on to the Resident in charge of the Province, urging a similar course. And, finally, the Resident, again after examination, has then written to the Secretariat asking for the necessary permission to change the assessment. In due course the reply comes back saying that His Honour the Lieutenant-Governor is not convinced that there is any adequate reason for making the change and therefore interdicts it.

*August 27th (Sunday)*

Road as usual like a river to-day. I had to walk all the way, the bicycle being unusable, and for a good part of the way my feet were under water. As it is Sunday I shall rest to-day and leave my initial enquiries into the murder until to-morrow. This is the seat of the District Head in whose District (Shitere North) the murder was committed, though the scene itself is a couple of days' trek from here up towards the Benue. I shall not trek to-morrow.

There is a well-designed and well-built mud rest-house here, but once again it reveals that characteristic lack of imagination. It is dumped down on the edge of a swamp at the bottom of a basin. Had it been built only a couple of hundred yards in either direction it would have stood on high ground and have caught whatever breeze was to be caught and would have given one a view over instead of into a wall of grass and bush.

*August 28th*

The local chief (District Head) is a tall man with a sensitive face and large restless eyes. He is called Tor Dwem, i.e. Lord Hyena; Hyena because in the days of his youth, when he was the personal guard and confidant of a previous chief, he used to prowl abroad at night time. He is said never to sleep at night time now, and to live in fear of black magic, especially of the black magic of the medicine men of a section (Tomba) of his District. He looks about sixty-five, but probably is not so old. He is a wealthy man: he has thirteen wives, over a hundred head of dwarf (tsetse-proof) cattle, and many acres of farm. Now, through the death of others, he is the most important man in the District—I mean the most important man according to Munchi social ideas and apart from his official District Headship. (The District Head appointed by us and the real and accepted chief are not necessarily the same man.)

There is good bird shooting here. I shot both guinea fowl and bush fowl this afternoon—as much as my men and I could eat.

After dinner to-night I had a long talk with my Senior Messenger, Mbaivo, on Munchi beliefs. They seem to centre around witchcraft and fertility cults (in which sacrificial blood may play a large part). He worked himself into a state of terror when talking about the operation of magic and witchcraft (though in daylight, due to his continual association with Moslem Hausas in Katsina Ala—Pagans have an inferiority complex vis-à-vis Islam—he professes contempt for such heathen superstition) and my own flesh began to creep a bit at some of his stories which he claimed to be derived from his personal knowledge.

*August 29th*

I resumed the trek this morning, going via Arufa. The four prisoners, suspected of the murder, are with me now. As they have been imprisoned at Wukari for some weeks and have been living together they will no doubt have concocted some story. The job of sorting out the truth looks harder and harder. I had a talk with all four to-day, each man separately.

*August 31st*

I am now in the country of the alleged murder and have begun the Preliminary Investigation.* It is an out-of-the-way corner: the

* A Preliminary Investigation is a technical term meaning, briefly, a preparing of a case for its subsequent trial before the Supreme Court. The

visits of Administrative Officers have been rare: according to the District Head and the local Elders it is years since the last man toured here. A marshy region, intercepted with low ridges running parallel to one another every couple of miles, I shall have to become amphibian when moving from point to point.

*September 5th*

I completed the P.I., or rather as much of it as can be carried out now so long after the event, yesterday afternoon, and trekked on to Akwana this morning, where there is a rest-house (I have been living in a leaky native hut for the last few days). Twenty-eight witnesses have been examined and the evidence and report run into fifty or sixty pages, but, as I have stated in the report, I am far from certain as to its value or its meaning. Given Munchi ideas on witchcraft, and given the lapse of several months since the event, it will be practically impossible now to establish a case sound in English law against the accused; but such evidence as I have collected prevents me from acquitting them at this stage. The story suggested by the evidence is as follows:

The principal accused (Agande), a man of fifty odd, states that he was returning to his home late one night and on the way passed an abandoned compound where he noticed (and could not fail to notice) three men performing certain sorcery rites around a *Mboyunga* (i.e. a human skull which is dressed in some way or other and is the central fetish in certain Munchi fertility and other rites). According to Munchi beliefs Agande had thereby done these men an injury: he had beheld what he should not have beheld and so incurred a flesh debt. They immediately jumped up and gave pursuit to him and overtook him. They said to him: "You have seen our *Mboyunga*. You shall expiate the wrong with blood."

Administrative Officer conducting a P.I. (as it is usually called) is a detective and a policeman in that he runs down and writes down the facts and then arrests the alleged culprits; and also a magistrate in that he holds a species of Court, charging the alleged culprit with the offence and taking evidence from witnesses both for the prosecution and the defence; and the counsel, at the same time, for both the prosecution and the defence; and, finally, the loca¹ expert who explains the alleged facts in the light of local customs, beliefs, etc. A P.I. is thus an onerous business and not courted by officers. An advantage of serving in the Emirates is that the Native Courts there can try major offences so that P.I.s are not necessary. Through P.I.s the Administrative Department does the "dirty work" for the Judicial Department.

They told him if he did not want them to kill him he must find some other victim. They suggested his nephew and ward, Aribo. Agande, however, suggested instead Aribo's wife, to which they agreed. The following morning they called upon Agande and insisted on his making the necessary preparations forthwith so that the sacrifice could be performed that night. Agande then went to one called Aban, a man of the woman's kindred, with a status in that Kindred equal to his own in his Kindred, in order to get him to make the formal handing over of the woman which Munchi conventions require on such an ocasion. Aban agreed provided his own senior, Uantor, did not object. Uantor did not object. Aban then went to a man called Ugar who also had some interest of kinship in the woman and who also agreed to join the party at the handing over for the sacrifice. He did not in fact appear, if his own and the evidence of other witnesses is to be credited, until after the woman had been seized and done to death. The other six—the three *Mboyunga* men and Agande, Aban, and Uantor—all met about sunset in the dense bush and elephant grass behind Aribo's compound of three or four poor huts. No one was in the compound at the time except the woman his wife; the rest of the family was out in the fields. They called out her name and when she came to them Aban formally delivered her to Agande and he formally delivered her to the *Mboyunga* men. Two of these seized her and apparently she was throttled by one of them while they were dragging her into the bush. Aban and Uantor departed as soon as the woman had been handed over and therefore did not see the actual killing. Ugar did not arrive until she was already dead: he says he saw Agande and the three *Mboyunga* men depart with her in the direction of the local river (a few hundred yards away). He then picked up a broken necklet which had fallen to the ground, apparently while the woman was being throttled, and walked back to his house some three miles away. The story up to this point is what has been told by five of the seven accused: they vary in slight or minor details in their telling, but the broad substance is identical. The two who dissent—they are among the *Mboyunga* men—deny that they played any such part as has been stated by their fellow *Mboyunga* man and the three other accused, and they claim to know nothing whatever of the whole business. The rest of the story, which follows hereon, is told by two of the four men alleged to have played it. The two dissentients above are also, of course, dissentients here: The woman's body was taken to the river, carried across it, and then laid down at a place in the bush on the outskirts of the abandoned house where, on the previous night, Agande had unwittingly come upon the other three. The leader of the three *Mboyunga* men then cut the body up, the appeasing blood was put on the *Mboyunga*, the rites were gone through, and the flesh then distributed. Agande declined to take his share. The other three took theirs and left for home. Four or five days later (the exact time is disputed by the two men) one of the *Mboyunga* men called upon Agande and showed him the bones and head wrapped up in the woman's cloth. Both of them then went off and threw them under a shrub near Aribo's house. On the following morning one of Aribo's friends, who had just returned to the neighbourhood after some absence and who was calling upon Aribo to offer condolences upon the disappearance of his wife, had his attention awakened by a smell near where he was walking, and looking down he observed the cloth partially covering the skull and bones. Hence the discovery of the body. The neighbours were informed, the body was buried, and at length the news seeped through to the District Head and thence to Captain Dickinson, my predecessor.

Is this a true account of what happened to the woman?

It is not enough that some of the accused should confess themselves guilty, as above. Munchi beliefs being what they are, a confession, no matter how convincing *prima facie*, is not enough by itself.* It is conceivable that Aribo, the husband, or some other person interested, consulted (against the law of course!) a diviner, and that the latter informed the consultant that that was how Aribo's wife came to her end. A Munchi, though innocent, can in such cases persuade himself into the hallucination of having done what is alleged against him. Another difficulty I am up against is that I do not know Munchi and have to use an interpreter: every statement made to me by the witnesses has to be translated from Munchi to Hausa, and Hausa is a very inadequate medium for conveying the ghostly twilight of Munchi sorcery and animism. Hausa has been subjected to Islam for too many centuries and has therefore purged itself of ideas belonging to its animistic past. In order to obviate as far as possible all misunderstanding in the

* Of course, a confession is not enough in itself to secure a conviction in English Criminal Law.

translation I always insisted on having three interpreters at work at the one time so that the translation of any single one could be checked by that of the other two. The interpreters were the Senior Messenger at Katsina Ala, the Scribe, and the school teacher at Shitere. A still greater disadvantage is that I am new to these people and know nothing of their intimate beliefs and ethnology beyond what I have picked up from a couple of months' observations and from reading files and predecessors' notes (some of which are excellent). I am thus suddenly called upon to move about in a world of ideas removed by some thousands of years of evolution from our own, a journey that cannot be made in two months.

All I can do is to put them on their trial and let the Resident, or whoever is going to try them, make what he can of it. They will no doubt be acquitted. So I am sending them and the depositions and exhibits (cloth, bones, human hair, etc.) and a report (stressing my uncertainty and inability to offer anything but a very tentative explanation) into H.Q. As I see it there is something in their story. So many witnesses have said the same (or substantially the same) thing; and, further, as I have shown in the opening depositions, this is the story that was told right from the start—from the very moment when they first went to the Chief and to Captain Dickinson and before the accused were sent to prison. Moreover, not only was this story given formally at the P.I., but also when I spoke to each man separately and isolated from the rest and in my own hearing alone.*

*September 7th*

Yesterday Chunk was shot. About ten days ago he became sick, and as the symptoms developed it became clear that the tstetse had got him at last. He swelled all over and had to be carried most of the way, and finally he went blind. He has been blind for the last week. There was no other choice than to put him out of his misery. I arranged for the Munchi running the school at Tor Dwem's village to shoot him with my revolver, careful instructions having been given as to precisely what was to be done. A grave

\* A further investigation was later ordered, and the D.O. who carried it out, after I had been transferred, came to an opposite conclusion from mine. He concluded that the woman had died from natural causes and that the statements made to me by the witnesses were due to "some form of compulsion" by the native chief and myself! I sought to question his proceedings, but was not permitted to discuss the matter. Previously the Resident had commended my efforts.

about seven feet deep was dug in the rest-house grounds yesterday afternoon. Just about sunset I tied him up and gave him a dish of his favourite food and then hurried away into the bush, the shot to be fired in his ear twelve minutes later. I heard the shot. Death was instantaneous, so my boys said (my boys liked him and were a little awed). When I got back he was buried and the whole black business was over. He had been my constant companion, as constant as my shadow, for the last two years. He was as affectionate and vivacious as he was good-looking. Several races were mixed in his blood, but all good. The dominant strains were from Hermon-Hodge's dogs and from Finch's famous (locally famous) beagles. In colour black, touched, symmetrically and prettily, with tan and white; smooth hair; and an unusually fine head. *Vale*, Chunk.

*September 8th*

This is the last stage of the trek back to Katsina Ala. I shall reach there to-morrow morning. I am spending to-day in the compound of an elder called Akabu, about fifteen miles from Katsina Ala. It is placed on a hillock and has a good view of the river. As I sit in the clean hut allotted to me I can hear the sound outside of the children and the domestic animals. A happy place: twenty huts; in them live Akabu and his wives and children and the wives and children of his married sons; and their fowls and goats and pigeons and cattle. The women are grinding the corn and singing at their work, the children playing and chattering in piping voices, the men talking, and the fowls clucking. Akabu, an old man with a merry eye and kindly face and rich in the stuff of our common humanity, tells me that one of his wives is in labour and that he bade her rest for a couple of hours this morning in case the forcing might kill the child. He has looked in several times to tell me that things are going on well. It is a sorry destiny that we should change all this and in its place set up men who will be concerned with the Gold Standard, gramophones, tailors' catalogues, the polity of the Totalitarian State, and our other civilized preoccupations.

*September 10th (Sunday)*

The boys at the school here (Katsina Ala) are keen footballers (also, I believe, keen cricketers). They play with good temper but with immense determination. I noticed the same at Wanune. The Munchi is a natural athlete and a natural sportsman, as are many other African tribes; though not the Hausa, I think, at least as far as ball games are concerned. I tried to teach tennis to several but with poor success.

*September 11th*

The hippopotami make themselves heard nearly every night, not far from the bottom of my compound in Katsina Ala. They give forth a deep grunting noise—rather like a pig, but very deep and long drawn out. I lie in bed and listen to them. They are doing harm to the crops and the local Chief has applied for permission to have some of them killed. Another characteristic sound in Katsina Ala is the squeaking of the bats. There are hundreds, probably thousands, in the trees near the house. Unclean creatures. And yet another characteristic sound is the singing of the Munchis as they bring their benniseed into the canteen. To hear a boat, manned by a dozen or score of stalwart lads, singing (perhaps chanting is more accurate) in good strong voices, and with a marked rhythm, echoing across the water, is to hear something not likely to be soon forgotten. The Munchis are enthusiastic and agreeable singers. Porters will keep up a song for the whole trek. Labourers cleaning up my compound yesterday morning sent a deputation to ask if they could sing as they cut the grass, for otherwise they could not work. I gave the permission—but it was the end of my work for the morning! During the benniseed season they are on the roads all night if there is a moon, and if there is not a moon they begin moving long before daylight, each man (or woman) carrying a bag of benniseed to the canteen at Katsina Ala. They move in groups. As soon as they get within a mile or so of their destination they break into song, shattering our sleep irremediably—I believe that one predecessor used to post Dogarai on the roads near the Station in order that the command should be given to stop singing until daybreak—a justifiable move. X——, of the Education Department here, complains that he is now getting no more than five hours or so sleep a night.

*September 13th*

The District at the extreme southern end of my Area, and marching with the Southern Provinces, has, as it were, declared war on the neighbouring tribe across the border, and amongst other unlawful courses has closed the road to the latter so that their men cannot bring their benniseed to the canteen at Katsina Ala. My opposite number down there has written a moving appeal for action. So down I go to look into the matter. I left Katsina Ala this morning and am spending the night at the rest-house in the hamlet of a District Chief, one named Ahom. His affairs are also somewhat disordered and will require a couple of days' attention. For one thing an election has to be made to fill a vacancy in the District Native Court and so far the five sub-sub-sections of the sub-section entitled to fill the vacancy have failed to agree: as usual each wants its own big man and refuses to agree to any other. The post is worth 5s. (or is it 7s. 6d.? I forget which for the moment) a month, a large sum in ready cash here. But by to-morrow I hope to have persuaded them to accept the man who, according to their own standards, is the senior among the five. The difficulty arises, however, that as he is an old man he himself will not act in his office but will select another. Munchi custom allows this: if a chief or other big man is too frail or for some other reason is unwilling or unable to perform the executive duties of his post he may appoint a regent (so to speak) or, to use the Munchi term, his "eyes-and-ears." It is taking orders from this regent to which the others object. The business is interesting because it shows how difficult it is to get below the surface to the reality of primitive man's actions, and it also shows the ignorance (more or less inevitable, at least in the beginning) behind our own Administration: for until quite recently (and in some cases even now) the chief we have selected has been, unknown to us, merely the "eyes-and-ears" of the unseen and real chief. Nothing harmful need result from such a position. But where it did become harmful was when we appointed a man who was not only not the real chief but not even his "eyes-and-ears." Considering that we have been in occupation of Northern Nigeria for over thirty years the ignorance of essential customs of the Munchis (as no doubt of other tribes) is remarkable. Even now the real facts of the *Mfe* cult are in doubt: the man who is accepted as the authority is now laboriously maintaining a thesis which is the exact opposite of what he was laboriously maintaining a couple of years ago. An officer who, up to the changes brought about by the depression, was acting as anthropologist and has made a special study of the Munchis, told me that he himself has not yet got to the bottom of the matter and is still uncertain what to think. That is to say, the spirit behind, as contrasted with the furniture of, their institutions is still unknown. Very few officers have learnt the Munchi language. The responsibility for this state of affairs belongs to the men at the top in the past and the quality of leadership and the direction they gave. A couple of years ago I was in the Secretariat at Kaduna going through old files and came upon a file written about twenty years earlier. In it was a report on the customs and ethnology of the Munchi tribe written by an officer on the spot at the time, an effort that drew forth a censure from His Excellency the High Commissioner of Northern Nigeria on the score that His Excellency could not waste time on the ethnological details of a primitive tribe. Then and right up until a couple of years ago interest was concentrated on the Moslem Emirates. The Pagans were of secondary importance. This again was understandable and largely justifiable in the earlier years of our occupation; but it lost all justification years ago. It was well known, though of course it would be difficult for a private person to prove it in a court of law, and I have no doubt it would be indignantly denied by the men concerned, but nevertheless every officer in the Service in Nigeria knows it, that promotion came via the Emirates and that if you wanted "to get on" you must serve and distinguish yourself there. Indeed, officers were punished by being posted to certain Pagan Divisions. One Lieutenant-Governor when peeved with a subordinate once, in a scene reminiscent of Henry II and the turbulent priest, shouted: "I'll send the —— to Kabba." (Kabba is a Pagan Area south of the Benue and Niger, for years the nightmare of Administrative Officers and the Devil's Island of the unsuccessful or the disapproved.) To be posted to a non-Emirate Division was, with certain exceptions, regarded as a calamity in one's career. Under such conditions not only were many of the best men kept out of the Pagan Areas, but anyone posted among them saw no reason to learn the language; rather, he tended to spend his time trying to get posted elsewhere. This has now stopped and the bias is precisely the other way: the Pagan Areas are exalted and the Emirates depressed.

Reverting to our ignorance of the Munchi, one special reason for it is that the great knowledge of their customs and mentality possessed by the Missionaries of the Dutch Reformed Church (of South Africa), knowledge garnered over a quarter of a century's lonely, devoted, and continuous work amongst them—the officer who has spent five years straight off amongst the Munchis is a rarity—has not been drawn upon. It is only lack of humility that enables officers to pretend that they can learn nothing from such men. As a matter of fact the two or three junior officers (all A.D.O.s) who really speak the language, know most about the tribe, and have the requisite education for arranging what they know in a way that is of some scientific and administrative value, do respect the Missionaries' knowledge and learn as much from them as possible.

*September 14th*

I have got the factions here to agree upon the selection of a new member for the Native Court, though of course time alone can show how far their agreement is real and what (if any) has been the arrangement among themselves. The basis of Munchi institutions is patriarchy: the most important man is the oldest man. That is the rough idea, though in practice there are many refinements. I have been much struck during the last three months with the evil of such a basis to a society. It is the unmitigated form of promotion by seniority. Not only does this tend to produce an ultra-conservative bias in the control and the development of the society concerned, but it also tends to kill progress negatively because the rulers (the Elders) have no energy, not even physical, let alone creative, energy, left. Thus to-day the Elders I have been dealing with are a set of senile wrecks (evil and cruel, too, were the faces of most of them). That leads to the weakness of the present over-anxious policy (a reaction from the previous ultra-Emirate policy) of re-arranging the administration of all these Pagan tribes on a basis of what purports to be their own indigenous institutions. There are some institutions which should not be revived, which should not even be tolerated. Most forms of rule by the Elders is one. If the policy is carried to its logical conclusion (which is likely, as practically no Resident or senior D.O. would risk his promotion by opposing it), it will be more harmful than the former pre-Emirate bias. The generality of a tribe, and especially the younger people, are better off under the Emirate structure than under senile Elders.

In any case there is danger of our building institutions which do not sufficiently guarantee the freedom or rights of individuals. We may set up a chief or a ruling group, but amongst Africans, even more than amongst other peoples, you can never be sure that the rulers will not abuse their position. Whatever course is taken must therefore be checked continuously by observing and studying the group concerned: that is why touring by officers, and sufficient freedom from routine work to allow them at least enough energy and time to watch intelligently the affairs of their people, are a *sine qua non* of sound administration here. Neither of these requisites exists at the moment. Here, the District Chief, Ahom, practices an oppression of his own kind: he seizes or otherwise acquires women to whom he has no right. At the present, I am informed by my Senior Messenger, who knows the facts, he has thirty-two women, and I see from the report of a predecessor that he once had forty odd in his compound. A woman complainant, greatly daring, came to see me this morning, who is one of the thirty-two. She went to Ahom as a litigant. He detained her on various grounds and forced her to become a member of his harim. When I come back I shall investigate the affairs of his harim, though such investigation is not only very delicate but also very difficult; he can easily hide the women or bully them into saying that they are not his women or are not there against their will. Also, to trace the history of a Munchi woman is almost beyond the wit of man: she acquires so many partners at one time or another, and the rights involved become so complex, that to run down the truth of any one woman's past requires weeks of research. Rough justice is the best we can do here. Another point about Ahom's goings-on is that as District Chief he occupies a position unknown to Munchi customs: they had no autocrats, only oligarchs (the Elders). Raised to a position unknown to them, this is how he uses it: it is certain that no Elder ever managed to get hold of so many women as thirty or forty. On the other hand, however, it is equally certain that Elders abused the liberty of individuals.

*September 16th*

I asked the local chief, a very old man of the place I am camping at to-night (Gidan Moi), through my Hausa interpreter, who built the rest-house. "Soap," he replied (Hausa "sabulu"). Further questioning elicited that one of my fairly recent predecessors, whose proper name had been forgotten, was still known by his nickname acquired through an honest Anglo-Saxon passion against dirt. It is illustrative of African mother wit that a dominating characteristic is singled out with a rapidity equal to its accuracy. Most officials acquire a nickname, generally fastening on a frailty in the person concerned with unerring sureness. The Hausa particularly is an expert at the practice.

*September 17th (Sunday)*

I arrived at the hamlet of the District Chief, called Jato Aka, this morning. The trekking throughout the last couple of days has been delightful, almost the most picturesque I have yet done in Nigeria. This country is one of wild hills, perhaps two thousand feet or so in height. Cycling towards them in the early dawn one has always a fine prospect before one: all around is green and on the horizon a rampart of broken ranges or fantastic peaks very blue in the morning light, the blueness often heightened by wisps of white clouds which lay in horizontal bands athwart them. There are magnificent sites for rest-houses in this country; to spend a couple of days with such views around one would be a tonic for body and mind after the steamy and sodden lowlands; but, true to form, the rest-houses are built in boggy hollows. I can't see why the new Divisional H.Q. should not have been built somewhere in this country instead of at Gboko. There is a Mission of the D.R.C. here, staffed by the head and his wife (who have been out for twenty years) and two unmarried women. They kindly asked me to tea; I enjoyed a couple of hours with them this afternoon. The head was particularly interesting on Munchi mentality.

The view from the Mission buildings is, after the view at Abuja in Niger Province, and perhaps some near Bauchi, the best I have seen in Nigeria. As usual the Missionaries looked healthy and were free from the "jumpiness" into which practically every official slips. This is partly due to the fact that they live better (not more expensively): quite the contrary; but they have gardens, and keep fowls, and live settled lives, in a place where they can count on making some kind of home or other, while we, on the contrary, are buffeted from pillar to post and never know from one week to another where we shall be; and, moreover, they are free from the harassment and strain imposed upon officials by the bullying and panic-stricken excitability of senior commands and by the preoccupation with career. Further, the psychological fact that they believe themselves to be doing the work of God, whereas we are not always able to believe that, gives them an inward tranquillity.

Jato Aka is not only District Chief but also President of the Parliament of Munchi chiefs. He impresses one favourably. His hamlet is clean and well laid out, and his administration of his District leaves nothing to be desired. He is intelligent, courteous, and firm; also, I fancy, a lonely and austere man. He is a keen farmer: his farm of about fifteen acres (a large one for such a hamlet) is excellent. He is very proud of his yams, which though monsters in size are sweet and light to eat. He presented me with some. My staff (one of whom was Jato Aka's scribe for some years) tells me that Jato Aka has only three wives and that they live in a fenced-off compound with him; no one enters the compound except near relations. He has two sons: one is married and lives here with the father; the other is a schoolboy at Katsina Ala.

*September 20th*

I arrived at Gidan Ayu two days ago. This is the hamlet of the District Chief whose men have closed the road to the neighbour tribe and have raided it. The Chief and his big men readily admitted the facts. They said they were acting in accordance with Munchi custom in doing what they did, and that they had taken similar reprisals in other years without mishap. As always, it was not easy to sift out from the welter of words and irrelevancies and claims and counter-claims what precisely had happened and why it had happened. It looks as though the trouble began over unpaid brideprice for a Munchi woman who was acquired by a hamlet across the border. Anyhow it has been made clear that the road must be opened and the quasi-war must cease, and they have been given a letter for having the case about the woman thrashed out in the Native Court across the border. I have also written a soothing letter to my opposite number there and to my D.O.

The D.R.C.M. runs a small Mission school here: about a dozen boys. Amusing to hear them sing dirge-like hymn tunes with the lilt and rhythm of their own native singing—an effect rather as if one sang *Onward, Christian Soldiers* to the rhythm of *The Volga Boat Song*, or to a sea shanty like *What shall we do with a Drunken Sailor?*

*September 25th*

I got back here (Katsina Ala) from the South yesterday. I have begun work on the end-of-quarter returns. The most troublesome are the returns of cases in the Native Courts: this job alone requires me to copy out the cases reported in thirty-nine different Native Court books, into twenty-six other Divisional books, and then to summarize the relevent statistics on a large double-sided form (Form 13) with forty-eight columns! If it were only the fairly straightforward but tedious labour of direct copying it would be bad enough that Government money should be wasted by Administrative Officers having to spend hours on such routine clerical work; but it is worse than this: the form is an old one and makes no adequate provision for the new Governor's orders about corporal punishment, so that one has to work out what these mean and whether the cases before one should be entered under this or that heading.

The words corporal punishment recall the pretty packet of trouble that has been caused by the recent orders thereanent. A common punishment, more particularly in the Native Courts, for certain minor offences has been to beat the offender with a thong on the buttocks, the usual number of strokes being from six to twelve. As most Africans, and especially those who commit offences usually punished by whipping, have little or no currency in their possession they cannot be fined, and the only practicable punishments have been either imprisonment or the whip, the latter naturally being given for all the less serious offences, as, for example, gambling or brawling or resisting lawful authority, as well as in conjunction with imprisonment for certain gross offences. A great merit was its expeditiousness and its cheapness: the offence could be dealt with and liquidated forthwith, and the punishment, unlike imprisonment, involved neither the withdrawal of the offender from ordinary productive life nor the Government in the cost of supporting him. Imprisonment, moreover, at least in the Native Administration prisons, was scarcely a deterrent to most offenders, and above all to the homeless roving scamps who go in for organized gambling and brawling in the markets, for they are fed more richly and more regularly in prison than outside, and, further, it casts little or no social stigma on the prisoner. There is nothing even remotely comparable to the stigma on Europeans who have been prisoners. The only noticeable hardship to most of the prisoners is to be deprived of women, and, up until very recently, arrangements were possible with the warders for circumventing this hardship. (It is only a few years ago that such arrangements were terminated in the big N.A. prison in Kano.) The whip, besides being cheaper and more expeditious, was thus also a deterrent; and, given the toughness of the Nigerian's skin, the low sensibility of his nervous system (it is rare to see a man wince or to show any signs of pain), and the moderation with which the strokes were usually laid on, it was not a brutal deterrent.* But it was (broadly speaking) unregulated and susceptible to abuse; and it is curious that next to nothing was done for mitigating the possibilities of abuse.

How far it was abused it is difficult to say. I have heard of a few cases; but speaking from my personal knowledge I have not so far come upon any abuse by a Native Administration authority (excepting a Dogari who, however, did it on his own initiative and for personal motives, and was punished adequately for it) and only once by a Political Officer. It is typical of the way control here is centralized in one person and of the ineffectiveness of Colonial Office supervision that changes in policy can be made from one extreme to another, as has happened in this connection now.

The present Governor's orders hedge corporal punishment around with so many restrictions that in most cases it will not be worth the trouble of giving it. It can now only be given in a prison, which in practice means at Divisional H.Q.; it is given on the responsibility of the D.O., who will naturally be chary of permitting it at all; it can be given only with a cane (the whip is abolished here) of a specified material and conforming to a certain weight and length and thickness; the cane must fall on a certain part of the buttocks; and the buttocks are to be covered with an antiseptic cloth.†

* Lord Lugard defended corporal punishment of the African, vide Annual Report on Northern Nigeria, 1902, p. 133.

† Later I saw the first of these reformed and hygienic canings being carried out in a certain prison: the prisoner was a primitive Pagan, whose offence was that in a burst of passion he struck a tax collector's representative. He had walked forty or fifty miles from his village to the H.Q. prison in handcuffs, and accompanied by two native policemen (who were the only Dogarai in the District, and were therefore withdrawn for the length of the journey to and from H.Q. from not unneeded work in the District), he had to wait a day in the prison until the D.O. could scrutinize his case; and then at length he was led into the prison yard, made to lie down, and finally underwent the horror of having the antiseptic cloth carefully arranged over his buttocks. It was this that broke him up: the antiseptic smell alone convinced him that some juju magic or other was being used against him. Sheer terror came over his face, and he did what probably had never been done before in the prison when a man was going to be whipped, he screamed and struggled. Two warders had to hold him down and another two held the antiseptic cloth in place, while a fifth administered six strokes with the regulation cane. The poor wretch was then released, firmly convinced that his punishment had been not the caning but the laying on of the antiseptic cloth, a juju of unknown and therefore the more terrifying potency.

There are other complicated regulations. The results will be that every D.O. in a Pagan Division will take measures to discourage Native Courts from using corporal punishment, even for the limited cases where it is still permitted. Not only will he naturally wish to avoid the responsibility and the trouble of answering queries as to why he sanctioned it here or there (he now has to submit a return of corporal punishments), but when, as is usual here, there are only two Dogarai at the service of a District Chief and its Native Court, he cannot afford that these men spend their time walking to and fro Divisional H.Q. with candidates for the hygienic whipping.

The whole affair is the work of a man with a defective sense of proportion and with no personal experience, and with an inadequate understanding, of the actual business of administering Africans in the bush. The tender conscience that was professed at the brutality of whipping would have been more convincing, too, had it made a move against the sordid and real brutality of capital punishment, an atavistic horror.

Such a straining at gnats, but swallowing of camels, is bound to show more than one inconsistency: thus while wrongdoers cannot be caned, schoolboys in Government and other schools can be beaten as you will.

Then the manner of introducing the "reform" was a model of confusion and countermanding. Before the regulations were finally drafted, approved, and gazetted, in such a hurry was the ruler, that there proceeded a series of tentative orders altering first this and then that. No one knew where he was. The file on corporal punishment in my office here contains twenty-two pages for just the last four months or so.

*September 28th*

It is very pleasant sitting out on the verandah of my bungalow in the late afternoon and early evening looking down to the wide waters of the river and beyond them to the hills on the horizon. When the dark comes there comes with it all the seething life of a tropical night—frogs, crickets, mosquitoes, and above all the bats. When I leave here I shall associate Katsina Ala with bats. There are hundreds or thousands of them in the mango-trees near my house, loathsome animals: loathsome to look at and loathsome in their dirty habits. If in the future and at home I hear somewhere a bat-like squeak, I shall see and feel again the nights at Katsina

Ala—damp heat, clammy clothes, fire-flies, the restless throbbing of distant drums, the grunting of the hippos.

The main affliction at the moment is the sandflies. These are minute creatures hardly as big as a pin's head and which would escape one's observation had they not such a sharp manner of attracting it. They rest at night-time, but from about ten in the morning until about five in the afternoon they are relentless. It is impossible to wear shorts or to leave one's arms exposed. Recently I have even had to swathe my neck in a scarf to protect it from their burning sting.

*September 30th*

I am on my way to Tor Donga. Some of the tax money has been stolen from the local Chief's house under circumstances which tend to inculpate the Dogari guarding it, if not the Chief himself, so I have to go out to investigate.

Last night was exceptional, even for Nigeria. A tornado blew up about five in the afternoon, and instead of the storm wearing itself out in a few hours it kept up all through the night until the morning. The lightning flashed and the thunder roared as only tropical lightning and thunder can, coming and going and then coming again, and so near where I was camping that I never knew when it might strike the hut (as the morning showed, a tree fifty yards or so away was struck), nor did I know when the roof of the hut, a flimsy thatch, might be blown off. Rain poured through it like a sieve, and I managed to keep comparatively dry only by putting a canvas ground-sheet over the mosquito-net rods of my bed. And now (the following afternoon) it has begun thundering again.

*October 5th*

I have completed the investigation of the theft of the tax money here and sent in the requisite report. Also inspected the road and bridges (it is the main so-called all-season road between Katsina Ala and the Divisional H.Q. at Wukari). Just around here both road and bridges have almost ceased to exist, so heavy have been the recent rains. Other routine inspections made.

There is a half-caste boy in the village here, about twelve years old. His features are Munchi in every respect, but his colour is that unpleasant dirty livid colour of the average African half-caste.

I noticed that it looked very light in comparison with the colour of his mates, but very dark in comparison with my own skin, so undiluted is the African's blackness. It is rare, even very rare, to see half-castes in Nigeria. I cannot recall seeing more than about half a dozen, including the natives seen around the mining areas on the plateau where, it might be assumed, liaisons with African women would amount to rather more than half a dozen. The fact seems to be that African-European liaisons are usually infertile, a matter of considerable biological, and more particularly genetic, interest.

*October 7th*

Back at Katsina Ala again.

*October 12th*

Orders arrived during the week for me to proceed to Idoma Division rather sooner than expected. My relief arrived to-day and I am to leave *en route* for Makurdi (whence I go by train to Oturkpo, the H.Q. of Idoma Division) to-morrow morning. The handing-over, which is generally a complicated ritual, did not take long as my relief has served in this area before and knows much more about it than I do. It so happens that he is the man who took over from me at Abinsi two months ago. Why the Resident could not have left me there all the time and sent him direct to Katsina Ala, when he returned from leave then, is not clear. Through this chopping and changing, I had only just got settled down in Abinsi and was just learning enough of the Area to become useful when I was sent off to Katsina Ala, to be relieved in less than two months by the very man who relieved me at Abinsi. And this is the fifth change in A.D.O. in charge of Katsina Ala since February, eight months ago!

If questioned, of course, such inefficient posting would as usual be ascribed to the "exigencies of the service" (a hallowed phrase in the mouths of our seniors). It is not the fault of the man in charge of a Province if the Secretariat chops and changes its postings, and no Resident could have suffered more than this one by such vacillation during the last six months (I believe there were no less than ten junior officers posted to his Province within this period whose posting was cancelled at the last moment and some one else sent in their places). But this particular matter shows that the vacillation goes further than the Secretariat. I have noticed in other Provinces where I have served an equally unplanned disposition of the personnel.

*October 13th*

I left Katsina Ala at daybreak this morning. At the water's edge my Munchi porters bade me farewell in their usual pleasant way. I distributed largesse and then entered a lorry for Makurdi, breaking the journey for a short rest at Yandev (where the agricultural experimental station is) and at Abinsi, and arrived at my destination at nightfall.

At Yandev the Agricultural Officer told me of a recent experience there with a python. He was awakened one night by a swirling noise and concluded that it was a tornado blowing up; but, on becoming more awake, he perceived that the noise was localized and near his bed. He switched on his torch and got out—to see the body of a snake extending through the door leading from the verandah, stretching the whole length of his bedroom, and passing out through another door leading to the next room. He did what we all do on such occasions: he yelled for his boys. They rushed up and brought him a shot-gun and the creature was at last despatched. It is said that it was fifteen feet in length. This is possible, as pythons out here have been found as long as twenty feet.

*October 13th*

Arrived at Oturkpo by train from Makurdi 9.30 this night. Met at the station by the D.O. (or rather the man who is acting as such) and an A.D.O. They drove me back to the Station by car. The car had no lights and the only illumination was a faint electric torch which seemed to show nothing of the road. As they had been having a cheerful evening together the driving was swift and curveful. I hoped they knew the road well. Anyhow we arrived at the D.O.'s house (an excellent house) without mishap. Another A.D.O. was waiting at the house. About midnight I was taken to my house.

*October 15th*

Oturkpo Station is situated on a ridge, along which it extends, and has a wide open view; but all around is a wilderness of bush and forest, so much so that you would never think the country was fairly closely settled. There is a well-built two-storey concrete house for the D.O. and two houses (also of concrete and two-storeyed) for the A.D.O.s, and about half a dozen mud and thatch houses. The Station, however, is, in my opinion, too close to the native town.

The present Administrative personnel consists of the D.O. and three A.D.O.s. There is no one else here.

The Division itself (of which Oturkpo is the H.Q.) covers about 3,400 square miles, running from the Benue down to the border of Southern Nigeria, and has a population of a little less than 200,000. There are a few Ibos and Jukons and a tribe called the Egedde numbering about 50,000, the rest being Idoma—about 150,000. These last have a bad reputation, the worst in fact of any people in Northern Nigeria.

*October 17th*

I have been allotted my Area here. The main work at the moment is to get in the tax, which is greatly in arrears, and to supervise the building of a new road which is to form part of a great arterial system linking up the North and East with the capital, Lagos. I left Oturkpo this morning for a few days' trek to get a general impression, especially of the work going on on the road. I have also got to begin a Preliminary Investigation on a murder committed by a boy on his playmate. Idoma Division is one of the most southern (I think it is the most southern) in the Northern Provinces—its most southern part is on a parallel of latitude which is only seventy miles or so north of Lagos, which is on the sea. This is a different world from the usual savannah country of the Northern Provinces, and different even from the bush country north of the Benue and Niger. There is bush here, but there is also forest: it is on the northern edge of the equatorial rain forests. To-day was my first experience of moving under these immense trees.

*October 21st*

I begin to understand how this place has got its bad reputation. The Idoma natives are said to be the lowest type in Nigeria: I have seen more disagreeable and at the same time excitable faces than ever before. They are surly and rarely salute or greet you (a rarity among Africans, who in general have an instinct for politeness), they are always quarrelling among themselves, and they are dirty. My second day out I was called upon to stop a brawl between two parties of men working on the road, numbering about forty all told. There were several teeth missing, eyes closed up, and cuts and bumps. My main difficulty, however, has been to get together the witnesses necessary in connection with the murder case. They are all in hiding and there is not a soul left in their hamlet (situated in deep forest) except a few old hags. Even the local Chief, the head of the sub-clan, is away and I cannot find where he is: his men hereabouts profess not to know! Also, no tax at all has been collected here so far, although it is three months since the collection should have begun. This, by the way, is one of the few Divisions where Political Officers are required to tour with an armed escort of Government Police. I have ten rank and file and an N.C.O.

*October 23rd*

I returned to Oturkpo this morning. Had to come back, because the quarterly meeting of the Idoma District Chiefs opens to-morrow. The Resident will be here. I am glad to get away for a few days from the work awaiting me out in my Area, though I am told that the work of attending to complaints during the quarterly meeting here will make me glad to return to the bush.

*October 27th*

As I had fever for a couple of days I missed most of the *Ojira* (as the meeting is called—it is Idoma for *the folk-moot*). What I saw of it, however, was enough. Purely as a spectacle it was amusing. Twenty or so district Chiefs, gaily caparisoned, sat under the presidency (officially speaking—the wretched President was completely ignored) of one of their members, the whole assembly squatting under a shed, without walls, especially erected for these conclaves. Outside, around the stone fence, were all the world and his wife (but particularly those with grievances), who happened to be about for the day, and, though they were supposed to be either spectators or suitors, actually they joined in the Chiefs' discussions when and how they felt like it. As I say, it was amusing purely as a spectacle; but to the overworked D.O. who had to run the thing and to get it to pass motions (such is the force of our ingrained Anglo-Saxon parliamentarianism) and to consider and decide on appeals to it from District Courts (it is also the Native Court of Appeal for the Division) and then to write a report on it showing its important place in the life of the Idoma and proving the progress that it is making, it must have been a nightmare. As a former District Officer, now retrenched but for many years the man who ran the Division and who knew more about it than any other, once wrote courageously in comment on a naïve memorandum from the Resident on the institution: "The Ojira is a mass meeting!" A mass meeting does not make a satisfactory Court of Appeal.

*October 28th*

Saturday night. So ends a memorable week. Two days of malaria; then the Idoma Ojira, the Parliament of the Idoma; and then three days devoted entirely to hearing complaints. We used to arrive at the office at seven in the morning to see the road lined with waiting complainants, all with their stories pat. From then until nine (when we went home for breakfast) and again from ten until 1.30 or two we sat and struggled with them. The Divisional Office here is a new one, built by the P.W.D., of concrete bricks. That is to say, it is a bad one and quite without any planning, hot to work in, no protection against the glare, and several hundred per cent worse than the old native mud buildings, which are generally excellent. It consists of three small rooms: the first is the D.O.'s; next to that is one about ten feet square in which there is the Local Treasury (here run by the D.O.), with its table, books, and safe taking up about a third of this space, and in which the three A.D.O.s have to work. As their work is mostly taken up with hearing complaints, there are thus three officers squeezed up in this tiny space each conducting a case, and each therefore with his interpreter and parties and band of witnesses. Add to this the excitable Idomas raising their voices and shouting out recriminations, the D.O. coming in every now and then to go to the safe or to call to the clerk (who is in the third room where he keeps up a rattle on his typewriter). The mere physical feat of hearing what was addressed to one, or of surviving the stench of Idoma sweat, was considerable. But what organization at the top! For £50 or less a very good mud office of the kind prevalent in Divisions lucky enough to have escaped the well-meant services of the P.W.D. could have been built. This building cost many times more than that. Such is the march of progress.

Apart from working under such conditions, there were the complaints themselves. From what I have been able to see, in this admittedly short time, it looks as though the vast majority of all the decisions given in the Native Courts of the Divisions are appealed against, such is the people's litigiousness and willingness to speculate on the chance of getting a better verdict next time. The cases were of the usual sort: the right to possess women or (the real point) the money due on them as bride-price; that is to say, they are questions of debt. As women tend to pass from hand to hand fairly quickly there is generally a number of outstanding claims on each woman, and amidst the welter of intricate native right and custom, and charge and counter-charge, and lying and perjury, and bad faith and bad temper, it is nearly impossible to determine the right claim. What makes it harder still is that you can never nail a man down to a direct reply (this applies more or less to all Africans I have had to deal with) and you cannot keep them to relevance. Ask a litigant a simple question of fact to which he must know the answer—as, e.g., Did you or did you not pay 2s. on such and such an occasion?—and make it clear to him when asking it that you want only Yes or No in reply, yet there appears to be no power on earth that can persuade or compel him to give you the simple reply. He will tell you anything, and at great length, but not the answer to that question. Though exasperating it is an interesting point on African psychology. Does he do this intentionally in order to mislead for his own purposes? Or does he do it because his sense of relevance, that is to say his general mental aptitude, is such that he is not aware of the irrelevancy? Perhaps he does it for both reasons.

*November 1st*

I left Oturkpo yesterday for a trek over my Area. I expect to be out for five weeks. In addition to supervising the building of the road (there are about thirty miles of it in my Area and it employs about one thousand men), and to expediting tax-collection and to hearing and settling appeals against the Native Courts, there is a number of special jobs to be done, the chief of which is to conduct three Preliminary Investigations into firstly the murder by the boy, secondly an alleged attempted murder, and thirdly a slave-dealing case.

*November 3rd*

I arrived here (Eke) this morning. The clan head (a sub-District Chief) lives here, the man who was "not at home" during my previous visit and who is now indispensable for getting together the absconded witnesses in this boy murder case. He was "at home" to me to-day, turning up at camp a few hours after my arrival, accompanied by nine of his clan Elders, not an attractive-looking bunch. He himself was rather an agreeable old man and lied pleasantly though shamelessly about his non-appearance before; but he wore a harassed air. The job of Chief (which is not an indigenous institution) among these anarchistic ruffians would be no sinecure. He says that although he has twice visited all the hamlets in his sub-District, which lies in deep forest, during the last six weeks he has not managed to collect more than a few pounds of tax. They all refuse to pay. He adds that they would do this in any case unless and until a Political Officer accompanied him with an escort of Government Police, but that this year the difficulties are going to be greater than ever because of the absence of currency in the villages. The depression has meant the loss of their old market for yams at the Oturkpo railway station, *en route* to the tin mines, and it is hard for them to sell other things to the extent of getting in the two or three shillings assessed on each adult male. There is no doubt that the loss of one of their main sources of currency supply has made it difficult for them to come by the pence needed for their tax, but, as the acting D.O. says, the root of the matter is their own unwillingness to make any effort to come by the money. The two or three shillings assessed is not much (they are under-assessed in comparison with Hausas) and it is still quite practicable for the adult male to acquire this amount in the twelve months. There is always difficulty in collecting tax among the Idoma tribe even in the boom years: normally it has to be collected by Political Officers themselves (which is irregular according to the principles of Indirect Rule) and with the aid of Government Police.

Having got as far as this in discussing tax I enquired after the witnesses needed in the murder case. He promised to have them in the camp first thing to-morrow morning.

*November 6th*

The Preliminary Investigation is over—finished it this afternoon. This is what happened: The culprit, a boy who looks the age of five years but is proved to be nine, was sent out one afternoon with another boy, a couple of years older than he, to cut reeds in a marsh a mile or so away from the hamlet. Just before sunset and after each of them had cut a bundle they fell to quarrelling, apparently over who had cut most reeds, and in the heat of the quarrel they struck at each other with their knives. The culprit received only a scratch, but he managed to stab his opponent two blows which proved fatal, though not instantly fatal. He then took to flight but the other boy managed to crawl to the hamlet. Too weak with loss of blood to utter connected sentences, the victim yet just managed to say that "Unamalu (the boy concerned) did it." He died during the night. Fortunately there is no difficulty in establishing these facts. The evidence is straightforward. There are other difficulties, however; firstly a legal difficulty, and secondly what might be called an administrative difficulty. As for the legal difficulty, the Criminal Code of Nigeria, following the general principle of the Common Law of Crimes, lays down that a juvenile of the culprit's age cannot be held criminally responsible for this murder unless it can be *proved* that at the time of committing the act he had the capacity to know that he ought not to commit it; or, in the words of the Common Law phrase, there must be *affirmative* evidence that the accused had sufficient reason to form a correct estimate of his conduct. Not only can I not prove this or obtain such affirmative evidence, but I have taken down depositions from his elders which in my opinion establish the contrary (although in any case it is enough to acquit him of criminal responsibility if the affirmative evidence is not available). On the whole, therefore, I feel fairly secure about this difficulty: I doubt whether our legal experts, to whom the depositions will be submitted, would try to establish the opposite. The second or administrative difficulty is another matter: According to Idoma ethics (and, within the lifetime of every adult in the hamlet concerned, according to Idoma practice) there is only one way of settling a murder like this and that is to hand Unamalu over for expiatory death. The parents or other family heads of the dead boy might, if they liked, exercise a right of letting the culprit's parents (or family heads) commute the culprit's death by the payment of a compensation, but where, as in the present case, bitter passions are involved, they would insist on expiation by his death. And the passions now are most bitter, and, as they embrace the whole clan, perhaps a little dangerous: the dead boy was the last survivor of the many children begotten by the father (who is too old to hope for any more). The father is now beside himself: he is practically insane with grief and the desire for revenge. He has not eaten a proper meal since the murder and has had to be arrested and committed to control, in case he himself attempts to kill one of Unumalu's relatives. The mother is also distraught: during the hearing of the evidence of Unumalu's grandfather (his guardian) she lunged at him with a knife and since then has also been under control. The most dangerous of the dead boy's relatives is an old woman who is one of the wives of the District Chief of Ogleo (a neighbouring District), who looks a very she-devil.

What exacerbates the tension is the memory of a similar case in this very sub-District four or five years ago (Odobi's case): The murderer, a boy, and, as it happens, a relation of Unumalu, was of course acquitted on the ground of criminal irresponsibility; but he was detained and sent to a school in Lagos. This seems an outrageous miscarriage of justice to the men here: not only were the parents of the murdered boy debarred from exacting any sort of compensation, but the murderer was taken away and taught to read and write and thereby given a big hoist up in the economic and social scale. The old Chief and Elders have been very frank in saying that in their eyes this is very wrong and that the people cannot understand it. When I concluded the investigation and announced that Unumalu would be detained pending further orders and would be sent under escort to Oturkpo there was an open outcry among the crowd of a hundred or so who have been hanging around throughout the hearing of the case. I thought for awhile that there might be a demonstration (the Acting D.O. was once demonstrated against in this very village and had to keep to his hut for a day; he has also been shot at with a cap-gun). So I had a shot at being (or looking) as firm as I could, and made a speech to the effect that they all knew very well that the British Administration did not permit the taking of life under any circumstances and that local custom was absolutely superseded in this matter; further, if any life were taken in revenge for the dead boy it would be a capital offence. I then made the old sub-Chief enlarge on the point. The crowd having seemed to cool down a little, I then tried to explain in friendlier manner, but all the Government Police remaining in military formation, why any such expiatory killing as they were demanding could not be considered for a moment and would be dealt with sternly (it is only a few years ago—1928,

I think—when a punitive expedition, though it was not called that, administered a severe lesson to the Idoma: the Obolulu Rising); but, of course, it is not easy to make such a point clear to them. The essence of the matter is that such a murder as this constitutes in their eyes a tort, not a crime, and as such is a case for compensation to an individual not a case for action by society as a whole. Also, the Idoma tribe is one of the last areas in Nigeria to be brought under effective control: I see from some of the old files in the Divisional Office that it was only in 1911 that somebody came along and made a "treaty" with what he conceived to be the Chief of these parts! (What the Chief thought of it all is not on record.) Little had been done over most of the tribal area when the war broke out so that active development would be suspended until after the war, only since when in fact can the tribe be regarded as having been brought under effective control. All the adults here can remember expiatory killing as the normal part of their life and morality, and there is probably not a man amongst them of thirty-five years or more who has not won his skull (they were headhunters).

*November 7th*

Arrived at Okwoga this morning. It is the hamlet H.Q. of the District Head of Okwoga District, one of the biggest Idoma chieftains. There is a Bush Dispensary here, and the R.C. Mission conducts a small school (seven pupils at present) under an Ibo teacher. Surprised to discover that there had once been an old European Station here and that it had been a Divisional H.Q. in the days when this part of the country belonged to Southern Nigeria. It is now overgrown with grass and bush and most of the buildings are ruins, or even just mounds. The rest-house is the remains of what had been the D.O.'s house. It stands in a fine ground. Later on I shall stay here for a few days, but to-morrow morning I must go to Obadigbo in order to do the P.I. into the case of one Dangoji, a hamlet Head, who shot (not fatally) Ochibu.

*November 8th*

I set out from Okwoga before dawn in order to get the trek over in the cool of the morning; but needlessly, as there was a dense fog until 10.30 or so. In places one could see only a few yards ahead. One somehow does not expect fogs in the tropics, but the local people here say that they are not uncommon towards the end of the rainy season. My servants, who are Hausawa and Fulani, knew of no words in their language for fog or mist other than the word used for a dust haze. Their homes being in the semi-arid savannah country south of the Sahara, they do not like the forests.

*November 10th*

The P.I. into Rex versus Dangoji presented few difficulties as regards establishing the facts. Dangoji is Head of a hamlet called Ogojubo which lies in a stretch of deep forest and is reached only after passing through a wilderness of bush and dense tall grass (eight feet or so high). Dangoji, who was arrested shortly after the shooting, and has been in Oturkpo prison since then (about two and a half months, I think) waiting until a Political Officer could be sent out to conduct the P.I., is with me here (a delay as long as this is very unfair to him; but so long as staff is as short as it is and so long as office work continues to be piled on Political Officers such delays are unavoidable). A depressed and anxious man, and feeling under a grievance. What happened was that a young man called Ochibu, an idler and a noted philanderer, continued to pursue one of Dangoji's wives. Adultery had been committed more than once, and the paramours had eloped on several occasions, apparently five. Dangoji grew more and more resentful of the scandal. A settlement along the lines approved by local Idoma morality and opinion, and desired by himself, namely the payment of the recognized adultery compensation (*kurdin chiki*: there appears to be no notion of moral offence in adultery among the Idoma; it is a question of paying due hire: the husband paid money for the woman; the adulterer paid nothing; he should therefore compensate the husband for the use of the latter's property), having been held up indefinitely by Ochibu's family continually attempting to evade the obligation, Dangoji gave himself up to brooding. Ultimately his self-control reached breaking-point. He set off one evening with a loaded Dane-gun (i.e. old-fashioned cap-gun) in his hand, resolved to bring the discussion with the adulterer to a final issue. The latter, when thus confronted, refused to discuss the matter at all and Dangoji in a burst of passion fired his gun. The pellet struck Ochibu in the thigh, the resulting wound requiring his despatch to the Makurdi Hospital. From the depositions I have taken I believe that, fortunately, nothing more serious than a charge of unlawful wounding can be entered against Dangoji, and on that charge I have committed him to stand his trial in the Provincial Court.

The interesting points about the incident are these: Firstly, why are these Idoma, who are admitted to be among the most excitable and truculent people in Northern Nigeria, allowed to have guns? In any case why are they allowed to have them without a licence? What is there in the Arms Ordinance that exempts Dane-guns from the necessity of being licensed? Secondly, there is the light thrown on local law and custom and practice: After the shooting the hamlet held an *Ojira* (i.e. folk-moot) and resolved that not only had Dangoji done no wrong in thus wounding Ochibu, but that had he actually killed him he would have been acting within his rights. The Elders actually tried to prevent Ochibu and his family from reporting the incident. Nor was this the first occasion when the local tribal authority intervened and intervened in a way that was *ultra vires* according to our laws: the hamlet folk-moot put Ochibu to an ordeal, apparently a poison ordeal, at an earlier stage of the matter (*na sha mugun rantsawa*). This shows, I think, what I am convinced is the case, that our rule here touches only the periphery of Idoma life and that in most of the essentials their old ideas and practices remain.

Thirdly, light is thrown on the status of women among the Idoma: the woman in the case was younger than some of Dangoji's daughters. Dangoji had paid the bride-price for her when she was a small child and her father had spent it long before she was old enough to marry. Not only was she not consulted, but when the time came for her to marry Dangoji it was not possible for her wishes not to marry him to be considered, as her family had no other means of satisfying the debt to Dangoji. Her marriage took place by her father calling her one day when Dangoji was in their compound and saying to her: "There is your husband." That was all there was to it. Further, when she was taken off to Dangoji's compound he did not give her a separate hut but put her in with one of the older wives (thus contraverting native custom and right: each wife has her own hut and *ménage* and purse); what the latter's treatment of her was like can be imagined.

I was much struck to notice in Dangoji's hamlet (it is officially listed as a hamlet; actually it is a populous and spreading settlement in the forest) that practically all the children (I noticed the children because they alone were naked) had sores over them. Whether it is syphilis or only yaws (I suspect the latter) I cannot say.

*November 12th (Sunday)*

I am spending a couple of days quietly here at Okwoga, a place I like very much. I have had all the grass in the extensive grounds of the rest-house cut down and the trees trimmed, so that I can trace what used to be the borders and beds of the garden fifteen years or so ago. Whoever laid out the grounds (he must have been the man who also laid out the Station, which was admirably planned) he had an eye for landscape. The hedge is planted with big trees, but there are no other trees in the compound (which is as it should be: trees break the breeze and shelter mosquitoes and flies and vermin) except some citrus-trees and a few ornamental flowering shrubs not too near the house. From the front of the house, which is situated on a ridge, you look due west on to a garden falling towards a stream, and across a gully to a prominent and well-wooded ridge. It is very pleasant sitting out in the late afternoon and watching the sun set beyond the ridge (at that hour the view is curiously like a view I once knew well in California—the Coast Range at the back of Stanford campus). When the dusk comes a night-bird begins singing in the hedge trees, his notes as clear and ringing as those of the nightingale.

I have been talking to my Messenger (called Itodu—"porcupine") for a part of most evenings. He is sharp and intelligent, though also, I fancy, a rascal deeply immersed in local graft; in fact the most intelligent Messenger I have had anywhere. He speaks Hausa, Igala, English, and Ibo, as well as Idoma. He is particularly interesting on the past and on the inception of our rule among his people. He first saw a white man about twenty years ago when his father brought him with a party of Idoma bushmen to Okwoga to sell yams to the soldiers (or Government police?) that were stationed here then. Three years later, that is about seventeen years ago, he got a job as a "small boy" to the Medical Officer in Okwoga Station—he says that there were six or seven Europeans here then—and after some years he was promoted to be a cook. (I can't imagine him as a cook. Abaivo, my old Munchi Messenger at Katsina Ala, said he was once a Missionary's cook, something even harder to imagine.) Then, after the war, Captain McCleod (who spent many years among the Idoma and who died in Zaria three years ago) had him appointed as one of the Government Messengers. Speaking of the Idoma head-hunting cult he says that there is scarcely an Idoma living of his age who has not killed a human being. Since every youth before he was eligible for marriage must get his skull no opportunity was missed of killing Hausa and Igala peddlers (there was a mild boom in native rubber after the war and most of the trading in it was done by Hausawa and Igalas). He says that one afternoon, he thinks about eleven or twelve years ago, he was sent off from Okwoga with a despatch of some sort to Igumale (about twenty miles south-east), and in the course of the journey he saw three corpses of men killed on that or the previous day, their heads and possessions both removed.

Within the kindred itself (tribes are generally divided into clans which are subdivided into families) a number of personal relationship tangles could be and normally were settled by killing (e.g. blood debts, unacquitted adultery, etc.), while war between different clans was carried on without limits. Add to this the fact that there were no real Chiefs and that the Elders had little power, nothing but the wild authority of the folk-moots where you would get an odd mixture of individualism and mob rule; and on the boundaries of the tribe was, on all four sides, the pressure, ever tightening, of the great Munchi, Ibo, and Igala tribes. The Idoma seems to have lived in something very near to the state of Nature written of by the philosopher Hobbes. Had our rule been established even only a generation later it is probable that the tribe would have been overwhelmed by (and ultimately absorbed into) the Munchi and Ibo tribes.

The District Chief (the D.H. of Okwoga) is a sorry creature. Takes no interest in what is going on: sits and scratches himself and yawns like an animal. I rated him yesterday when, during a meeting of the Native Court, he got up and urinated four or five yards away. He seems enervated: like most of the Idoma Elders he is an alcoholic and smokes continuously, and as he has many wives (Itodu, admittedly a prejudiced witness, says twenty-seven) he is probably also stupefied with excessive concupiscence. In two days alone here I have had to deal with seventeen appeals against decisions of the Native Court. I have told the Native Court members that in all cases where one of them is a relation of a party to a suit he must withdraw from the Court and leave the decision wholly to the other members. This follows on the discovery of a case where the District Chief (who is the President of the Court) used his influence in the interest of a relative. Given the prevailing mentality it is not likely that they will observe what I have told them—litigants themselves would be the most surprised if they did: favouritism and nepotism are recognized as a family obligation. A far more important cause of the weakness of this and other primitive Native Courts is its lack of force: the Munchi Courts and the Idoma Courts will both remain ineffective until they have sufficient Dogarai at their disposal for seeing that their verdicts are carried out.

*November 13th*

Trekked from Okwoga to Orukpa this morning, rather less than fifteen miles, I should think. Orukpa is a small District, and, unlike so many of these Districts in Idoma Division, not an artificial administrative unit set up by us without sufficient understanding of the relations of the various kindreds or clans that we lump together therein, but a homogeneous group. The Chief, too, gives one an excellent impression: he is a manly-looking fellow and is that rare bird among these people, the person who smiles and laughs. Most surprising of all, the collection of tax is finished!

This morning several of the porters fell when crossing an improvised bridge over a stream (it was dark at the time) and much of my crockery was broken. For the rest of this trek I shall have no cups.

*November 14th*

Pushed on from Orukpa H.Q. to Orukram H.Q. this morning. Again could not use my bicycle and had to walk all the way, but not (as yesterday) because of the streams but because of the sand. A road has been constructed from Orukpa to Orukram, but, I am told, has never been used. I don't see how it ever could be used. It is all sand. Before you reach Orukram you get on to a plateau some hundred feet above the surrounding country: there is a fair view; clumps (almost coppices) of magnificent forest trees; and cooler air.

Orukram is also a small District, but its Chief was "elected" as President of the all-Idoma *Ojira* in October. He seems sulky and surly as though he has a grievance. A crop of complainants, too, and among them the usual noisy, excited, belligerent group who want to get rid of their Village or Hamlet Head and put another in his place—a phenomenon confined to the Idoma as far as Northern Nigeria is concerned, I fancy. What a pack of cut-throats they look, too: bleary eyed, usually partly drunk, and all shouting at once. This is the fifth such deputation I have had in the last thirteen days. During the *Ojira* I saw the D.O. trying to deal with two opposing groups from some village or other: there was about a score on each side: he was completely ignored while the two groups fell into a war of words, yapping and snarling at each other like pie-curs. It looked as though it would become a war of blows at any minute.

The rest-house here is the first I have encountered in the three Divisions of the Benue Province in which I have served that makes use of a good site. It is elevated, open to the breeze, with a view, and stands in an acre of cleared ground. I wonder who is responsible.

*November 15th*

I trekked from Orukram to Otukpa this morning. There is a good road (motorable in the dry season) and the country, consisting mostly of clumps of forest trees and cleared ground (at this season generally covered with grass six to eight feet high—but there is none of the deadly bush) looks extremely fertile. Bananas seem to grow like weeds, and coconut palms everywhere.

Last night the Corporal (the African N.C.O) of the Police got drunk and quarrelled with three of his men. I was awakened by shouting in the Police quarters about midnight and went over and arrested him. As he is normally well behaved and a trier I shall not report him. I don't think there will be a recurrence. They are good lads these Police: well-disciplined, intelligent, and cheerful. But it is hard in a country of bibbers like the Idoma to keep some of them from an occasional indulgence: they get so bored.

There are twenty tax-collecting units with sixty-eight sub-units (several hamlets to each) in Otukpa District. The tax due this year is £487 12s. 6d. Not a penny paid in yet. This is one of those Idoma Districts where tax is paid only when the white man, accompanied by a squad of Police, assists at the functioning of Indirect Rule. I foresee some wearying days ahead in beginning the collecting campaign.

A pretty incident here this afternoon: after I dismissed the Chief and his men an altercation arose between him and a young man with a pitcher of palm wine. Apparently the Chief took a swill and did not want to pay for it. The young man then became Idomaish—abusive and threatening; a Dogari pushed him back; he struck the Dogari; then the Chief, although in his best ceremonial clothes, cast all dignity aside and went for the young man, belabouring him with the Staff of Office presented to Chiefs by the Government, a use quite unmentioned in Secretariat regulations.

*November 16th*

A disturbing day. The tax-gathering has opened. Before daybreak I went off with the Police, twenty of my porters, my Messenger, the District Head, his three Dogarai, and about a dozen of his followers, to Effugo, a hamlet about two to three miles from the rest-house and scattered over a stretch of forest. It had been arranged the previous afternoon that the Elders of Effugo, who are responsible for the collection of the tax there, and who had excused their not having collected a penny to date on the grounds of being persistently ignored by their men, should meet me. Not a man appeared except the Hamlet Head. He assured us that the rest would be there any minute. I waited half an hour, in the course of which one other appeared (the remainder, as it was later discovered, were busy hiding their goats, fowls, etc.). So action then began; and it continued for the next four or five hours. I left four of my porters and four of the District Head's men and also four Police (with orders to draw bayonets but not to use them) where we were, in the *Ojira* meeting-place, to look after whatever distrained property was brought to them. The rest of the party was divided into two: the District Head, together with the solitary Elder and eight of my porters and three of his own men and four Police, went in one direction, and myself with the Hamlet Head and the rest of the porters and Police went off in the other, to distrain all the movable property found up to the value of the tax due from every household. By about eleven we had collected as much as we could cope with—about eighty goats (their most valuable movable property), sixty fowls, yams, oil nuts, and odds and ends like cloth. The labour involved was formidable: many of the households werē deserted, or only the old women were left behind, the other occupants hiding in the forest or in clumps of banana palms (to look for them was as hopeless as looking for a needle in a haystack), and most of the livestock was concealed.

Again and again men running off with the family goats, or hiding with them, were tracked down; and again and again fowls were found "planted" beneath large earthen pots. The chasing and scurrying and shouting of absconding taxpayers and their lawful pursuers and the bleating of goats and moaning of fowls brought pandemonium to Effugo; but it was all kept within hand and also within the rules and regulations and the current theology of Indirect Rule.

A record was kept of every item distrained and from whom; and the distraining was done not by myself or the Government Police, but by the District Head as President of the local Native Court, or his lawful representative the Hamlet Head—an important issue according to the contemporary theory of Indirect Rule. In theory what happened was that every man whose property was taken had been proceeded against in the Native Court for tax default and goods to the value of his default were distrained. There were some blows of course, but not many and nothing serious. The worst mishap is that five or six of my men have trodden on short stakes driven in the ground hidden amidst the grass around some of the animal pens. They protest that the villagers put them in in anticipation of this visit and that they are poisoned; but though the latter is probable it is also probable that the stakes form a normal device against possible thieves. No huts, not even of those who had absconded with all their property, were burnt down (a sure means of dismissal from the Service), though how, given all the circumstances that prevail, the willing defaulters can be punished otherwise is not clear; nor did I resort to a method once recommended by an ingenious colleague—to have part of the walls of huts needing such treatment rammed in with a piece of wood. This is as efficacious as burning but can be covered in any subsequent discussion by explaining it as an accident when moving timber.

Having mustered men and animals, and being surrounded by a good crowd of villagers, I made them a short speech pointing out that they knew that their tax was overdue, that the sum necessary was easy for them to come by if they exerted themselves, and that unless the tax was paid beforehand all the property distrained would be sold to-morrow afternoon at an auction and the money would be used in discharging their tax obligation. Our procession, noisy but not unimpressive, of men and animals then moved off.

*November 17th*

This afternoon I auctioned (on behalf of the Otukpa Native Court—we continue to observe the formulas) such of the goats, fowls, yams, etc., as were not recovered by their owners; that is to say, about a half of what we distrained yesterday (the significance of which is that at least half of the defaulters had enough cash to pay their tax, but declined to do so until this stimulus was administered). The auction was an ordeal even worse than the distraining. The District Chief was caught twice trying to steal distrained goods; my Messenger, Itodu, who belongs to this District and who interpreted my Hausa into Idoma, was up to tricks in getting things sold to his relatives cheaply and was sulking because I refused to let him buy anything himself; the police were sulking for the same reason; the three agitated and bewildered Dogarai mixing up the different parcels and adding a confusion of their own to the general confusion; competing buyers shouting out their bids against one another; goats bleating and fowls screeching; and some of the ex-owners crying (one, when his goats were offered for sale, came into the ring and said that he was going to do "this"—"this" being conveyed by running his hand across his throat). Then, just before sunset, when I refused to accept the bid of the District Chief for a parcel of goats offering about half of their current value (his interest in the business all along has been the possibility of scooping up a series of bargains: its connection with the collection of tax-money has scarcely entered his head) he jumped up in a passion and left in the direction of his compound. I retrieved him. I let him off lightly—as it has been a trying day for him too: the hoped-for bargains have not materialized, and that matter of purloining the women's cloths and of having a grinding stone carried off to his compound privily was not only exposed but payment was exacted at a price that was not a bargain.

The prices realized averaged out at only a fraction below the current market price.

I was just leaving the scene of the auction and walking towards the rest-house when I heard the sounds of quarrelling proceeding from there. My own household was falling in with the spirit of the day. It turned out that the wife of my cook, a Nupe woman in full possession of the bellicose qualities of her race, and the wife of my first steward boy, a Hausa woman with a past and now rather frayed, were having one of their periodical fallings-out.

Tongue lashed tongue and shriek rose above shriek and at length the slappings began. The efforts of the two husbands to separate and pacify them were without result. This female quarrelling is about the most disgusting thing one can see or experience in the country: it is more revolting than can be conveyed on paper: something suggestive of animalism gone wrong.

I had them arrested by a couple of Government Police and sent them off to spend the night as prisoners with the quarter guard. That might sober them down a little, though from past experience I know it is impossible to frighten them.

Nor was that the end of the day. After dinner, while I was sitting outside in the moonlight, smoking, a tumult arose from the District Chief's compound, which is only a few yards away from the hedge around the rest-house. It sounded like a pack of pie-curs: I could hear voices raised against one another, women's as well as men's, and sticks at work, and cloth being torn. Another Idoma discussion was obviously in progress. I sent a couple of my men to run off and see what was happening; they returned calling for me to come. I hurried there with three of the Police who were on guard and found one of the four members of the Native Court clutching at the District Chief (whose gown was in tatters). The valuable Staff of Office was lying nearby on the ground, fortunately: I picked it up—and also put it to uses unmentioned in Secretariat Regulations. Peace being restored the causes for the incident were enquired into. What happened was that the District Chief's son had committed adultery with one of the Elder's wives, and ultimately they ran off together. The Elder was now on one of his periodic visits to the Chief for the bride-money that is thus due, and having once again received nothing but promises he threw formality aside.

*November 18th*

This morning I went to a village called Epiga, also about two or three miles from the rest-house. As the doings at Effugo have been a lesson to the villagers they did not run away or hide their things. Instead, when called for they all came. They brought some currency—all in pennies or halfpennies or tenths, as usual—in earnest of their good faith and asked for seven days' grace. As I am going off to-morrow, but will be back about a week hence, I agreed.

The Village Head of Epiga was dismissed at the instance of my predecessor last March because of his part in a theft of tax money. The village has been told several times that they should now elect another Head, and send him into Oturkpo for confirmation. They refused and still refuse to do this. They decline to have any Village Head except the expelled one. He in fact has been (and still is) collecting the tax! The best thing under these circumstances seems to be to give him another chance, which I shall recommend.

In the afternoon I attended a meeting of the Native Court. It was held in the open air under a tree. There are fourteen Native Court members, but only five were present this afternoon in addition to the District Head, their President. The proceedings were typically Idoma: disputants shouted recriminations at one another, drowning the voices of the Court. At one point there was a scuffle in which a Court Elder played gamely. The wonder is that such Courts ever accomplish anything; yet they do accomplish something and are valuable for their promise in the future.

*November 19th (Sunday)*

Set off from Oturkpo before daybreak in order to reach what is going to be Mile 27 on the new road, at a place where I arranged yesterday for my tent to be taken on ahead and pitched. A trek of about twelve miles, and as most of it was over sand we had to walk nearly all the way; it descends from the plateau.

I had again to reprimand my Messenger, Itodu, for his insolence and sulking when given an order uncongenial to him. As it was Sunday he did not want to trek to-day; he tried to dissuade me with various transparent pretexts. It was interesting over the trek this morning to notice the amount of deference he gets from the Idoma: the white man gets a surly stare, sometimes an *a ga ba*; Itodu is saluted with *Jachi* (*Zaki!* Lion!). He enjoys a certain influence, at the least. It is extremely unsatisfactory that a European official cannot commune with so difficult a people as the Idoma in their own tongue, instead of having to fall back on an interpreter: under the circumstances interpreters are bound to acquire an undue power. Itodu volunteered the information the other day that during his seventeen years' contact with Europeans he had so far worked with only one Government officer who knew the language. A few could say "Come," "Go," "Bring," etc., but only one could understand a complaint or follow a conversation. X——, for example, who has now been here for five or six years, has not learnt the language, no doubt for the reasons mentioned previously.

I have had my tent pitched on a hill which commands a good view. In order to give an open view I have had trees cut down.

*November 20th*

My motive in coming here was to spend a few days in seeing how the building of the road was getting on. The work is being done by contractors, each of whom contracts to do a length of a half mile, making the necessary banks, digging the necessary cuttings, etc., for a fixed sum plus supplements for various extra work, and he also contracts to pay such labour as he employs a certain wage (averaging about 4d. per day). There are fifteen such contractors, and another engaged in building culverts. The number of men working as labourers varies from day to day, but is now about seven hundred to eight hundred. When I came here all the contractors were Ibos or Yorubas, Southern Nigerian literates, typical products of a system which teaches men to read a little and to write less, and to speak pidgin English and to wear European clothes, and at the same time creates in them a spirit which makes working on the land or performing manual work contemptible. All are bearers of Biblical names—Joseph, Josiah, Caleb, Paul, and the rest—and all adding the Mr. to them, as "I am Mr. Josiah." Every Nigerian town of any size has its colony of them.

If Southern Nigeria produces them it can keep them is the policy I follow as far as it touches me. Hence all but four or five (who are decent responsible men) have been discharged (or will be as soon as their contracts are finished) and the contracts are being given or will be given to responsible Idomas who, I find, do the work just as well, more honestly, and with less strife between them and the labourers. The labourers are all local men who come to the work as a means of getting a little cash (for tax, it is hoped). Seven or eight contracts, which are not going to be renewed, are finished and await inspection prior to being paid off.

There is also an Overseer called Audu, whose job is to keep a general eye on the work and especially to see that no tricks are being played. He is an old man, a Hausa from Bauchi—was one of Lugard's original soldiers—and, Hausa-fashion, is full of good spirits, laughter, and chaff. His hair is nearly white, but when covered you would not take him to be more than forty or so, so unaged and youthful is his face and manner. He employs a Southerner as clerk (useful rather than necessary to him) who writes me delicious notes in pidgin-cum-dictionary English.

>                           At Miles 28,
>                               Okpokoro Station,
>                                   Oturkpo Section,
>                                       Nigeria.*
>
>                                   December 18, 1933.
>
> Dear Sir,
>
> I have the honour to write you this amiable epistle, which I deem it will meet you in a good Sanity. I sincerely beg your honour to say something Re— to one of the Chief of Okpokoro by named Oseke, said that he is willing to get half a mile for himself why simply because, the rest of the chiefs got the same when the road got to their towns, and at the same time, I beg to say, that the chief has promised to supply labourers to the whole contractors, and he has supplied labourers to the contractors that are herewith me at present. More particularly, I beg to say, that I told him I am unable to supply him, not untill the Sanction was accepted by your honour, Sir.
>
> Hope to hear from your honour very soon.
>
> Prolate my best greetings of the Winter Season to your honour and much to your workers.
>
> A merry Xmas and a happy New year to you Sir.
>
>                   I remains,
>                       Fraternally Servant,
>                           AUDU, Road Overseer.

>                           At Miles 29,
>                               Oturkpo Obolo Rd.,
>                                   Nigeria.
>
>                                   December 29, 1933.
>
> Dear Sir,
>
> I am fain to write you this courteous anagram, which I deem it will meet you in a good Attitude. I am sportive to say that the Chief of Obokoro has supplied the whole

---

\* These letters were written in the following month.

Contractors, from miles 29½ up to 35, his people as labourers to the Contractors.

I have the honour to be Sir,
                    Yrs Obedient Servant,
                            AUDU, Road Overseer.
                                P.W.D.

> At Miles 29,
>     Oturkpo Obolo Rd.
>         December 25, 1933.

Dear Sir,
    I have the mirth to write you this amiable anagram, which I reflect it will meet you in a good pose. Your anagram sent to me through Contractor Joseph Warri, were accurately penetrated. More particularly, Re to the tools your honour Ordered me to shear among the Contractors, I have done so with a great pleasure, and at the sametime, it remains the tools for the three Contractors that are coming after Xmas, in the stock. I beg to give my best wishes of the Winter Season to your honour and much to your workers.
    I am always at your Service.
            I remains,
                Yrs Obedient Servant,
                        AUDU, Road Overseer.

*November 21st*

Spent to-day in examining the road from the furthest point reached up to the last point examined on last visit. As expected the Ibo contractors have been playing tricks: pegs have been removed and then re-posted, but in such a way as to make the road narrower than the specified width; and instead of covering it with a five-inch depth of laterite gravel, as contracted for, they have covered it with two or three inches, etc. Four contracts accordingly have been condemned: no authorization for payment will be made until the specifications are fulfilled. The contractors' job, however, is no sinecure. The Idoma labourers turn up as and when they feel like it, and are not easy to command. I doubt whether a contractor living as he is out here, alone in the bush, would take the risk of trying to underpay them.

There were complaints, two or three score of them, hanging around my tent all day—both to-day and yesterday. It looks as though every man in the sub-District who has been unsuccessful in the Native Court during the last decade is coming here. Several cases went back ten years (and one to the childhood of an aged complainant—about bride-price too!) and all for trifles (trifles to us: not to them of course), like a debt of a goat or two due on a woman's bride-price. There were also the usual deputations in rebellion against their Village Head, notably a more than semi-drunken crew from a village called Eibida-Obukura. Also a deputation from the sub-District of Amajo asking that one of the four to five Dogarai attached to the District Chief (D.H. Okwoga) should be an Amajo man. Their spokesmen said that they felt it as a slight when a Dogari who was not an Amajo man was sent to arrest one of them! The District Head in fact had already complained that when the Native Court sent a Dogari to bring a man, either a witness or a defendant, from Amajo he was beaten off and driven away.

*November 22nd*

This morning I retraced part of the way I followed on Sunday and then struck across to a place called Obu. As there was a strong head wind blowing and a steady up-hill grade on to the plateau, and the track lay through stretches of sand, the twelve miles were slow and heavy going. But again much struck with the richness of the country, especially on the plateau: yams, guinea corn, maize, beans, benniseed, oil palms, and bananas were growing in abundance, and every here and there were stretches or clumps of magnificent deep forest. Obu itself is in the middle of such a clump—I skirted it for about three miles and then moved into it for about half a mile. Monkeys were chattering and leaping in the trees. The Obu villagers have, on their own initiative, built a rest-house, and quite a good one too. Their motives? A gesture against the present District Head of Otukpa. The Head of the strongest clan in Otukpa lives here and was the chief rival to the present D.H. before the appointment. They lose no opportunity of showing that they regard themselves as apart from the District Head.

The tax due from the village is £39. As the Elders had collected nearly half of the sum since my talk with them a week ago I decided not to distrain. They are to be given ten to fourteen days' grace, which will give them time to take palm oil or other saleable goods into Oturkpo, and so enable each defaulter to raise his half-crown.

Itodu, the Messenger, whose home is here, turned up drunk this evening. His legs, which are always stained with a reddish dye, were stained with a wild uncompromising scarlet.

*November 23rd*

Trekked from Obu to Otukpa H.Q. early this morning, doing tax work in two villages *en route*. This afternoon, without any warning, the District Head and I, and our respective contingents, proceeded to Effiom, a village about three miles away in the direction of the Southern Provinces border. The tax due from the village is £8. They have collected only 8s. since my last visit. So a distraining campaign. We managed to get hold of thirty-eight goats and fifty or so fowls and some odds and ends; many goats had been hidden in the dense undergrowth or in thickets of banana. On the way back to the rest-house a party of our contingent entered the next village, Effole, where so far not a penny has been collected, but there was not an animal or any movable of value to be found, and all the inhabitants except a few decrepits and some children had absconded.

*November 24th*

The goats and other property distrained yesterday were sold to-day. Significantly enough, everything was bought by its Effiom owners: they thus had enough currency to pay the tax. Effiom tax collection is now finished for 1933-4, but no doubt there will be the same pother for the 1934-5 season just as there has been for past seasons.

Also proceeded to Olai-ochogbahe, but every goat had been hidden (the Village Head swore great oaths that they own no goats in their village—the tax assessment lists, however, show that they own many) and nothing was left but a few fowls and yams. There were not six adult males in the whole village. It is clear now that these distraining raids cannot be usefully repeated in this neighbourhood for a while: every village is expecting one, and so prepares for it by concealing its property, an easy measure in a country of forest.

*November 27th*

The last three days have been spent in investigating a case where it is suspected that a young woman has been sold into slavery by her husband and parents. The woman in question disappeared, and her disappearance has not yet been accounted for. Her parents, a couple of months after her disappearance, reported the matter to the D.H. and alleged against her husband and the husband's brother that she had been sold. I have examined twenty-odd witnesses, some of the main ones again and again, and have used every tittle of whatever cunning and penetration I could muster. I believe that what happened was as follows: The marriage had been arranged in discharge of a debt (despite what is said to the contrary, a wife in Nigeria is normally a purchased chattel) when both husband and wife were children, and when the time came for her to become his wife he not only had no liking for her but considerable distaste. The woman in fact appears to have been an imbecile. His elder brother, and/or others, suggested a solution: why not sell her and use the money for paying the bride-price on a more suitable mate? It is true that her parents would learn of the arrangement, but they could easily be satisfied if a percentage of the price she realized were paid to them. Various discussions followed between the girl's family and the brothers, and also between these and the Village Head and Elders (the Village Head is certainly implicated). One can imagine these discussions: their leisureliness, their obliqueness, and at last the edging in of the essential points as though they were an afterthought, at the end of a couple of hours' generalities on the crops and weather and the like. Subsequently an Igala (living at Utonkon, and against whom a predecessor attempted to work up a case, but had to abandon it, on a similar charge) agreed to buy her and to take her into Ibo country and to sell her there. One night he arrived at the village; the woman was gagged; and he set off with her. As the village where this happened is in a rather out-of-the-way part, the matter could easily have escaped observation had not one of the parties revealed it. Apparently the brothers did not pay the parents anything (perhaps because the Igala paid them nothing), and they finally, in pique, went off to the D.H. and reported the case to him.

As I say, I believe that this is what happened. But it is impossible to work up a case which would fit the rigid requirements of the English Law of Evidence. The outstanding characteristic of the English Law of Evidence is, very properly, to give the prisoner the maximum benefit of the doubt and to cast the whole weight of establishing guilt, which must be unassailable, on the prosecution.

But in England you have a system of detectives and police whereby a man's movements can be traced from day to day, often from hour to hour. You have not them here. Again and again one has no doubt as to what has happened, but one dares not attempt to help the party wronged. There is thus a premium on the wrongdoer: the dice is often so heavily laden in his favour that only the bigger crimes or those committed in big settlements can be run down. An exception is in the Emirates and some of the Northern Pagan tribes. The difficulty becomes greater the more literate and litigious the population is, e.g. the Ibos. The confidence in being able to circumvent the effects of wrongdoing by use of a lawyer and his manipulation of technicalities is as unbounded as, socially, it is pernicious. The "professional liar"—the lawyer—enjoys implicit trust. Behind the trust is much of the primitive man's faith in supernatural processes: legal technicalities are fetishes or jujus.

*November 30th*

I am now back at Eke *en route* for Oturkpo (which I shall reach on December 2nd) inspecting the new road as I go, and also stimulating tax collection. As for the latter, it had been arranged some days back that all ten Village Heads of this sub-District (Edumoga Eke) should meet me this afternoon and report what they have done in tax collection. Only four of the ten appeared, and of these four only two had collected anything at all, and what they collected was only 8 per cent of what is due. Yet within the last month or so over £50—more than the tax due—has been paid out in cash to local men working on the road.

Eke is in deep forest, a clearing amidst the great trees. The path leading into it which I followed this morning had a series of shrines on either side, with offerings of food in them, and at the entry into the hamlet the trunk of a banana palm, newly cut, was laid and on it sacrificial blood had been sprinkled.

*December 5th*

I have been in Oturkpo for the last three days.

I discover that in the servants' quarters to the three two-storeyed P.W.D. bungalows here there are no latrines. The servants (counting wives and children they would average about ten to each bungalow) use the tall grass, which is everywhere fifty yards or so from the bungalows, as their latrines. A disgusting feature of the Station is that one never escapes the stench of human excrement: one sultry night it was so sickening that I had to sprinkle eucalyptus oil over the bed and mosquito net. It is not merely that the servants use the neighbouring grass as latrines, but the native town is also too near the European Station. The significance of all this is that sensibility tends to coarsen under the conditions of life here and men come to acquiesce in things which previously they would have believed themselves incapable of acquiescing in.

During the evenings the Station (all men) has met and talked, sitting out in the cool, swapping yarns.

*December 6th*

I left Oturkpo again to-day. I shall be out for only a couple of weeks, but I am sent back partly because various odds and ends have to be attended to on the road and partly because the results of my tax-collecting efforts are adjudged insufficient.

Yesterday and the previous day in Oturkpo I spent wholly in hearing complaints brought into Divisional H.Q. or in "reviewing" cases of prisoners tried by the Native Courts (who are always brought to the D.O. with the warrant committing them before they are actually convicted). The D.O. puts this formula (it is censure-proof) to every such prisoner: "Do you admit this charge?" The Idoma (for that matter any other African) who admits a charge is a rarity. If the charge is denied, it is the officer's job to investigate and to establish whether the accused did or did not commit the offence, an undertaking that is quite beyond achievement unless one has the witnesses concerned before one. These would take days to collect, and in any case the pressure of other work would prevent any such course as a regular thing. So if X—— (a good man warped by the lashing of several stupid and unjust censures) is not about, I venture to turn the formula from "Do you admit this charge?" into "Did you steal eight goats (the number mentioned in the warrant) or only five?" or "Did you actually beat this man with a hoe (the charge mentioned for aggravated assault), or did you merely hit him with a piece of wood?" Invariably the reply comes that only five and not eight goats were stolen, or there was merely a hitting with a piece of wood.

*December 8th*

I was lying down on my bed about 2.30 this afternoon, when a rabid dog entered the thatch and unwalled shed serving as a rest-house here. I did not know at first that it had rabies. It drank, quietly, some water in a bowl on the floor; and then I heard excited shoutings outside to the effect that it was rabid. It so happened that I had a loaded revolver, but it was on a table the other side of the dog. Seeing the animal coming towards the bed, I leapt up on to an overhanging beam (a possible and probable home for snakes) and shouted for the boys to come in with sticks and drive it out; which they did. I had two longish shots at it with my revolver, but missed: the crowds, standing and running about in all directions, made shooting dangerous. The dog was finally killed, but three people have been bitten. The local Chief tells me that there were four deaths here last year through rabid dogs.

Complained to the Chief of the condition of the rest-house. It lies in his compound, some of his huts being not three yards from it; no grass is cleared away and on one side it grows right up to the doorway; the refuse dump of the compound is a couple of yards from one end of it; pigs and fowls come in and out and grub or scratch at will; and there is an insupportable stench of human excreta from the grass around the compound. It is odd that such standards should have been tolerated here, for they would never be tolerated in the Emirates.

*December 10th (Sunday)*

A pleasant day on my hill-top at Mile 27. I was besieged with complainants all morning, but refused to listen to any this afternoon. To-day is Sunday. From four onwards I sat out on a long-chair in front of the tent enjoying the view of the surrounding hills and forest clumps, green and blue in the late afternoon and evening light.

The three Police on guard keep up an endless but cheerful chattering under their shelter; my own boys do the same in the shelter serving as a kitchen; and from below the hill, where the porters and the rest of the Police are camping, come animated sounds; and from nearby villages the restless patter of the drums.

*December 12th*

Back at Obu. The promises about collecting a reasonable amount of the outstanding tax not having been kept, I carried out a distraining campaign among the defaulters this morning and auctioned the distrained goods this afternoon. As a result only 15s. out of the £39 due remains unpaid. As always, the Chief is delighted to have this assistance. We have set these men up, often an exotic institution, and demand of them certain work, but we fail to give them the force necessary for doing the job. So we ourselves have to come in with our force.

I always make a point when distraining of leaving food supplies alone, or, if a few yams are carried off, of seeing that ample remains for food needs.

Just before sunset I was out for a stroll and saw on the path the sequel to an ant war. For the length of three or four cricket pitches there were ants dead or in the last stages of dying, black ones about half an inch long. The victors were rather bigger and their soldiers had jaws at least a third the size of their whole body, monstrous-looking creatures; their workers were now gathering up the corpses of the vanquished.

*December 15th*

At Otukpa District H.Q. When I left the District Head 2½ weeks ago I gave him a carefully mapped-out programme as to which places to go to, and when and how, for collecting tax. He hasn't done a tap—he has not budged from his compound. So three strenuous days of distraining. Of the £478 12s. 6d. due from Otukpa District rather more than £100 has now been collected.

Every rest-house in this Area, I notice, is infested with wasps, about two inches in length, building mud nests in which they insert both eggs and a worm (for the food of the former when hatched). At this one moment there are eleven in the room, all busy and buzzing about their occasions. When I bath a boy stands by flapping a towel in case of eventualities.

*December 16th*

Am spending the day at Obu *en route* for Oturkpo, whither I have to return. I like Obu. It is clean (as African villages go; many of the Idoma villages are clean) and well spaced and well drained. This afternoon, about 2.30, I heard an instrument being played which sounded not unlike a xylophone. As I had seen or heard nothing like it in Nigeria before, I went out to look at it. I found in a clearing in the trees not far from the rest-house two green boles of banana palms, freshly cut and about four or five feet in length, placed parallel to one another separated by about one foot. Across the boles were placed stems fastened somehow in position by leather thongs. When struck the stems emitted a clear musical note, the pitch being higher or lower according to the position of the stem. As there were six (I think six) different stems, there were six different notes. Three men played the instrument simultaneously and produced an effect not only of vivid rhythm, but also of melody and here and there of simple harmony. With the exception of the *Algeta* (Pan's Pipes) in the North, it is the most attractive native instrument I have heard. I fancy that it belongs to the forest country and would not be heard north of the Benue and Niger Rivers. One of the Police in my escort, who comes from the Cameroons, tells me that it is heard there. I recollect seeing something like it in Freetown (Sierra Leone) once.

At its sound men and women and children foregathered to the dance. I left them to the revels. When I reappeared, about five, a dance was in progress. About twenty women (young women) walked round a ring, slowly and then more quickly, and then went through certain motions with their bodies, the drummers beating out an accompaniment.

I have heard of improper dances before, but, excepting this and one performed by porters $2\frac{1}{2}$ years ago in Bornu, all when seen turned out to be dull. So was this dance after the first ten minutes. African dances (of which I have seen many, as I have made a point of seeing them) are monotonous to our tastes: the same simple (fairly simple) stereotyped rhythm or motions go on and on and on. Also they are without pattern or discipline: there is no real director, and people come and go haphazardly. The only dances that have not struck my taste as being both ugly and tedious are those of the little girls in Hausa country—they used to be a common sight in Kano on moonlit nights—where they clap hands and sing a chorus. African dancing is uninteresting to us (it is little more than wriggling the body in a simple rhythm) not because of its strangeness to us (it is not so strange: the connection between our modern dancing and African dancing is obvious), but because of its intrinsic ugliness. The truth of this seems to be suggested by the appeal that the better but far stranger Asiatic dancing makes to us. Anyone who has seen a Japanese Geisha, for example, would agree that African and such dancing is separated by unbridgeable gaps.

*December 20th*

Arrived back in Oturkpo this morning. J——, who was my D.O. in Abinsi Division, is here as our D.O. now. A grand fellow: generosity itself. Unfortunately, is rather a sick man at the present and has been grossly overworked. But in any case my days in Idoma are numbered: after the New Year I am being transferred up North to Bauchi.

*December 22nd*

I am up in Makurdi for three days, taking a language examination.

*December 26th*

Yesterday was Christmas. I was awake before sunrise, so after a drink of tea I got up and went for a walk of six miles in the cool. The rest of the day I spent quietly in the bungalow, declining J——'s invitation to have lunch with him but promising to come round to dinner in the evening. There were three of us there for dinner: J—— himself, a P.W.D. Engineer (recently arrived in order to build some bridges on the new road), and myself. A good evening. After dinner we sat outside in the moonlight, and when we had yarned for an hour or so J——, who has a passion for music, brought out his gramophone and played off and on until we left, about 2 a.m. Somehow the music, despite the manifest defects, seemed music at its best: perhaps because it was freed of the distracting associations of a concert or opera hall. At midnight some of J——'s boys lit a bonfire at a distance of about fifty yards from where we were sitting, sufficiently far away to spare us its heat while amusing us with its flames.

*December 30th*

An interesting case here at Oturkpo. On Christmas night, while we were at the D.O.'s house, the place occupied by the P.W.D. Engineer was broken into and various things were stolen. As a result of the searches that have been made some of the stolen property was found concealed in the hut of a Dogari serving as a warder at the Divisional prison; and from the investigations following on this discovery it transpires that the Sarkin Dogarai—i.e. the head of the Native Administration Police in the Division—having previously ascertained that we should all be at J——'s house for the evening, let out of prison an Ibo (serving a term for burglary) in order to go and burgle the Engineer's house. It further transpires that this is not the first occasion on which the head of the Dogarai had done this. In fact the Divisional prison under his direction appears to have been an organized crime centre. A few years ago there was a similar case in Ilorin, I hear; and no doubt others elsewhere. It shows how unceasing must be the vigilance of Administrative Officers if happenings of this kind are to be obviated, and how difficult, even with unceasing vigilance (the prison has been rigorously supervised here), it is to obviate them entirely.

Moreover, my relief has just arrived from England to find that his house has also been burgled. His camp equipment (bed, bath, etc.) had been stored in the house that he is to occupy. A jolly way of beginning a tour.

### *1934, January 5th*

My transfer to Bauchi Province having been decided on recently, I joined the northward train at Oturkpo on the evening of the 3rd, *en route* for Bauchi. All my porters and other protégés were at the station to see me off. Arrived at Kafanchan, the junction, about ten in the morning and got out there in order to catch the train for Jos, which, however, did not leave until about four the following morning. As the rest-house at Kafanchan was already occupied, I had to spend the whole of the day and night on the station platform. An old follower of mine happened to be there, Corporal Adamu of the Nigerian Police (I believe my commendations were mainly responsible for his getting his corporalship), who was sent down from Jos in connection with the investigations into the suicide a couple of days ago of a railway foreman. He helped me by getting water and wood, so that I managed to have tea to drink and baked beans to eat.

Fever came on during the night, probably partly as a consequence of the heat and fatigue. When I arrived at Jos, about 8 a.m. this morning, I could stand up only with difficulty, and was dizzy through high temperature. On getting out of the train, a clerk from the Station Magistrate's Office (one of the numerous duties of the Station Magistrate is to arrange for the meeting of officers arriving and for their accommodation in Jos), dressed in the height of African clerk dandyism, came up to me in a simpering way, and said: "Is your name Crocker?" I replied (faintly) that it was. He then said that the Station Magistrate had sent him to tell me that I was to go to the rest-house, where a room had been reserved for me. Assuming that he was sent to help me with my loads, as would have been usual (to get them off the train—never a simple business in Nigeria), and to show me where the rest-house was, I gave him the weighbill, which he took and then went off. Meantime the motor-lorry which was to take me to Bauchi turned up. On its arrival I sent for the Station Magistrate's clerk; having noticed him for the last ten minutes or so promenading up and down the platform, ogling women and shaking hands with others of the African clerk class, I concluded that he had attended to the unshipping of my things. On my asking him, however, he replied that the Station Magistrate sent him to tell me to go to the rest-house, and that seeing to the loads was not his work; and handing the weighbill to one of my servants, he then walked away. There was nothing for it now but to do it myself. As my servants were all Northerners, it was useless sending them: all clerks and subordinate officials in Nigeria, including Northern Nigeria, are Southerners, and in general not only do they not attend to what a Northerner (though a servant of an official) asks of them, but they go out of their way to humiliate him. First I went to the Stationmaster or his deputy (the Stationmaster himself was not on duty, I think). He said that he was too busy and that it was not his work to see to off-loading, but directed me to the clerk in the goods shed. Having arrived at the latter's office, I was told that he could do nothing until a clerk in another part of the station had seen the weighbill and had accounted for the off-loading. I then sought out this third clerk, and eventually found him in the middle of having his breakfast; he also attempted to excuse himself, but unsuccessfully this time. I threatened to telephone the Resident then and there, and that moved him. I went off with him. We could not find the van in which the loads had come. It had been shunted away from the platform and was now somewhere in the yard mixed up with many other similar-looking vans. When at length he found it, he had no key to unlock it and had to walk back to his office to find the keys. Eventually, after what seemed hours, the van was unlocked, the loads taken out and checked, labourers found for moving them, and everything placed on the lorry. Nor was this all. There are two rest-houses here. The clerk from the Station Magistrate's office had omitted to inform us of that, and had also omitted to inform the lorry driver (a newcomer to Jos) in which of the two accommodation had been reserved for me. After making what was pretty well a complete circular tour of the extensive town of Jos, the lorry driver at last delivered me to my destination. It is now midnight: the attack of fever is nearly over, and I have had some sleep. I leave for Bauchi first thing to-morrow morning, a run of eighty miles.

*January 6th*

The lorry driver turned up about three-quarters of an hour later than ordered. Also he came without a sufficient supply of oil and petrol or water, so that twenty minutes or so were further wasted at Allen's garage getting them. The driver and his assistant (there is no conceivable job in Nigeria, especially a job held by a Southerner of the clerk or mechanic type, which has not an assistant or assistants) were Ibos. All signs like "closed roads," "dangerous curves," "slippery descent," "narrow bridges" were, of course, entirely ignored; and, as usual with these gentry, whenever a group of women were passed the driver withdrew his attention from his driving in order to be free to stare at them with a minimum of distraction. At one stage he stopped in order to give a woman a ride, the manner of paying the fare being well understood; but I intervened with a veto. After a couple of hours on the road sounds of a struggle at the back of the lorry pulled us up, and I found my head servant, Mohammadu, assisted by his wife, pummelling the driver's assistant. The latter, it turned out, had attempted to relieve the monotony of the journey by interfering with Mohammadu's wife. And then fifteen miles from Bauchi the engine broke down temporarily! Instead of arriving at the Station at midday, and before the afternoon heat, as planned, we reached it about three in the afternoon.

*January 7th (Sunday)*

It is good to be in the Moslem country of the North again. There are many Pagans in Bauchi, but they are not of the Idoma kind, and moreover the rulers and the dominant races are Moslem and Fulani-cum-Hausa. The country of dark forests and dark looks is two hundred or three hundred miles to the South. Here and there are herds of cattle wandering from point to point in the charge of their tall, slender, handsome Fulani owners, and all the old familiar sights and sounds of the Moslem North: donkeys braying, and the cark! cark! of the *hankaka* (crow), and flocks of graceful white egrets, and the whistling note of the vulture, and flat-topped square-shaped buildings, and the mosques and prayer-calls and date-palms and Kuka-trees, and people who can smile and laugh. It is nearly two years since I left it, and I feel an odd exhilaration to be in it again. My boys are beside themselves with joy: they can now get their own food and enjoy their own customs and speak to men as brothers. Bauchi itself lies on a plain, surrounded with hills of odd shapes, and in the distance are views of ranges picturesque in formation and still more picturesque in their purplish-blue colouring. The native town is walled and sprawling (as is the way of the old Fulani strongholds) over a large area, the Emir's quarters being in the middle. The Station (i.e. European quarters) is about a mile and a half from the native town, and is well laid out over a park-like stretch. The houses stand far apart, and for bush houses are well built. The best place I have been posted to in Nigeria.

Went for a walk about sunrise this morning in the direction of, and beyond, where a 9-hole golf course has been laid out. Noticed two lots of antelope feeding quietly. The Resident has the reputation of being interested in Nigerian wild life and inspired with a proper sense of the desirability of preserving it.

In the Station, which fortunately is not a big one and is off the railway, and avoids that atmosphere of a Bexhill-on-Sea which the sophisticated Stations somehow contrive to fake up out here, there is the Resident, the District Officer in charge of the Emirate, an Assistant District Officer helping the latter in the Divisional Office, another Assistant District Officer now out on tour in the bush, and myself, and also another Assistant District Officer who is in charge of the Provincial Office—six Administrative Officers in all; there are also the Medical Officer, three Officers of the Education Department, and a P.W.D. foreman who is seconded to the Bauchi Native Administration workshops. And there are four or five wives in the Station, not necessarily or even normally an unmixed blessing.

## *January 10th*

I arrived at Zaranda this morning from Bauchi, a place about twenty-five miles away. I spent Monday and Tuesday reading up files and getting together and studying maps and generally preparing myself for the job of expediting the collection of tax in Lame District (one of the senior Districts in the Emirate) which has been handed over to me. It looks as though it is going to be hard work. Despite the fact that collection has now been going on for several months, less than a quarter of the tax is paid in. I suspect that the District has been over-assessed this year and that it will not be possible to collect it all; but I am looking forward to the tour very much. It will take me through rocky hill country lying on the broken side (not the escarpment side) of the Bauchi Plateau and among a hotchpotch of peoples—Fulani, Hausawa, Berri Berri, and various Pagan groups.

*January 11th*

Yesterday I was met at Zaranda by the District Head himself, a round, fat, tubby man a shade more light-hearted than the affairs of his District seemed to warrant; Zurebu, who will accompany me as the Emir's representative (the theory of Indirect Rule being that the Emirate is a quasi-sovereign state, and that Political Officers are the representatives of the British Administration which, broadly speaking, does nothing but advise the Emir, and then always through the recognized channels of the Emirate hierarchy, and in such a way as to preserve at least the form of the Emir's authority); a Government Messenger from the Bauchi Divisional Office; and three Dogarai, one mounted on horse, one mounted on a cycle, and one on foot, loaned by the N.A. In addition the District Head is accompanied by his four scribes and an entourage of servants and followers, some of whom will be mere hangers-on in search of prey. We are all mounted on horses—the land of the tsetse and the bicycle is miles to the south, happily.

The District of Lame is a large one—over 2,000 square miles in area and with a population of 35,000. It is cut up into twelve sub-Districts (*gunduma*) or "village areas," as the very unsuitable official term is. I spent to-day in investigating what had been done so far in the Zaranda sub-District. The Head of the sub-District and the fifteen Village Heads therein turned up. They are a poverty-stricken lot, clad in old tattered *rigas* (gowns) which would have been scorned by even a Gwari Village Head. A certain sum was set against each man's name which is to be brought to me—i.e. in theory, the District Head—in fourteen days' time. That gives them a definite objective; it also gives a chance to their villagers of selling whatever they will have to sell in order to raise their tax.

The *harmattan* was blowing to-day. Except for the last few days before leaving there was no *harmattan* south of the Benue, and there have been only slight signs of it since I came north; but it looks as though it is now setting in. The *harmattan* is a wind from the north-east, i.e. off the Sahara. It is dry, and while it lasts the nights are cool, sometimes even cold (they seem cold to people who are thin-blooded and recently suffering from the heat of the tropics), and it is also laden with a fine dust. Everything becomes covered with dust, and one can smell it in the bedding or in one's clothes. When the *harmattan* is thick it is not possible to see more than fifty yards, if that, away from one, and the air seems stale and slightly choking and one's membranes become irritated. People respond to it differently. Some like it, some dislike it. It is a matter of choosing between evils: you get cool nights (and how much that means!) and a freedom from clamminess; but you also get rhinitis and, at its worst, a sense of suffocation. It varies from year to year, both in the time it begins and ends, and in its intensity. When I was in Bornu it began in the middle of October, which is exceptionally early; it usually begins early in December or late November and lasts until March; but in some years it is shorter, and occasionally there is none at all. The dust is said to have a fertilizing effect: the natives say that the crops are better after a heavy *harmattan*. The wind is usually gentle, sometimes scarcely perceptible; but the current is always from the same direction—the Sahara and Europe under winter. The dust is carried hundreds of miles; I believe it goes as far as the sea.

*January 14th (Sunday)*

On Friday morning I trekked from Zaranda to Nabordo, on Saturday from Nabordo to Jauru, and this afternoon from Jauru to Guka. When at Jauru on Saturday, I was awakened about midnight by the sound of a motor pulling into the rest-house compound. I got up and found that it was a trader from Jos, who had run the eighty or so miles after dinner and was proposing to spend the night at Jauru and to shoot the next day. I was not very pleased at being disturbed: strictly speaking, the road is closed and he should not have come at all. As an official I was entitled to keep the rest-house, which consists of a single room, for myself and to tell him to make other arrangements; but that would be a degree of inhospitality fortunately rarely perpetrated out here. I therefore asked him to come in and share the room I was sleeping in. He got up before sunrise and went off for his shooting, saying that he would be back for breakfast late in the morning. He got back sometime before midday. I gave him breakfast-lunch. Just after we had finished the meal his men arrived with what he had shot. They brought in three beef: one was male, and, to my discomfort, the other two were females, in the shooting of which he had committed, as he well knew, an offence. The Resident, to his credit, takes a stiff view of these game offences. But whatever might have been the correct attitude for me to take, I somehow was not prepared to be official after giving him hospitality: all I did was to indicate my disapproval and then to leave him.

At Jauru there are the ruins of an old walled town covering an area of about one mile square. The site has now been entirely abandoned and the new Jauru is an untidy village, much smaller in population than what must have been the population of the old town. The local Head says that they abandoned it about a decade ago on account of continued sickness and premature deaths. This often happens, especially in the tsetse zones: after an epidemic, or after heavy mortalities from some endemic disease, the old town or village is abandoned and they move on to a new site.

The ride this afternoon from Jauru to Guka was through wild uninhabited bush, the haunt (like much of Lame District) of much and various game (X——, the huntsman, told me on his arrival last night that he had seen a lion cub a mile or so back on the road). Guka itself, situated in a basin of high rocky hills, is exceedingly picturesque, quite as picturesque as Abuja, the best standard of comparison in Nigeria. I was much struck with the way the trees managed to grow high up on the boulder surface of some of the hill rocks (inselberge): it is as though one saw trees growing on a cement wall. In the late afternoon I sat out on a long-chair and enjoyed the sunset and the scene—and thought thanks for being out of those hemming pestilential forests and bush and swamps of the South.

*January 18th*

On Monday morning, the 15th, I rode the short span between Guka and Lame town, the H.Q. of the District. As the H.Q. of the District it is also the seat of one of the four Alkali's Courts of the District, and there is a Government school here (sixteen boys).

It is, further, the H.Q. of a sub-District, the Head of which is a son of the District Head. A mile or so from the town I was met by the various dignitaries and the usual concourse that meets a Political Officer on tour when nearing a town in the Emirates.

I have spent the last four days in examining the tax situation in the town and sub-District, in inspecting the records and doings of the Alkali's Court, and in meeting and making the usual conventional admonishments to the local Village Heads. I have finished my programme here for the time being and shall leave to-morrow afternoon.

The town is untidy and dilapidated: not at all like the seat of an important District Head in an Emirate. The houses are seldom built of mud, instead mere thatch huts, and in either case in poor repair. Compounds are surrounded with zana mat hedges which are generally broken and crumbling. Very surprising too is the fact that there is no market here: not far from the school there are a few small sheds used as market stalls by a handful of sorry-looking fellows. Nothing of the usual hum and vitality of the Northern market. Moreover, in the country adjacent to the town walls only a small area—small relative to the size of the town and to what is usually found around such towns—is cultivated. It is clear that not enough grain is grown locally for its needs. The population comprises 220 adult males, 198 adult females, 72 male children, and 67 female children, according to the tax lists; but there are quite a number not on the lists.

The tax situation illustrates the nature of the community. The tax due from the town is about £68. Only £4 has so far been collected! In the rest of the sub-District the tax due is about £290, of which over half has been collected by the twenty-one unpaid Hamlet Heads who are responsible for its collection (incidentally far the biggest proportion collected so far in the whole District). The significance of all this is that here we have a fairly characteristic African phenomenon and still more characteristic Emirate phenomenon (unless checked): Lame town is just a sink of idlers, wastrels, and hangers-on, all unproductive and all parasitic. According to the information collected, about half the households do not even grow their own food, and a disproportionate number claim to be servants or officials of the District Head (who is not vicious but lazy and self-indulgent and prone to the flattery and servilities of the adventurers) or his son the sub-District Head or so-called (officially)

"Village Head," a youth of no character and manifestly with few thoughts beyond those of "enjoying" his office.

In the mornings about sunrise I have taken my gun and walked out in the country surrounding the rest-house. Very pleasant—inselbergs here and there rise out of the plain on which Lame town is situated, and further back a rim of hills all round the horizon. On the inselberg behind the rest-house, about one-third of a mile away, there is a colony of baboons. They live in caves, and sit out sunning themselves on the rocks, every now and then barking their sharp deep calls.

When out walking late the other afternoon my attention was struck with the sight of what appeared to be a huge bird striding behind a clump of bushes. After looking closely for a couple of minutes and walking towards it, I saw that it was a man. He was bent almost double and held in his right hand the preserved neck and head of some big bird (I couldn't identify it). He thus simulated the movements of a big bird and so frightened a flock of guinea-fowl, not sufficiently to put them to flight, but sufficiently to make them keep edging away from the monster until at length they edged into a tangle of string which trapped and held the unlucky ones. An ingenious method. Effective too: the hunter had already caught three.

Yesterday was "Sala" day, i.e. the main Moslem holiday following the termination of the month of *Ramaddan*. For the last month these people, following the Mohammedan rite, have tasted neither water nor food between sunrise and sunset and have observed several lesser penances, an extremely severe test in this climate and when leading this life. Now, in reaction, comes the joy-making. After a sort of "State" service at the Mosque calls are made upon the local big man (in this case the District Head), and he and a concourse then make a call upon the Administrative Officer if there is one about. At the seats of the Emirates the ceremony is impressive; at Kano, for example, it can be described as memorable. Here it is a little tedious. As part of the holiday, gifts are exchanged (one usually presents a sheep to one's servants), various games are played by the lads, and the girls dance; and everyone dresses in his or her best. The rigas of the "big" men are magnificent, and some of the girls make a comely sight. The African's taste in colour seems to me rather good in general—making allowances, of course, for the brightness which tends to offend our tastes but which is justified and even required by the colour of his skin. (His taste in smells, on the other hand—witness the scents that are used so copiously by the "big men"—is execrable.) In the afternoon yesterday the District Head arrived at the rest-house with his entourage and a troupe of *Sala* entertainers—a woman and two men. The entertainment consisted of a little dancing but mostly of singing accompanied by a little action. The woman (the leader) composed "poems" about someone present and sang out the words in a reedy falsetto, the men keeping up a more or less rhythmical movement and acting as a chorus. The necessary prelude to any "poem" was a gift from the person about whom it was composed. Thus the District Head would send over a servant with sixpence, and she would then sing out to the effect "Behold our great Chief! What a noble ruler is he! And how handsome!" etc.; comparisons would then be made between him and various of the larger fauna, to their disadvantage; his horsemanship would be extolled, and some trifle or other would be thrown in referring to certain recent topical happenings (e.g. his horse tripped and broke a leg). All this would elicit rapt attention and enthusiastic applause from the audience, and the entertainment would go on for so long as the necessary money was forthcoming.

*January 19th*

A longish trek this morning from Lame to a place called Nassarawa (a common place-name in Hausaland). Left before sunrise and passed through hilly, rough, and sparsely populated country, but again uncommonly picturesque. On the right hand (the north) the path skirted a reserve of the Forestry Department which is several hundred square miles in area and quite uninhabited, but which abounds in wild game. The villagers complain of depredations by the elephants. There are said to be some giraffe and rhinoceros in the forest too, though I should have doubted the latter. Both are very rare in Nigeria and, I thought, practically confined to the eastern border. The rest-house here is well placed, and the surrounding view is interesting.

The nine Village Heads of the sub-District presented themselves and their tax books this afternoon. They have collected about a third of the £220 10s. due—better than the average. I discussed the situation in detail with them, sketched out a plan of campaign, and arranged a further meeting. Here, as in every other place visited, there are pleas of poverty and of the great difficulty of finding the money for tax. Not only have prices fallen greatly, but the harvest was a poor one. It looks as though they have been over-assessed.

*January 20th*

Trekked from Nassarawa to Sabon Gari, the Forest Reserve still on my right (to-day my right was the east, not north) and the country sparsely populated. Noticed many of those reddish-brown monkeys. At Sabon Gari I was met by the Head of the sub-District and his ten Village Heads. A little more than a quarter of the £222 due has been collected. I shall have to spend a couple of days here and in the neighbourhood. A letter has arrived from my D.O. urging me to more drastic action and to make examples.

Much struck with the change in appearance between these Village Heads here and those whom I have previously met in the District. These are genuine Hausawa, and more like those one meets in Kano. Their superiority in dress, in manners, and in appearance is outstanding. One of my visitors (Sarkin Zuna) is a quiet, dignified, handsome old man with the appearances of a benevolent character. How he and his kind in the North contrast with such people as the Idoma or the Ibos. What other elements have they in common than a dark skin?

The Gamji-tree: there is a tree in N. Nigeria, mostly in Hausaland, which grows either by rising from the base of another tree (e.g. the Boabab and the Locust-bean tree), or even from the branching point of the bole. It grows fifty feet or so in height and generally right around and right into its host as though it were part of it. Many of them in this neighbourhood.

*January 21st (Sunday)*

The day has been devoted to the painful business of conducting a house-to-house campaign in Sabon Gari and in assisting the Emirate authorities to distrain where advisable. There is no doubt that many here are if not unwilling at least unconcerned to pay their tax; but there is also no doubt that many are experiencing hardship in trying to acquire the necessary cash this year. Their condition is quite different from that of the Idoma.

*January 24th*

Back at Nassarawa. Spent the last two days in riding round the surrounding hamlets and in trying to find out precisely what the paying of the tax this year involves for the people. I rode alone, unaccompanied by Messengers or Dogarai or anyone, so as to get on as free and easy a footing with the villagers as possible. A pleasant friendly people, but not as intelligent as the Hausawa. Much of their poverty is due to themselves. They grow few "exchange" crops (e.g. cotton, tobacco, even few ground nuts); and, more surprising still, they keep few, if any, goats.* They managed to get along in this fashion in former days (pre-depression) because they could always sell their surplus guinea corn in the mining camps, and if, after doing that, they wanted any cash, they would send some of the young men to work on the mines for a few weeks. On account of the fall in the price of tin and the restrictions in production brought about by the Government's Tin Quota system, they have lost both the market for their surplus corn and the chance of earning cash at mine work.

As everywhere in Lame District there are numerous herds of cattle and the accompanying camps of their Fulani owners. There is such a camp across the small river which runs at the bottom of the rise on which the rest-house stands. I have gone along and had a chat with them the last two evenings. The head of the household is ill (it looks like pneumonia). Various others had ailments and asked for medicine. I gave them quinine and some other drugs.

*January 25th*

I trekked from Nassarawa to Zelau this morning through the wildest country I have yet struck out here. For a couple of miles I had to dismount and walk, so rocky and steep was the way up a gorge.

The usual tax work routine took up the day.

There is an Alkali's Court here, which functions well.

*January 27th*

Arrived at Badiko this morning. Had all the Village Heads of this sub-District up, and also the twenty Village Heads of the

* The goat is one of the most valuable agents in the economy of the Moslem peasant in Nigeria. The Nigerian goat skin makes some of the best leather in the world. "Moroccan leather" is said to have originated in N. Nigeria, whence it was transported by camel across the Sahara to the Mediterranean coast.

sub-District of Ribina. Only one-sixth of what is due has been collected in the former, and less than one-quarter in the latter. Badiko town, like Sabon Gari, is an old settlement of Kano Hausawa. The races of Lame District are extraordinarily mixed: there are Hausawa (mostly of Kano or Zaria extraction); Fulani (both nomad and settled); Berri Berri; a people called the Habe (here probably the "autochthones," the aboriginals); and several distinct tribes of Pagans, not to mention their sub-Divisions. Generally these various groups live by themselves in their own villages. Some of the Pagans still live in what to primitive man would be impregnable fastnesses on the hill-tops, and their women wear nothing but small aprons made of leaves or some other scanty cover before and behind. Though there has been some intermarriage, in general they all keep apart, Hausa marrying Hausa, Fulani Fulani, and so on, and such mingling of blood as there has been dates mostly from before our advent, thirty years or so ago. By taking and examining each main group separately one could reconstruct the main outlines of the history of Northern Nigeria in the last century or so, for this one small area, standing as it does at one of the old natural cross-roads of the migration of primitive man, shows deposits left by all.

The main movement in Northern Nigeria in recent historical times was the *Jihad* or Moslem Holy War, waged by the Fulani at about the same time as Napoleon, become Emperor of the French, was astride Europe. The Fulani, a slender, light-complexioned, non-negro race of presumed Near-Eastern origin, were electrified into a crusading zeal by a remarkable personality named Dan Fodio.\* Not only did he possess himself of the Sultanate of Sokoto, but his armies and emissaries acquired practically all Northern Nigeria excepting the territories of the Sheik of Bornu, pushing across the Niger as far down as the Yoruba country of Ilorin, 400 miles or so south of Sokoto, or to Kaffi (north of the Benue), about 500 miles south-east, or into Adamawa, about 600 miles to the south-east-east. For years subsequently the Fulani were like the Maráthas of eighteenth-century India. To this day the rulers of the Emirates are, with the single exception of Abuja, which was retained by the old Hausa family of the dispossessed Emirs of Zaria, and of Bornu, descendants of Dan Fodio's men. The only limit to their conquests seems to have been those natural conditions which formed a barrier to their horses—zones of bad tsetse or mountain fastnesses. The

\* See Arnett, *Rise of the Sokoto Fulani.*

burst of energy that threw a relatively small number of men from one end of the country to another, and kept them there, may be only a small ripple on the great stream of human history, but it is a remarkable and significant ripple.

Thus when Lord Lugard subjugated Northern Nigeria, 1900-3, the great bulk of the country had for about a century been living under the rule of the Fulani Emirs (who in turn owed common allegiance to the Sultan of Sokoto as the head of the Mussulmans) either as direct Moslem subjects, or as non-Moslem tributaries, or as recognized infidels against whom, in theory, perpetual holy war was levied and against whom, in practice, slave raids were conducted as often as convenient. Some of the Pagan tribes—especially a great tribe like the Munchi—suffered scarcely at all except for occasional sallies on their periphery, because horses could not be used against them. Others, especially certain tribes in Bauchi or Gombi Emirates, or the Gwari tribes near the Emirate of Kontagora, lived under the constant shadow of raids. The population in parts of the present Emirate of Kontagora, for example, was decimated.

The Fulani, however, were not inept at ruling;* and not only did we retain them and guarantee them in their religion and rule, but we often brought hitherto unconquered Pagan tribes within the cadre of their Emirates. This was perhaps unavoidable at the time, and on the whole it was a good arrangement for the Pagans. But Lugard left for the governorship of Hong Kong in 1906 when, after all, nothing much more than the foundations (though most admirable foundations) had been laid. He was succeeded by two men of different quality, and when he returned in 1912 his time and energy were taken up with amalgamating the two colonies of Northern and Southern Nigeria, under himself as Governor-General; and when that was consummated, in 1914, the World War broke out and queered the pitch pretty well until his retirement in 1919. His two next successors again were not of his quality. The plight of the Pagans thus became more or less overlooked, and the twist given to the theory and practice of Indirect Rule by a dreary series of second-rate Lieutenant-Governors—a theological formula to be discussed only by the hierarchs, a delphic mystery beyond the

---

* Lugard's very favourable testimony, possibly a shade too favourable, can be seen in his reports to Mr. J. Chamberlain, then at the Colonial Office. His impressions are worth comparing with those of Barth fifty years earlier.

understanding of all but a handful of oracular seniors (some of them had acquired the monopolist mentality of the Medicine Man)—turned it into a pro-Fulani and pro-Moslem creed of a fervour and a singleness unseen since Dan Fodio's days. The Pagans already within the cadre of Fulani rule were not discussed, while those like the Idoma which lived a separate life were regarded chiefly as penal settlements for officers who were out of favour.

The Governor is now heading a reaction in the opposite direction. He wants, or appears to want, not only to concentrate attention on the long-neglected independent Pagan tribes but also to resurrect and revivify the "traditional" ways of rule of the Pagan groups now incorporated within the Fulani and to detach them and make separate "Native Administrations" of them. Every such Pagan group is now being reported on, and its fate—whether to be separated and turned into an independent "Native Administration" —will then be decided in the Secretariat. The idea of giving attention to the long-neglected Pagans is sound; and the idea of administering them according to their own traditional institutions has something to be said for it; but if the movement is pushed too far, as seems possible, it will be mischievous. Some of the tribes have been so broken, and for so long, that they themselves no longer know those of their traditional institutions which it is now intended to revive. They have been living for a generation under their chief as a Village Head or as a District Head in an Emirate. Nor has this necessarily, or even generally, interfered with their intimate and local life: their religion and folk customs and local government are free, and the Fulani rule touches them lightly and more or less indirectly.

My D.O. (who is a Resident by status and draws the emoluments of a Resident, but is acting only as a D.O.) has just sent out the Secretariat questionnaire on Pagan tribes, which is now going the rounds and asks for particular action with regard to Lame District.

## January 28th (Sunday)

Rode from Badiko to Ririwai, leaving the District Head and various of my own entourage to tour Badiko sub-District. Much struck with the quantity of cotton passed *en route* that has perished or has not been worth picking. This morning alone I have seen several hundreds of acres. The local Chief informs me that throughout his sub-District (where more exchange crops are cultivated than in most of the Lame District) not only the cotton but also the sweet-potato crop failed practically in entirety, and the ground nuts amounted to about a fifth of what was expected, on account of the poor rains and the locusts. The guinea corn, their staple, will just suffice for their food until next harvest. It is possible that he is exaggerating the failures in order to excuse the slight proportion of tax due that has been collected; but there is no doubt as to the truth of the general crop failure. One has only to look round and see it. Nevertheless, there will have to be some action to-morrow: I have my orders. Bauchi Province was the last Province last year to finish its tax collection, and is reported to be furthest behind again this year. The Resident and D.O. are getting restive.

Ririwai town is Berri Berri. It is strange that their forefathers should have migrated all the way from Bornu and settled here. A stranger case is that of the town of Lafia Berri Berri in the Benue Province—a trek of at least three hundred and fifty miles from the Berri Berri frontier and through a variety of Pagan tribes.

*January 30th*

From Ririwai back to Zelau. On the way we passed a host of Pagans with spears and bows and dogs out on a hunting foray. This communal or semi-communal hunting is seriously wasteful of the game. A favourite dodge here is to resort to burning the grass or bush so as to "drive" the animals. In areas where communal or semi-communal hunting has been practised for some time the game is now nearly all gone, as in the Munchi country.

In the late afternoon I went out to a tin mine about four miles away to have an early dinner with the solitary manager, a vigorous Cornishman.

*January 31st*

Back at Nassarawa.

What a contrast there is between the vulture on the ground and the vulture in flight: such power and grace as it soars high in the empyrean, yet so mangy, shuffling, and dirty when scavenging for carrion on the ground.

*February 4th*

Back at Lame town. A mail from Bauchi waiting for me.

A Secretariat circular for the Administrative personnel has arrived. In it Residents are directed to send in the names of

Administrative Officers in their Province whom they recommend for posting to the Secretariat. The circular records that it is His Honour's opinion that only officers who are strongly recommended by their Residents as having ability above the average and a flair for office work should be employed in a Secretariat. A copy of this circular has been sent to each Administrative Officer in the Province; those who wish to be considered for posting to the Secretariat and who regard themselves as coming up to the standards desiderated are to apply to the Resident.*

*February 5th*

From Lame to Guka.
How restful and contenting to hear a horse at night-time champing his jaws over his provender. One of the best sounds in nature.

*February 6th*

Rose about 4 a.m., and after a cup of tea pushed off. It was pitch dark, but as we rode along we could hear the baboons barking on the steep inselberg to our left. At sunrise we passed a small bedraggled hamlet; but saw no sign of human habitation again until we reached our destination at Sum, two or three hours later. The trek lay through a wilderness of sterile bush country. Yet well stocked with a variety of game. The Village Head at Sum, a friendly Pagan, told us of a week's hunting visit paid by two W.A.F.F.s from Kano a few months back, when a lion as well as much antelope were bagged. They brought a gramophone with them, the first ever seen by the village. The old man and his villagers were still talking about the wonder: "You could hear a man's voice inside, and yet there was no man inside. It was a marvel," he said. Visits by Europeans are rare in this out-of-the-way place.

*February 8th*

At Kwambo. Another Hausa town; full of scallywags too; but Hausa scallywags who because they can still laugh, can be forgiven much. During the last few days I have been camping in native compounds, there being no rest-houses. I was watching

* All but two or three of the officers to whom it could refer in the Province applied. The Circular is No. 10259/544, Kaduna, January 19, 1934.

the *hankaka* (crows), here in great numbers, when sitting out having a drink around sunset this afternoon. I asked Umoru, my second steward boy, a bright lad, whether they ever ate them. "No," he said, "not we Moslems. The crow helped Allah once and since then crows are regarded as Moslems" (is this a version of Elijah and the ravens?). He then went on to add that among the crow's supernatural characteristics is this, that it never lays eggs. "Where do its young come from, then?" I asked. "They hatch eggs, but they never lay them. They steal the eggs of other birds and sit on them and so get their young."

"Do you mean to say that if a crow takes a sparrow's or a bustard's eggs and sits on them the hatch will be crows and not sparrows or bustards?"

"Certainly, Allah has caused it so."

Privily, a little later, I asked separately first the cook and then a Dogari and they all told the same story.

Likewise a snake-bite: the other day one of my porters was bitten by a snake. When I asked how he was getting on, his friends told me that he had been bleeding badly, but they had removed two of the snake's teeth from his leg the previous night and one that morning! They had been gouging the wound. What had they got hold of as the snake's teeth?

It is interesting because it bears out what for a long time I have been much struck with—the remarkable lack of observation in the African, even of the everyday things around him. Things they handle habitually or which form a part of their actual living—e.g. domestic animals or the ways of their food crops—they know to a detail; but, excepting the larger obvious things, the rest escapes them. This accounts for their surprising ignorance of Nature lore, a matter in which one would expect them to be learned.

This same slowness or dullness of perception is to be seen when one tells an African to bring to one some easily observable object lying close to his hand: he will look and look and at length blunder on it by mere process of trial and error. So, too, with noises, portentous noises, that elude them entirely.

It seems to suggest that primitive man as well as being deficient in power of deduction is also deficient in perception. Probably a large part of his ignorance of that section of the Universe lying around him, and his consequent resort to superstitions or to super-

H

natural rather than rational explanations of cause and effect, is due to sheer not-seeing.

All this might throw light on a bigger problem, viz. why is it that a human device or institution (e.g. certain medicines) can go on being used generation after generation when its effects are not merely inefficacious but sometimes even harmful?

In fairness to the African it should be recalled that naturalists like Richard Jeffreys and Hudson found striking examples of ignorance in English farm labourers as to elementary facts about birds or animals living in their neighbourhood.

*February 10th*

Back at Zaranda. My time is up. I have to go up to Jos for a few days and then back to Bauchi *en route* for Katagum Division. I am now writing the two necessary routine reports on my tour of Lame District. The first is general, dealing with the working of the administrative machine and the conditions, economic and other, of the District; the second deals with the real purpose of the trek, viz. to get in the tax for the year 1933-4.

When I arrived in the District nearly five weeks ago about a quarter only of the tax due had been collected. As the result of my tour another £700 has been brought in. The whole Emirate of Bauchi is very behindhand, and since it was last and lowest on the list for all Northern Nigeria last year the Secretariat is beginning to be pressing. The Resident and the D.O. are consequently becoming urgent for action which will expedite payment. The latter has been calling for arrests and prisoners who might serve as an example to tax defaulters, a call that I have resisted. The truth is that the administrative machine in Bauchi Emirate has been running creakily for some time, and it has been running creakily because the continuous oversight and encouragement and checking that are essential to the functioning of Indirect Rule has been lacking here for several years. The root of the trouble lies in the chaotic and capricious system, or rather lack of system, of postings. In 1931 the Emirate was for some time in charge of a second-tour Cadet, all of whose subordinates were Cadets newly arrived in the country! Since then it has been run mostly by an A.D.O. (it so happens a very competent A.D.O.) acting as D.O., also assisted by newcomers, and recently he has handed over to a man who has long been away in a Department in Lagos, and is not only out of touch with administrative details, but lives in a continuous panic fear of the Secretariat and its censures.

Hence, it emerges that Lame District is over-assessed. Since the fall in prices from 1930 to 1931 onwards the assessment has been reduced about 19 per cent, but prices have fallen, as the numerous statistics I have collected and summarized and sent in for the D.O. show, not less than 50 per cent and over a large field of commodities as much as from 60 per cent to 100 per cent or even more. Had the life of these people been affected by no more than such a steep slide in the price of their commodities, even the reduced tax represents a much heavier burden than before the slide in price. But their life has been affected by much more. In the first place the partial cessation of work on all the tin mines and the complete cessation on some, has deprived the Lame people of much of their former natural market for whatever surpluses they had to dispose of; further, it has deprived them of their former means of coming by such cash as they needed and could not otherwise acquire (by sending some of their men to work as labourers for a few weeks). In the second place there has been a local failure in the crops, a total or nearly total failure in some (cotton around Ririwai) and a marked insufficiency in others. For the vast majority of the people —I should say 90 odd per cent—there is no other way of obtaining currency needed for their tax this year than that of selling some of their corn, and to do that will mean selling a large amount of it (prices are already slumped), and it will also mean short rations for most and in some cases hunger. From hundreds of house-to-house visits throughout the whole District I am convinced of the reality of their absolute poverty: they have nothing but a few fowls, a handful of old ragged cloths, and just about enough corn to keep them going until next harvest. I do not believe the District can pay the full amount at which it is assessed—except by depriving the people of their food. It is the most highly assessed District in the Emirate, and the fruits of their simple economic system (revolving around the prosperity of tin mining) which once justified a high assessment no longer exist, because their economic system has been broken up by the crisis. And this year there is in addition the special fact of the local crop failure.

One effect of the extreme poverty that has come over the Lame people is that the bride-price for a virgin never reaches more than 10s. (it used to be £3 or upwards), and in many villages nothing at all is paid now. As the Head of Tama said, if they do not let them go for nothing there can be illicit relationships only and no marriage.

No officer has toured the District since last June—eight months ago and before the probable crop yields could be known. Consequently, the above facts, which should have been known before the tax season commenced so that appropriate modifications could be made, were not known.

Another notable fact is the frequency and degree of disparity in incidence from hamlet to hamlet. I have recorded dozens of such cases. Thus in Badiko town the incidence works out at 9s. 6d. per taxpayer (one hundred and twenty-four adult males to pay £58 3s.), that of the village of Dan Bako at 7s. 4d., and that of the sub-District in which both are situated at 7s. 8d. In the neighbouring sub-District of Ribina the incidence works out at 7s. per taxpayer. Within the sub-District of Ribina are discrepancies like this: the village of Tudun Wada, with forty-three adult males, pays £16 10s., while the village of Matani with two more adult males pays 20s. less.

I am therefore venturing to decline to do any wholesale arresting. I am sending in three or four men to Bauchi whom I have got the Alkali to convict because they do appear to have been slack, and their imprisonment might stimulate others who are not putting forth an effort; but I have seen that their sentence is only for a couple of weeks, and I send even them in with some misgiving.

*February 15th*

I have been up in Jos for a few days. As it is on a point on the plateau about four thousand feet above sea-level the nights have been cold. In fact the morning I arrived I was so cold from sitting in the lorry for several hours that M——, an old friend from Balliol days, who gave me breakfast, added brandy to some hot tea.

I have been living in the rest-house that used to be the old hospital. There is accommodation for six or eight couples, I should think. It is now full. All the other occupants, with one exception, are W.A.F.F.S. A camp or manœuvres of some kind is being held at Bukuru (nine miles away), and, also, promotion examinations in Jos itself: as a result the bulk of the entire W.A.F.F. Officer force seems to be about. The club is filled up with them in the evenings. Many of our defenders are better not looked at in a batch; they tend to a type with such faithfulness as to suggest that each had been poured into the one mould: the same moustaches, the same sartorial preoccupations, the same manner, and above all the same air of vacuity. It comes as a shock to see one with a newspaper in his hand: it somehow never occurs to you that they can read.

Last night I did not get back to the rest-house from a dinner party until after midnight. I was just getting off to sleep when a pack of W.A.F.F.s arrived from the club. First the gramophone was turned on, then their boys were shouted for (as they were naturally asleep a good deal of shouting was required, though not more than the W.A.F.F.s were capable of), and dinner was ordered. After 3 a.m., when the meal had begun, and in the middle of it, two more turned up. The gramophone kept up its crooning and jingle all the time, of course. At something after five I gave it up and left the bed.

Of course not all the W.A.F.F. are like this. Some of the best men I have met out here have been among them. Cameron, who trekked across the Sahara, one of the most gallant and least advertised ventures of recent times, was a W.A.F.F.

One of their major problems is that they have not enough to do. In fact, how exactly they all spend their time defeats Political Officers. Why have them? The West African Frontier Force in Nigeria costs the Government over £300,000 a year. It cannot be denied that they are expensive. Subalterns begin on £600 or so per annum (unless they have not been in a regiment for six years, I think), and they have allowances in addition. The time served out here by the N.C.O.s is for some unexplained reason treated as double (if a man is out here for five years it is regarded as ten years in computing his pension). Probably there is some arrangement between the War Office and the Colonial Office, otherwise the Police, which is already really a militia, could do whatever the local army might do.

It is significant that while, owing to the depression, the outfit allowance of civil officials was reduced from £60 to nil, that of the W.A.F.F.s is reduced from £60 to £50.

*February 21st*

After breakfast this morning I left Bauchi in a motor-lorry for Azare, my new Station, about one hundred and forty miles to the north-east, and arrived there around 4.30 in the afternoon. Besides myself and the driver there were the driver's assistant and four of my servants, two of whom had wives, all packed in with the loads at the back. We stopped for twenty to thirty minutes on the way, partly in order to let all hands have something to eat and a rest, and partly to enable the driver to put in enough petrol, oil, and water to get us to Azare. As usual he did not do so, although he assured me he had, and less than a mile from our destination the petrol gave out, and—again as usual—the petrol being placed underneath the loads, the lorry had to be unloaded to get it, and then nearly half an hour was taken up with trying to get the vacuum tank to function again—all within sight of the Station!

On arrival there I went to the D.O.'s house and presented myself. The D.O. is an ex-soldier and with a handsome muscular military gait. He took me to the hut I am to occupy temporarily. There is no other house, not even a bush house, vacant, and I shall have to live here for two months until the other A.D.O. goes home on leave.

I had dinner with the D.O. to-night, but left him for bed almost immediately afterwards. These long journeys on ancient lorries are wearing: one is cramped up in the same position for hours on end and the being out in the sun (the glare is more wearing than the heat) for so long and without food or drink take it out of one. Also the *harmattan* was blowing strongly all day: the dust was choking and the wind eye-cutting.

*February 28th*

I have been in bed with malaria for the last three days. For the four days prior to that I was busy making myself familiar with the elementary facts of Katagum Division and its H.Q., Azare.

Besides the D.O. there is an A.D.O. (now two A.D.O.s—myself being here), a Medical Officer, an Engineer seconded to the Native Administration, and an Inspector of Works similarly seconded. The Engineer is here for only about half his time: we share him with the Bauchi Native Administration. The M.O. is married, but his wife leaves for England next boat. The Inspector's wife arrives from England some time next month. I have now seen enough of the people with whom I shall have to live—with some of them for nearly twelve months (when I am due to go on leave, assuming I'm not moved again)—to form an idea of what the ordeal is going to be like. The supreme strain for all in life out here is the being thrown together with a group with which and in which you not only have to live for a long time, exclusively and separated more or less wholly from outside contacts, but with which and in which you have to live an intensive social life. You cannot escape one another. Such an existence would impose the severest psychological strain on a group who were all friends and of similar social and cultural interests, even in a *milieu* where the climate was tolerable and food was normal. Here the climate makes neurasthenics (more or less) of all but a few, and the food, conjoined with more or less endemic malaria, wrings out our vitality. Under such conditions let the accident of official postings throw half a dozen people together of different antecedents and tastes and interests and the stage is set for strife. The remarkable thing, however, is not that animosities should occasionally break out but that people manage to keep them down and live so long in peace. A high tribute is due to the people out here for their good sense and self-restraint in this respect. This is the thirteenth Station I have served in and I know of only one case where the animosities took an uncivilized form among the men. In general, where there are men alone they will manage to make the difficult arrangement work in some fashion or other. Fortunately there is no evidence of dangers here: the D.O. has a strength of character and a sensibleness equal to his uncommon physical strength; the M.O. is sanity and cheerfulness themselves; and the A.D.O., Engineer, and Inspector are three sound men. Fortunately, too, all are free of that gregariousness which makes a man think that an evening in his own sole company is an intolerable penance.

The outlay of the Station, however, is another triumph of the urban mind. Although there were thousands of acres at the disposal of whoever in the past was responsible for its lay-out he yet contrived to make a slum in the bush, and at less than half a mile from the native town. The D.O.'s house is a palatial structure in the Kano Hausa style and stands in adequate (though not over-generous) grounds; but right in the front of it, and shutting out his view to the west, is the Divisional Office; and next to the Divisional Office are dumped down the houses of the two African clerks, and next to them, again, the Christian African cemetery; and two other sides are hemmed in with the A.D.O.'s and the Engineer's house. All can hear one another's musical instruments as easily as though they were living in an American flat. The hut I am living in (it is officially described as the Resident's rest-house) is built at the back of the D.O.'s house, practically adjoining his servants' compound and within a few yards of their latrines. Had the Station been built a quarter mile to the north it would have stood on a ridge with an open view and free to the breeze, and at the cost of not a penny more. As it is we lie in a heap at the bottom of a sand pan which, clearly, will be a swamp and mosquito reserve in the wet season. The giant of the past who did it all is probably now a governor.

One of the D.O.'s servants had a marriage a couple of days ago. When the bride was brought to the compound in the evening she was accompanied by the usual horde of people in search of free refreshment and by the professional musicians—two drummers, three guitar players ("molo"), and the praise-singers. They kept up their din until the moon sank, in the early hours of the morning —the same rat-tap-tap of the drums and strumming of the guitars, and the same refrain being sung over and over again; and they began again in the morning, keeping it up only until all the money for tips had been exhausted. As an exhibition of sheer physical endurance African merry-making is impressive: drummers will keep up a passionate percussion for hours, in fact all night.

The Division itself is interesting administratively as it consists of three separate Emirates, one, that of Katagum, being of some importance; the second, that of Misau, is smaller in area than the District of Lame (in the Emirate of Bauchi); and the third, that of Jama'ari, is a tiny little state smaller than most of the Village Areas in Lame District. The area of the Division amounts to 5,123 square miles while the total population is about 334,000.

These are distributed among the three Emirates in this way:

| Emirate of | Area, Square Miles | Population | Official Salary of Emir |
| --- | --- | --- | --- |
| Katagum | 4,064 | 234,000 | £1,300 |
| Misau | 910 | 85,400 | £750 |
| Jama'ari | 149 | 17,000 | £400 |

Contrast them with some of the big Emirates:

| Emirate of | Area, Square Miles | Population | Official Salary of Emir |
| --- | --- | --- | --- |
| Kano | 12,200 | 2,000,000 | £6,000 + £2,500 |
| Sokoto | 25,600 | 1,324,000 | £6,000 + £1,000 |
| Bornu | 33,160 | 715,000 | £6,000 + £1,000 |

The Division lies north-east of the Plateau and of the hill country. It forms part of that great stretch of sandy plain of the Central and Western Sudan which merges into the Sahara. There is only one hill in all its five thousand square miles, they tell me. It is a vast expanse of sand and laterite, often covered with stunted bush but sometimes open and park-like, with here and there a river course. At this time of the year, the height of the dry season, the country looks parched; but four months hence it will be green and fresh and productive.

The population is nearly all Fulani, but they have given up the nomad life and now cultivate the ground. There are a few Hausawa in the towns, and here and there are remains of the old pre-Fulani aboriginals, but the Fulani comprise about 90 per cent of the total population.

*March 1st*

Apropos of the haphazard way postings are managed out here: I see from the records in the Divisional Office that our previous subordinate clerk was transferred from here *four days* after returning from leave. Being a Southerner his leave was spent in the South, as would be known in the Secretariat, and yet he was allowed to come the nine hundred miles or so from Lagos to here, and was then, four days after his arrival, sent back more than half that journey. This little piece of blundering cost the Government a not insignificant sum in the transport of himself and family, not to mention the loss of time involved. Multiply the instance by what no doubt is the several score of such cases in a year and it will be seen that the absence of planned staff dispositions is expensive as well as being unsettling to those personally concerned.

*March 2nd*

This morning, about 7.30, the D.O. took me down in his car to look over the native town and the various organs of the Katagum Native Administration—the Treasury and Central Office, the prison, the workshops, the market, the animal clinic, and the hospital. At the prison he found that the scribe had not turned up although the appointment had been made, one of the many samples of slackness, disobedience, or incompetence which the scribe is said to show, and that the head-warder was continuing in irregularities that he had often been warned against; at the hospital he found a good deal of filth, including that the hedges surrounding the hospital grounds were being used as latrines and rubbish depots, despite the fact that two N.A. officials are paid to attend to the sanitation; and in the town he found comparable irregularities. The D.O. complained that while none of these was sensational the point was that for the last year or so he had noticed the unfitness of these (and other) functionaries and sought to have them dismissed, yet, being relatives or special protégés of the Emir, the latter had refused to take his advice.

Theoretically the D.O. could insist on the Emir's taking his advice, especially if he liked to push the matter right to the top, the bias at the top being now what it is. But had he insisted, or attempted to insist, at one time (and the Emir continued to resist) he would have been branded as non-"Indirect" and his career would have suffered. He would almost certainly have been removed from an Emirate, and have been given "easier work" in Kabba or some Pagan area.

This illustrates the unsound side of Indirect Rule as it tended to be interpreted and practised here until recently: the Emirate of Katagum existed, in effect, not for the benefit of its quarter million inhabitants, but for the family (a very large polygamous family) and the friends of an obsolete Moslem Chief.

I have been discussing with my boys what to us are superstitions. Thus many Nigerian tribes refuse to eat roan antelope on the ground that if you eat it you go mad, and, oddly enough, one of the P.W.D. Inspector's boys here recently ate some, against the warnings of his mates, and is now raving. . . . Various trees are the object of superstition. The *Roko*-tree is believed to contain evil spirits and must be avoided at night time. Some *Rokos* do actually make a noise: the *Roko* at Kuta (just below the Chief's house), in Niger Province, is known to all who have served in Kuta Division for its weird noises. To rest under a *Tsamiya* either in the middle of the day or in the dark is accounted dangerous. There is also a snake (called *gamshaka* in Hausa)—some of which are reputed to live in the Baobab-tree at the Kofar Galadima in Zaria—which does not bite, but if you see it you go mad.

*March 3rd*

By accident to-day I stumbled across a file containing the Governor's comments on the Annual Report of the Kano Province for the year 1931. I did a number of weeks devilling when in Kano for the writer and the writing of that document. The Governor's criticisms go, in my opinion, to the heart of the unsoundness of the old Indirect Rule policy here, especially in its spiritual home, Kano. Much was made in the Report of the degree and extent of the devolution of responsibility which had been carried out in the Emirate, the proof of the devolution being held to consist in the Emir's Council (composed of the Emir himself, the aged Waziri— the Vizier or a sort of Lord Chancellor—the Madaki, or senior Councillor, the Galadima—the Mayor of Kano City, and the Treasurer). It was surprising what praise had been claimed and given for this contribution which, in fact, was not new,* and also was an obvious unavoidable adaptation of a traditional institution. No single Emir ever did or ever could perform all the work of so large an Emirate. Nor is there an Emirate of any size in the country which has not some kind of Council *de facto* if not *de jure*. Yet when a certain "Fifteener" was promoted to a Residentship in 1931 he was sent to Kano for about a week to study this "devolution" prior to his taking charge of the Sultanate of Sokoto. The Governor in his comments on the Report says, in effect, that this is not devolution and that the real approach to the problem of delegating responsibility is through and to the village. That is as shrewd as it is sound and as it has been neglected out here. Unfortunately, however, in the spate of explanations and memoranda that the criticism produced the Governor virtually accedes to the Kano claim and drops the point about the villages.

And at the end of 1932, too, he promoted the D.O. who had spent practically all his career in Kano and was identified with all the wonders of that Province, to a full Residentship in a very short time.

*March 5th*

Our motor-lorry, which had been sent into Jos (our railhead, two hundred and twenty miles away) early last week, arrived to-day, three days late. Like nearly all the fraternity of African motor drivers the driver of this lorry is reputed to be completely unreliable and untrustworthy. He gives rides (in return for money, of course) contrary to explicit instructions, and overloads the lorry in doing so, thereby breaking springs, causing blow-outs, etc., and he overstays his time in the Vanity Fair of Jos. This time he had to make

* Barth, when in Kano eighty odd years ago, spoke of the Emir's Council. See Barth, Vol. 11, 145.

a clean breast of his misdeeds: While dallying along the primrose path in Jos he made the acquaintance of the wife of a policeman and when he left he took her with him. Providence intervened against the sinners, however, for on the road, when descending from the Plateau, the lorry crashed into a bank (he had omitted to have his brakes adjusted though he knew that they were needing adjustment) and the woman was injured fairly seriously. When he arrived at Bauchi he had to take her to the hospital; and it was while on the way thither that the Engineer (who is in Bauchi for a few days) ran into him and demanded an explanation of why he was in Bauchi at all. He has now had to confess all this again to the D.O. on his arrival this evening. The D.O. told him that he will probably have to have him arrested as if the woman dies the driver is probably liable by the terms of the Motor Ordinance (referring to unlicensed vehicles carrying passengers) to a charge of manslaughter! And in Jos the policeman, the injured husband, is waiting for him!

*March 6th*

The D.O. and I were in the town before breakfast this morning inspecting various of his building works that are going on, the chief of which is the new gate, a handsome *Arc triomphale*, in local design, over the main road leading to the centre of the town.

This evening, or rather late in the afternoon, when I was out walking on the Gadau road, the D.O. overtook me in his car and we motored to Gadau, eleven miles away. It is one of the District H.Q.s of the Katagum Emirate; also the Sleeping Sickness Investigation have their H.Q. out there. We did not visit the latter to-day, but looked at various things in the native town. The D.O. is very much the kind of Empire-builder who likes constructing roads and bridges and houses and so on, as keen as can be on it, and his plans and enthusiasms seem sound. The new Court House for the Alkali and the new lock-up are both excellent, as also a new type of rest-house which he designed and has had put up on the outskirts of the town. He has also had a splendid camp constructed for the numerous sleeping-sickness patients who foregather about here and has put order into what previously was chaos.

While inspecting the rest-house, which is nearly finished, I noticed that the two "painters" working on it were Southerners. The usual excuse brought forward in justifying these imports, that not sufficient of intelligent or competent local labour can be found, will not hold, because the work of "painting" could be done by an ape or a trained dog. It consists merely in smearing oil over the wall. It is a reflection on the quality of the past controllers of policy in the North that such a position, which is now nearly universal, has been permitted to arise. Ninety per cent (in some cases more) of all the Government artisans and motor drivers and clerks and railway servants and post-and-telegraph men employed throughout the Northern Provinces are foreigners from the unpopular South. Although the Northern Provinces comprise two-thirds of the area and more than a half of the population of Nigeria, and although any man who has had experience of both the Northern and Southern native would not hesitate for a moment in his general preference of the former over the latter, yet the effect of policy has been such that the Southern, and the least desirable of the Southern, races are getting a lien over the country because they have had opportunities for learning, along with pidgin English and the wearin' of the white man's clothes, various crafts. Hausawa and the other Northern people can be taught to be artisans and clerks as well as the coast negro.

*March 7th*

The M.O. has a good deal to contend with, as we saw when down at the hospital this morning. As head of the hospital he has Government stores (medical) to account for. Pilfering done by his staff is of course continuous, considerable, and irremediable. Certain commodities, notably soap, cathartics, medicine for gonorrhoea, etc., all of which are in great demand among the African, draw like a magnet. It is impossible wholly to check the usage of medical stores because to do so would mean that either every dose given to every one of his hundreds of patients must be measured minutely and recorded, or, otherwise, it must be given only when he himself is present. Which is not practicable. As an example of the length to which the thieving will go the Doctor told the story of how one day he was working in his dispensary and he handed to one of the nurses (nurses are nearly all, like the one in this story, Southerners and males) an ounce of brandy to take to a patient in a bad way. For some reason or other the Doctor stepped into an adjoining room and when doing so his gaze strayed through a window—to see the nurse gulping down the brandy.

At the moment he has on his hands the little scandal of the *Sala* loans. *Sala* is the Mohammedans' Christmas (only there are two Christmases—the "big" and the "little"), the season when he feasts and gives presents and dons his finery, and, in general, lives gloriously beyond his means. A necessity of his life at this season is to have ready money. Out of kindness, and in keeping with a common practice, the Doctor agreed to advance to all the staff their monthly salary in the middle (instead of at the end) of the month so that they would have the requisite cash in hand. The dispenser and all the "senior" or skilled or semi-skilled staff at the hospital are, as usual, Southerners, while all the menial work is done by Northerners. One of the "senior" staff acts as the manager for the Doctor. It transpired that this man (no doubt in league with the other Southerners) had represented to the non-"senior" staff, the Hausa labourers, that he was paying them their salaries as a loan made by himself, and consequently when at the end of the following month their salaries were paid out he collected interest from each man on the alleged loan. The truth leaked out because one man, greatly daring, refused to pay the interest, and when the "senior" threatened to have him dismissed he complained to the Doctor, who thereby ran down the whole story. (A common dodge of native foremen is to collect a portion of each labourer's wages on the ground that if this is not paid he will have the defaulter sacked. Try how you will you cannot wholly eradicate such irregularities. "Graft" and trickery are so deep-rooted in the African's character that he considers it a normal and natural process for anyone in any sort of power to make use of it: to "eat" it, as his expression goes.)

Part of my work at present is to supervise the repairs that are being made to Government buildings at this time of the year when new thatch and new walls are constructed in readiness for the wet season. There are three or four such houses occupied by the "senior" staff of the hospital. I notice that at each house the grinding and beating of the corn—the hardest domestic work in the African household—is done by a bevy of women patients (mostly venereal patients) from the hospital. It is probable, if not certain, that they have been told to do it, though if the women themselves were asked they would no doubt deny it stoutly, and would probably even add what they have already been told to say in the event of such questioning taking place, viz. that they were being paid for the work. So one sees a group of slender Fulani women working briskly in these compounds while the fat Southern negresses, the wives and concubines of the "seniors," loll in the sun.

*March 8th*

The four walls (once ten to twenty feet in height, though now mostly mounds seldom more than six to eight feet above the ground) of Azare are surrounded by four roads lined with rows of trees on either side. Under these, any day, and especially any afternoon, of the week you can see dozens of boys learning the Qur'an. Their passage is written out in big characters on a piece of paper or over a slate, and they sit on the ground poring over it, bending forwards and backwards, as though the motion helped the effort of mouthing it out.

It is pleasant to hear the piping voices of the smaller boys intoning the passage that the *Mallam* (Ulema = Doctor) has set them to memorize. As they are generally given different passages, and as each recites his own at the top of his voice, and, boylike, they cannot resist putting various yodelling and similar extraneous embellishments into the exercise, it is remarkable that they ever learn anything. It is to be feared that the birch is in frequent use.

There is among the Hausawa an undoubted enthusiasm for and respect of learning—as they understand learning—that is to say a memorizing, often no doubt an unintelligent memorizing, of the Qur'an. They make notable efforts to acquire it. The usual custom is for parents to send a son to a well-known *mallam* in whose house he is to live for a period, normally for a year or two. A small fee is paid and from time to time the recognized presents are given; moreover, the pupil works for the *mallam*, hoeing his farm, begging for him, and so on. A severe discipline is exacted. My second steward boy was a pupil in one of these schools, and, as such, having graduated, is entitled to the honorific of *mallam*. His parents sent him to a well-known *mallam* in Kano. After a few months in the *mallam*'s house there all the boys went off with him (the *mallam*) to Hadejia, over one hundred miles to the north-east. They stayed in Hadejia for six months, long enough to sow and reap crops on ground lent to them as an act of piety by the Emir of Hadejia. The whole party of twenty-seven then moved off to Kazaure, about the same distance to the west, where they stayed for five months. After that they returned to Kano, and as after three or four months longer he could do the required amount of reading and writing and reciting of the Scriptures he returned to his home. It was a hard life. They were beaten frequently; and, presumably because the venture was conceived of as a pilgrimage and an act of faith differentiating them from their less pious fellows, the *mallam* allowed them to eat only once a day, and permitted only a few hours sleep, forcing them to begin study before daylight and to carry on long after dark, and interdicting all merriment. The boys were afraid to laugh in the hearing of the old man.

There are several thousand of these schools in Northern Nigeria. The supreme merit of this kind of education is that, having undergone it, the boy does not regard himself as henceforth too good for the ordinary work and life of the village. No rupture is made in the indigenous culture. Of the scores of boys intoning their Qur'an around the walls of Azare at this moment, probably over 90 per cent will go back to live as ordinary farmers. The boys in the South who go to schools and learn to speak pidgin English and to read and write (after a fashion) regard themselves as above the life and work of the village: they go off and swell the number of that growing class of parasites which will soon form one of the major problems in the country. They are already a problem. Every town has its little colony of these Southern literates, the local crime centre. Of course, considered as education, the Qur'an schools leave much to be desired. But, then, what is education?

*La îlah ill' Allah! wa Mohammed rasûl Allah!* What religion has evolved a ritual more effective than the muezzin's call to prayer? Islam seems to belong not to the forests or the mountains, but to a landscape of sand and bare rocky hills and an open sky and a light without mistiness. Yet there are fifteen to twenty million Moslems in West China, many in Georgia, etc., and converts are rising in African forests. The Yoruba Moslem is devout enough.

### March 9th

Apropos of the question of the lack of Northern artisans and also of the former drift of Indirect Rule here: I see from a file that last year there was a vacancy for a pupil in the technical-cum-artisan courses that are conducted by the P.W.D. at Kafuna. It was suggested that the Emir of Katagum should send a man. But he refused, and no reason was given beyond that he was unwilling. His refusal was acquiesced in without comment.

On my return home this afternoon I found the cook and his wife fighting, the disgusting business being accompanied by the usual shouting and shrieking. As she is as big as he is small, he was being roughly handled. I stopped them immediately and tried to shame them. For all his cheerfulness the African is quarrelsome.

*March 10th*

The Annual Reports for 1933 of the other ten Provinces in Northern Nigeria are now coming our way on their circulatory rounds. In reading them one is struck again, as one has been struck in the past, with the universal tone of gratulation and complacency: "steady progress," "everything is excellent, considering," . . . and so on. Why cannot at least one of the eleven Residents have sufficient courage, truth, and originality to say that one of his Native Treasurers is incompetent and untrustworthy; or that this or that Native Administration is honeycombed with corruption and nepotism; or that the burden of tax on the peasantry in this or that area has just about touched breaking point this year. The Chief Commissioner, who does know the country and its people and their conditions with intimacy, must smile cynically and a little uneasily as he reads through the piles and piles of stereotyped whitewashing and window-dressing. . . . If the Reports were published, or in any way made accessible to the world outside the Service, there would be much to be said for such an attitude, for otherwise a watchful section of philanthropic opinion at home would be misled, and in its misunderstanding of the situation might cause a good deal of mischief (for even at the moment there is no denying that the native is better off in every way than has ever been his lot in the days prior to our coming). But for purely inter-Service and unpublished documents to be written thus seems indefensible; another step from reality.

*March 11th*

The D.O. has been away on tour since Friday and I am alone in the Station. Last night there was a drum band performing in Charo Charo, a village about half a mile from here, and, as the breeze was blowing from that direction and the jollification of a hearty kind, the ensuing din was tremendous. It lasted all night.

## March 12th

It is odd how the African, and more particularly the Hausa, tends to avoid being in front of you when speaking or being spoken to. Thus Messengers or servants, instead of placing themselves in your line of vision, sit or stand at the side or even as far back as they can get so that without turning your head to an uneasy degree you cannot see them. It is comparable to that silent padding walk some of them have.

Another Secretariat Memorandum, circulated for and on the Administrative Staff, has just arrived.* It is entitled *Anthropological Investigations*, and informs the Service in the North that some Administrative Officers are going to be set aside for anthropological investigations (this follows on the recent burst of enthusiasm for and discovery of the Pagans). His Honour regards proficiency in work of this nature as the surest road to accelerated promotion, and he invites applications from officers who desire to be considered in connection with it. In the last Memorandum dealing with these matters we were informed that it was His Honour's opinion that only officers having ability above the average should be employed in a Secretariat. At the moment there is also a premium on officers with legal qualifications. What of the plain Administrative Officer who actually administers? Is there anything left over for him—the linchpin of the whole system, the hard core of reality at the bottom of all the gingerbread?

Once again the effect of a Service Memorandum will be to encourage just those vices and to discourage just those qualities which make the Service what it is. The effect will be that all the careerists will do the requisite window-dressing by putting out an anthropological report, while the D.O. and the A.D.O. who are carrying on the Administration and decline to think out ways of producing a show of "ability above the average" or a report on Pagan tribes bearing out the thesis congenial to the present régime—in short the very men who bear the heat and the burden of the day—are ignored.

## March 15th

The *harmattan* is still blowing. It has lasted for an unusually long time this year. The air is so thick with dust that one cannot see further than twenty or thirty yards ahead sometimes. But the

* 13474/127 of March 2, 1934, Kaduna.

cool nights and less hot days are nevertheless beginning to disappear: yesterday the thermometer at the hospital went as high as 105; and to-day was just as hot.

While at the office this morning, about 7.45, I heard a shouting and holloaing, and on going out to see what it was about observed a fire in the direction of my house. It turned out to be my kitchen. By some miracle the house itself escaped.

*March 16th*

The Agricultural Department for the last few years has been pushing a policy of what it calls "Mixed Farming" (the term is a misnomer: what is meant is "animal husbandry"—the use of cattle in cultivating the land), and on the whole it is being supported by the Administration. The Agricultural Department has written numerous memoranda on the policy and the file thereon in any Divisional Office is a bulky one; yet it is doubtful whether they have really worked out the subject. Taking one of their recent memoranda, I see that they claim that by employing cattle for ploughing the land and by using cattle dung as manure, (1) the yield of any given piece of land will be increased two-fold, and (2) a farmer can cultivate about four times as much as he now cultivates with his own unaided body; that is to say, a total increase of 800 per cent in the farmer's income.* The real point in favour of considering some such scheme is that the farmer, if supplied with manure, might be able to cultivate the same piece of land over and over again and need not therefore resort to his present method of restoring soil fertility, by the wasteful and tree-destroying practice of "shifting cultivation" (though, *en passant*, I cannot recall ever seeing this point put forward by the Agricultural Department). But could the few oxen that a farmer would keep supply him with so much manure? It is doubtful. The main criticism of the policy, however, is that it is unmindful of the economic and social basis of native life; and, further, assuming its predictions to be correct, it has not worked out the necessary administrative and other preparations which would be required to cope with the immensely revolutionary effects of an eight-fold increase in the farmers' productivity. That the villager's productivity will be increased

* The Governor, as reported in the *W. African Review*, June 1934, goes even further: he says an income of 10s. can be increased to at least £10, i.e. 2,000 per cent!

four-fold, let alone eight-fold, by such means is extremely unlikely. It is unlikely, too, that there is four times as much profitably arable land available as is now under cultivation. And what is the use of increasing his productivity eight-fold? What can he do with the crops? He already has as much food as he wants, and sells such surplus as he has with difficulty.

In 1931 I was touring in Rano District (in the Emirate of Kano) where the Agricultural Department was running a much advertised "mixed farming" scheme and I was required to look into it, and there had an opportunity of comparing what was actually taking place with what the Agricultural Department represented to be taking place.

A few henchmen of the District Head had been compelled by him (he himself compelling them in order to placate the troublesome importunities of the Agricultural Officer) to accept the small bullock teams and ploughs. The whole business became ludicrous, and in fact was abandoned some time later, yet glowing and in effect quite misleading reports had been written on it from time to time.

The Mixed Farming policy illustrates the need of limiting and supervising the activities of technical departments, and especially those activities which might impinge upon the very basis of native social and economic life; but still more does it illustrate the practice in Nigeria of failing to think out fundamental policies and the effects of that failure. There should be a group of men available who can examine and check the claims put forward by technical experts— i.e. a real staff. The Mixed Farming controversy has now been going on for years, but it is still not decided upon definitively.

The present D.O. is opposed to the policy and to the suggestion of the Secretariat that the Native Administrations here should pay the salary (or part) of an Agricultural Officer to be seconded to them for the purpose of teaching the local natives Mixed Farming.

It is probable that there are certain local areas in Nigeria where the policy would be a boon, but it is quite improbable that it can have any real interest for Nigerian farming as a whole.

*March 16th*

I spent my entire working day to-day in going through, and checking, and then arranging for the payment of, the invoices sent to the Katagum Native Administration. These referred to a variety of goods bought—medical supplies for the hospital, cloth for the

Dogarai uniforms, spares for the motor lorries, equipment for the prison, cement and nails and screws, etc., for the workshops, petrol, and so on, and so on—and bought from a variety of places (about a dozen different firms and sometimes from three or more different branches of a single firm), to say nothing of goods ordered from England through the Crown Agents. I suppose the Katagum Native Administration alone would receive not less than a thousand invoices a year, probably more; and in this Divison there are two more Native Administrations besides the Katagum. Nominally and according to the theory of Indirect Rule the invoices represent transactions between the relevant trading firms and the Native Administration. Actually, however, everything is done by the Administrative Officer: he has to order the goods, check them when they arrive (a single order may take as long as two hours to check, though ordinarily of course much less), check the monthly statement from each firm when it arrives, prepare and remit the cheque for and from the N.A., and attend to the receipt.

And dealing with invoices is but a small proportion of the time that an Administrative Officer gives to purely clerical or mechanical work connected with these so-called autonomous N.A. Treasuries. In a Division like this probably about a third of the A.D.O.'s working day is on the average given to Treasury work, while in the large Emirates (e.g. Kano) an Administrative Officer (the A.D.O. Finance) spends all his time at it—and even then considerable leakages of money take place. D.O.s and Residents each in their sphere are also required to give much time to the N.A. Treasuries. There is the preparation of the N.A. estimates of Expenditure, and of Revenue; the writing out and supervising of the Vote Service Ledgers; at least once a month every entry in the Daily Cash Book and the Abstract Book must be checked (it takes a full day's work to do this for the Katagum N.A. alone; the investment of N.A. savings made abroad through the Crown Agent (e.g. in Ceylon or Kenya or Australian stock); fixed deposits in the local banks; the current account in the local banks; and so on. A remarkable thing is that this control—virtually full control—of N.A. money and accounting has never been subjected to auditing until 1932, when a certain case exposed the obvious possibilities of fraud (to the credit of the Service, be it said, possibilities rarely if ever taken advantage of).

To anyone with a knowledge of African mentality it is a foregone conclusion that, for the time being, non-corruption no less than ordinary competence necessitate a European control over N.A. Treasuries, so strict that at the best the autonomy must be the thinnest of façades. This, however, though a big point, is not the main point. The main point is that to ask these Beit-ul-Mal (what the N.A. Treasuries were called originally and are still called in the Moslem country) to run modern finances is as though one were to ask the modern Treasury of England to be run by the old checkerboard and notched-tally-stick methods of the Medieval Exchequer. In any case when they were established about twenty years ago the work they were called upon to do was very elementary and simple—receive taxes, pay over Government share, and hand out salaries. Now they handle thousands of pounds (the annual revenue of Kano is about £220,000 and of Bornu about £75,000), and run a complicated system of accounting with Vote Service Ledgers, revotes, vouchers, and the rest, handle numerous and intricate payments and receipts (take alone the remuneration of European seconded technical staff, with the labyrinthine system of allowances, passage money, contribution to pensions, etc.), etc. Mr. Temple, the man who was mainly responsible for the Beit-ul-Mal idea, is no longer alive. One wonders whether he would have suggested it had he been able to foresee later developments.

There seems to be a case for abolishing the Native Treasury system. The so-called financial autonomy is pure pretence (supplying, in passing, an interesting example of the way a formula will continue to be saluted when it has ceased to be either practised or practicable). Every item in N.A. expenditure and receipt is arranged and checked by Administrative Officers, and even all their efforts fail to prevent large irregularities, in even the most developed N.A.s, as at Kano.* I have asked several Residents and senior D.O.s what in their opinion is the value of retaining the N.A. Treasuries and the most they could think of, after critical discussion, was their educative value to the N.A. staff concerned. This seems a weak case, firstly because the number of N.A. staff concerned is a mere handful—in a fair-sized Emirate like Katagum there are only two men devoting all their time to it. Who else in the Emirate is educated by the Beit-ul-Mal? In my opinion a reform that is needed with some urgency is the abolition of the N.A. Treasuries and the handing

* A few months after the above was written the Treasurer in the Sultanate of Sokoto decamped into French territory, his defaults turning out, it is said, to be more than £2,000.

over of all the accounting and other treasury work to the Government Treasury. This would not be incompatible with allowing N.A.s a measure of financial autonomy (and no financial autonomy exists at present, despite the existence of the N.A. Treasuries): the mere handling of money and the mere book-keeping are not a necessary part of controlling the raising and the expending of money (after all the Government Treasury does not determine the receipt and expenditure of Government money: this is done by the Government in its estimates and budget). And it would release a number of Administrative Officers who are now spending all their time in petty book-keeping. (In addition to the A.D.O.s Finance in the larger Emirates there are three full-timers at Kaduna, one of whom is a senior D.O. on a thousand pounds a year doing work which at home would be done by a clerk on about a hundred and fifty), and would also release that half (or more) of the Administrative personnel in the Northern Provinces who now spend hours every week in the work.

Any such release from office work would be welcomed by all. I see from the Touring Returns that in the June Quarter of last year my colleague did only fifteen days' touring out of ninety-one days: seventy-six days were spent in Divisional H.Q., where he was kept by office work! The proportion should have been exactly reversed: instead of spending five-sixths of his time in Station the A.D.O. should have spent five-sixths on trek, getting down among the people, putting the hand of the Administration on their pulse, so to speak. All this paper work stands like a screen between the real people and their real rulers.

As an illustration of the ever-mounting barrage of paper, the following list of returns which have to be sent in by our Divisional Office—sixty odd!—may be quoted:

### WEEKLY

1. Locusts Report.
2. Hopper Destruction.

### MONTHLY

1. Accounts: Payment and Receipt Vouchers: Copy of Cash Book.
2. Cash Balance.
3. Mail Carrier's Sub-allocation.

4. Postal Agent's Account.
5. Small-Pox and Vaccinations.
6. Postal Statistics of Business.
7. Births and Deaths—One Copy to M.O. Azare.
8. Cattle Disease—One Copy to V.O.
9. Rainfall and Crop Prospects.
10. Cause Lists (Protectorate Court).
11. Departmental Fines.
12. Expenditure on Allocations.
13. Nickel Coinage.
14. Dispositions (18th of every Month).
15. Government Revenue and Expenditure.
16. Juvenile Offenders.

### QUARTERLY

1. Native Court Cases, Form 13.
2. Return of Touring.
3. Board of Survey on Treasury Chest.
4. Government Revenue Paid into Treasury.
5. Check on Native Treasuries.
6. Revenue and Expenditure N.T.S.
7. Forestry Expenditure.
8. N.A. Bank Deposits.
9. Lorry Traffic (Dry Season).
10. Transport and Transport Allowances.
11. N.B. Prisoners. Daily Average and Deaths, to be Rendered when Something Outstanding Occurs.

### HALF-YEARLY

1. Arrears of Revenue Returns (June 1 and December 1).
2. Arrears of Income Tax (August 1).
3. Advance Proposals, N.A. by August.
4. Half-yearly Reports.

### YEARLY

1. Annual Reports.
2. Statistics of Province, Form 7.
3. Protectorate Court Criminal Returns, Form 11.
4. Table of Sentences—Protectorate Courts, Form 12.

5. Native Court Cases, Form 13.
6. Prison Statistics, Form 15.
7. Return of Freed Slaves, Form 16.
8. Return of Touring (in Triplicate), Form 17.
10. Capital Sentences.
11. Livestock Return.
12. Statement Showing Emirates, etc., and Area in Square Miles per N.C.
13. Arms Registered in N.P.
14. Board of Survey on Government Furniture (December 31).
15. Population, Area in Square Miles.
16. Roads—Annual Report on.
17. Mohammedan Schools—Annual Return of.
18. Statistics of Juvenile Offenders (to go with Provincial Annual Report).
19. Counterfoil Books—Return of (end of Financial Year).
20. Employment of Army Officers in Time of War—Conf.
21. Return of Graves.
22. Return of C. of O.s and Temp. Occupancy Granted by Residents.
23. Taxation Statistics.
24. Return of Juvenile Offenders in Protectorate Court.

### DUE 31ST MARCH

1. Direct Taxes (after Taxes completed).
2. Assessment Register, Form 1.
3. Revenue for the Year, Form 8.
4. Native Treasury Accounts (Estimates).

### DUE FEBRUARY

1. Return of Floggings by Native Courts.
2. Slave Traffic in Cameroons.

### DUE AUGUST

Typewriters, Report on.

*March 17th*

There has been some correspondence between the D.O. and the Resident about the N.A. Estimates of Expenditure for 1934-5. The

D.O. (who has a number of what in my opinion are very sound general principles, and not a little of the Scot's dialectical talent) is all for breaking up the tendency, now deeply entrenched, of spending the bulk of N.A. revenue at or near H.Q. Much of it admittedly has to be spent there because there are centralized the prison, the Emir's office and scribes, the Treasury, the Central Emirate Court, and other institutions serving the whole Emirate.

But how much does old Audu out in the bush see for his money? Of course he, with the rest, has enjoyed the freedom from slave-raiding and war and the more anti-social caprices of his former rulers that our régime has brought to the country; but that has been the minimum, and, it might almost be said, a negative effect of our coming. It is not much to ask that, having suppressed slave-raiding and the grosser interferences with personal freedom, we should spend the tax money in a more equitable fashion. Kano (which is always the *locus classicus* of our good works, but still more of our lack of imagination, our deficiencies in Administration, our over-centralization, and above all our letting Indirect Rule become a formula run to seed) supplies a good example of the mal-distribution of the expenditure of the N.A. money. Compare the proportion of Development Funds spent in or near Kano City with that spent in the rural areas. In particular, take the Kano Electric Light and Waterworks Scheme which cost about a third of a million pounds (I have heard engineers criticize it as unsoundly conceived and extravagant. In 1931-2 it was not raising enough revenue to pay what would have been the interest charges on capital) which serves a permanent population of less than 75,000; yet out in the rural areas, as every Administrative Officer who has served in Kano knows, and as the Beeby Thompson Report has recently enabled others to know, there is a serious shortage of adequate wells. Had even only 10 per cent or 20 per cent of the huge sum disbursed on the Electric Light and Waterworks Scheme been expended on digging and walling wells in the Northern villages, and in constructing water troughs for the animals, a reform of quite unusual beneficence would have been wrought for several hundred thousand people.

*March 18th*

The *harmattan* is back this morning. The air is thick with dust: you cannot detect trees or other biggish objects three hundred yards away. Three days ago it stopped and the air cleared to such an extent that we thought it had at last finished for this year. But here it is again, as strong as ever.

There is no doubt as to there being a strong degree of slave-mindedness in the subjects of the Emirates; probably because they have been dragooned into it through generations and generations of cruelty and caprice on the part of their rulers. The stories collected by Edgar* from Moslem savants all over the Moslem country, many of them relating to times just prior to our conquest, are evidence of what the commoner might have to endure in a Moslem autocracy.

On the other hand it is easy to exaggerate this side. Wherever I have been I have always made it a point to ask as many men as possible who remember the days before our coming (which was only thirty to thirty-three years ago) about the past life. There may have been gross iniquity here and there, and there is no denying that brute force and corruption sometimes existed to a degree unknown to-day; yet against this there was a strong sense for and a strong measure of justice.

Nevertheless, in general, the Pagan is the Moslem's superior in absence of slave-mindedness. The Pagan's society was seldom an autocracy: authority was generally conciliar: the rulers were a witenagemot of the Elders; in some tribes (e.g. the Idoma) the rulers were even folk-moots. The Moslem, however, is on the whole (though not always) superior in intelligence. The Qur'an and its teachings are, for all their defects, a better rationale of, and rule for, life than fetish and animism: monotheism is a stupendous simplification of the mystery of life and nature. The Moslem prohibition of alcoholic stimulants, a first-rate evil in most Pagan tribes (the Gwari men are chronically fuddled with drink; the Idoma are also sunk in the vice), is another great advance. Nor does the Moslem's rule of life make demands too great for his moral strength. The effect, too, of feeling that he is a member of an international brotherhood—a feeling kept alive by the pilgrimage to Mecca—gives him a pride which saves him from the inferiority complex of the Southerner.

But whether the Moslem or the Paganis the more slave-minded is of secondary importance, for the real point is that the women of both are the true slaves. They are not without rights, especially

* Cf. *Litafi na Tatsuniyoyi na Hausa*, by Major F. Edgar, 1911.

among some communities, but their status is markedly inferior to that of the men. Certain individuals of great force of character may rise above it, carving out their own status; and the weakest and most foolish possess a weapon in their tongues which is not lightly tempted into use by the average man. But the almost universal prevalence of bride-price illustrates her true status: the man buys his wife. She is his chattel. Thus she carries loads while he walks empty-handed. The other day I saw a man and woman walking along, the former carrying nothing, the latter with a baby on her back and with a large load on her head. I indicated them to one of my boys and asked him whether he thought it right that the husband, the stronger of the two, should carry nothing while the woman was overburdened. "Yes, that's all right," he said, "because the man has paid money for her."

*March 20th*

Umoru, my "first small boy" (i.e. he is second in the hierarchy of three steward boys), came and announced this evening that he wants to get married. He met the lady—a divorcée who has just completed the requisite three months at the end of which it is lawful for her to re-marry—two days ago. Asked when he proposed marrying her he said to-morrow. After my pointing out the swiftness of the affair and urging caution he agreed to delay the event by a day! My part is to finance the match: there is 30s. to be paid to her late husband, this being the bride-price he paid to her father; the usual two or three cloths and head-gear to be presented to the bride; tips to her father, mother, and other relatives; a marriage fee to the *mallam* who conducts the rites; and finally money for the professional drummers and praise-singers. I don't think I can get out of it for less than a fiver

Praise-singing is a calling. Whenever there is a marriage or some other festivity praise-singers come and keep up a shouting and a crying out of the merits and virtues of those present whenever they slip a coin into their hands. It is a point of prestige (*gsirma* = "bigness") to tip them: the more you give them the bigger man you are. To illustrate: at this impending marriage feast my cook from time to time will rise, with some dignity, and strut towards the troupe and slip in a penny or so; he will then walk slowly back and the praise-singers will call out (accompanied by song and dance), "Behold the cook, the white man's cook: here goes the greatest cook in the world. Oh, his cooking! etc." The praises might even extend to the beauty of his person, and then on to the deeper beauties of his character.

Big men, e.g. Emirs, District Heads, and the like, when in public are often accompanied by their praise-singers. In any case there will be those in their entourage who at certain points will ejaculate: "Oh, do be careful how you walk," "Don't slip," and so on, the implication being that here is something too precious for injury, for injury would deprive the world of its essential prop. It loses its freshness after a while when riding with an Emir in his motor-car to have to listen to some menial commiserating or felicitating him on each bump, or recovery from a bump, along the road.

## March 21st

I have been amusing myself by going through old files and records here, as I have done in all other places to which I have been posted. Once again I find that they are very incomplete. There are no annual or quarterly reports for the years prior to 1907–8, though there are a few pages referring to those for 1904 and 1906. The earliest assessment report is dated 1910–11. It is a pity that early documents have been allowed to perish like this. The documentary records for the first ten years of our occupation in Northern Nigeria are fragmentary, and its historian of the future will note big gaps in his original sources. In the Secretariat the losses are, I was told in Kaduna, mostly due to a fire some years ago; in the Provinces the losses are due to there being no system of storing or archiving old documents—periodical burnings being the accepted method for keeping their bulk manageable. When serving in the model Province, Kano, in 1931, I found, while rummaging through old files, Lugard's original letter of appointment (or, confirmation of appointment) of the Emir of Kano of that day. This very interesting paper was mixed up with a bundle of old gazettes and routine forms. The Resident, who had a sense of history, immediately had it sent to the Secretariat for safe keeping; and such of the other early documents as could be found were put together and filed.

## March 22nd

Umoru's marriage took place to-day. Mahomadu and the cook, representing Umoru, went off and met the representatives of the bride; both groups of representatives then went to the *mallam* who performed the ceremony. The bride and the bridegroom do not take any active part. At sunset, the bride, escorted by a body of women (not only friends—the prospect of free food draws many well-wishers from beyond the circle of kith and kin), drummers and praise-singers, came to the compound.

The ensuing din reminded me again of the point as to whether the African is musical. My impression is that he is not, or at least that he is not more so than other people. The general hubbub, be it on drums or on instruments, has the monotonous regularity of a gasoline engine, but made more aggressive by syncopation. Is the African more musical than the Chinese or Persian or Fijian? To my own tastes his music is not agreeable with the exceptions of (*a*) a certain Gwari instrument, the name of which I have forgotten—there are some in the Pitt-Rivers Museum at Oxford—but which is tuneful, especially in a band; (*b*) the Idoma xylophone; and above all (*c*) the algeta played throughout the Moslem country, but especially by the Fulani. This last—a sort of Pan's Pipes—can be a lovely thing. I shall never forget a late afternoon towards the end of the rainy season, when out shooting in Kano once: across the valley, sitting on a rock half-way up a hill, was a Fulani lad herding cattle and drawing delicious notes from his algeta with all the "fine careless rapture" of a blackbird in song.

## March 23rd

Have just come across another case of one man giving "medicine" to another to make him love him! When at Gwada two years ago, there was a European foreman on the railway who suddenly developed acute stomach trouble and had to be sent up to the Kaduna hospital. After some days' treatment he recovered, and in due course returned to his work. He was not long back before he received a letter from a charm-seller, a Southerner, requesting him to deduct 7s. 5d. off the monthly wages of his cook, and remit same to the charm-seller, being money due for medicine supplied for putting in his master's (the foreman's) food. From the enquiries that followed it emerged that the cook, a Southerner, had a brother, a carpenter, who was out of work. The purpose of the medicine was to overwhelm the foreman with love for the cook, thereby leading him to acquiesce in any little requests he might make, such as giving his brother a carpenter's job. As the foreman refused the request, the cook refused to pay for the medicine. Hence the direct appeal. The foreman had been poisoned (unintentionally) by some muck in it.

The birds in Nigeria are as numerous and interesting as the trees (the variety of trees of edible produce is remarkable). Some of the birds are excellent songsters, and others are handsomely coloured. Occasionally one sees English birds here: when trekking across Bornu from Chad to the Kano border I recollect seeing a number of Wheatears. Just around here are Bustards, making themselves heard about sunset; they are difficult to see, being so shy.

*March 24th*

When the Governor returns from leave formal letters are sent by the Emirs and Chiefs welcoming him back, a job I am now engaged on. Formal letters are also sent by the Emirs to greet him after the *Sala*. We instruct them to send the letters, we tell them what to put in, and we send them off. They are written in Arabic, translated into Hausa (in Roman characters) and then into English, the whole business taking up many hours both in the Provinces and in the Secretariat.

Great commotion this morning. As soon as I got up I was greeted with the news that a burglary had been committed during the night in the servants' quarters of the other A.D.O.'s house. It turns out that the hut of his head boy had been entered and practically everything in it (i.e. a couple of boxes containing clothes, a few odds and ends like a mirror and scissors; and a blanket and gown hanging on a peg) was stolen, and—the very mosquito net strung up over the mattress on which the boy and his wife were sleeping! It is another of many such instances one runs up against of the heavy stone-like sleeping of natives. A characteristic which simplifies the profession of burglary.

The D.O. and I called on the Emir and his Council this morning. The Emir is not regarded as a satisfactory ruler, but, like most of these Moslem chiefs, he is a "gentleman": he has manners and self-possession. On leaving the Council we went and had a look at the new gate which is in building. As usual, the artisans—builders, carpenters, painters—are nearly all Southerners, and, as usual, all were elegantly dressed in topees, woollen golf-hose, and the like (no English artisan of the highest standing at home could approach them), and all were addressing one another as Mister (e.g. Mister

Josiah, Mister Solomon, Mister Paul, etc.). The unskilled, their subordinates, are local men. I directed the D.O.'s attention to a sight unhappily common throughout the Northern Provinces, and one that partly explains the antipathy of the Northern officer to Southern natives: a painter was "painting" the mud plaster with the oil that is put on to counteract the effects of the rains: he was extravagantly dressed and worked his brush in a leisurely manner while one local Hausa held up the ladder on which the "painter" was standing and another local Hausa held up to the "painter" the pot containing the oil. The only Hausa "painter" on the job (paid less than the others, being a "learner") held his own pot and tended his own ladder just as any English artisan would have done at home. The D.O. intervened as actively as the situation required. Yet no one dares to do much: they cannot be dismissed because they are Southerners. If they were dismissed they would petition the Governor who, correctly or incorrectly, is reputed throughout the country, by the Service no less than by the Southerners, to read their petitions and generally to constitute himself their special protector—their Abraham Lincoln as the *Times* (Nigerian) described him.

The *harmattan* has gone again: the sun is now hot and glaring.

## *March 25th (Sunday)*

Dinner to the Engineer at X——'s last night. X—— supplied the victuals and I the beverages. After dinner X—— played his bagpipes (though not a Scot he is a doughty piper), marching up and down by himself; after a while I joined him with a drum. Later we sat on the top of the house which is flat-roofed. The moon was at the half: a perfect night. In the distance was the glow of the iron-men's furnaces at Charo Charo. X——, a tall man, fair-haired and blue-eyed, looks like a Viking (he has a passion for boats, too, superior even to his passion for music), and is an example in life of "the mad dog of an Englishman who goes out in the midday sun." The bush is his element. After the office closes at two or two-thirty, he goes home, has lunch, plays his pipes for a while, and then in the heat of the afternoon wanders off into the bush. As he never loses his temper, and is as courteous and pleasant as he is firm the natives adore him. It is a reflection on the present condition of the Service that such men, made for running the Empire's outposts if ever anyone was, cannot be kept. They say that if one has to be an office clerk one might as well be one in the English climate.

This afternoon X—— called for me in his ancient car at 3 p.m., and we motored off to the river at Jama'ari for some shooting. The heat was terrible; but motoring back after sunset in the moonlight made up for it, for here again was the Nigeria we shall never forget.

*March 27th*

While going through some old files this morning I found a correspondence of over twenty years ago between the Resident of the day and an A.D.O. here. The A.D.O. had been touring Misau Emirate, and, when discussing tsetse, of which little but their dangerousness was known then, wrote in his touring report that he was told in the south-west of the Emirate there were two villages, and that the inhabitants were continually dying of sleeping sickness. He visited these villages and made enquiries. He was also told that tsetse flies were numerous on the banks of the Kobe River, but as he could not distinguish Glossina Palputis from Glossina Morsitanso he determined that it would be taking useless risks to examine these flies at close quarters. He had already shown his courage by visiting the two infested villages; moreover at the time there was a M.O., a Dr. Chesnays, engaged solely on this very work of investigating tsetse in the Division, so that for an uninstructed Political Officer to attempt collecting tsetse specimens was a useless risk. Notwithstanding this, however, the Resident, who years later became a Governor, and is still enjoying the successes of his career, wrote him a reprimand imputing cowardice, a copy of it being forwarded to the Deputy-Governor of the day, who also wrote a sneering minute on the A.D.O.'s "excessive caution."

This is one among the illustrations which come one's way from time to time of the fact that a characteristic tone in the relations between brother officers of the Service goes back some distance in our régime.

Somebody brought me a leopard's skin to-day. The last time one was brought to me was over two years ago when the D.H. at Gogwada in Zaria gave me one. Chunk, my dog, had, I am able to swear, never seen a leopard up to then, yet as soon as the skin was produced he leapt back, bristling with fear and anger, and barked at it. He kept this up for an hour or so and would not be pacified; and even when the skin was rolled up and put on a rafter in the rest-house he kept looking up at it, sniffing and uneasy. Surely here is an indubitable case of inherited memory.

An official of the Veterinary Department has been here. He is outstanding as he really and positively likes his life here: he prefers the African bush to a European city and the simple native to modern sophisticates, and to such an extent that the disadvantages like climate, food, etc., become secondary; a feeling I share. But then his work gives him the bush and the most interesting natives, and he has no office work, and his Department is small and allows him some individuality. . . . He is a hunter and a naturalist, his special hobby being snakes. He collects them, removes their fangs, carries them about, and in general is on as easy terms with them as any favourite careerist with a Lieutenant-Governor.

*March 28th*

The hot weather is on us with a vengeance. Walking the fifty yards or so between the office and my house in the middle of the day *feels* dangerous, as though one might be sun-struck. The glare is as bad as the heat. Swarms of flies have come too: for an hour on either side of sunset or sunrise they are as fearless as they are numerous: you can't shoo them away, they must be *brushed* away.

*March 30th*

I have been in bed with an attack of malaria for the last two days, and this afternoon an attack of malarial nausea came on. But one soon recovers and the D.O.'s visit this evening has brought me new life. Next week his relief arrives here, the D.O. and X—— both being due to sail for leave about three weeks hence.

*April 1st (Sunday)*

Still in bed. Have been reading a couple of books: one a history of the war in West Africa by a Brigadier-General and the other Gwynne's Life of Mary Kingsley (and also part of her *Travels*). Mary Kingsley's *Travels* give one the "feeling" of West Africa (south of the Niger and Benue—West Africa of the Rain Forests and the Coast) as few other books have done. (There is a poverty of literature on Africa: so far it has stimulated nothing like what

Asia—take India alone—has stimulated.)\* The Brigadier-General's book in comparison is thin stuff, though generous. Also, apparently, his experiences are not wholly representative. In a discussion on the life of Europeans in West Africa he states that in the course of fifteen years' service he had never seen a British officer the worse for drink.

Mary Kingsley said of the Moslem in West Africa, "judged by the criterion of every-day conduct the Mohammedan is in nine cases out of ten the best man in Africa." Conversely she was contemptuous of the Europeanized native, "that perfect flower of Sierra Leone culture who yells your bald name across the street at you, condescendingly informs you that you can go and get your letters . . . while he smokes his cigar and lolls in the shade." Her limitations, however, come out in such things as her quixotic idealization of the Coast trader (who would not have recognized himself in her pictures), her attitude to the hut-tax controversy in Sierra Leone (money had to be raised for revenue and this was not an unfair way), and above all in her attitude to the importing of liquor among the negroes. She argued for importing it on the ground that European alcohol was more hygienic than African! Assuming for the moment that this is true, how many natives could (or can) afford to buy trade spirits? Only chiefs, clerks, and the like; never the man in the bush. The price of a single bottle of gin would supply him with palm wine for months.

The Medical Officer returned from Shira to-day, bringing the bodies of nine hyenas with him. The hyenas have been a pest in parts of this Division for some time, but the M.O. has entirely freed Azare from them. I forget how many he has got, but it is a large number, thirty or forty, I think.

## April 3rd

The African has the same facility in picking up a language as the normal child. Bilingualism is common. In the town of Misau nearly the whole population is trilingual, speaking Hausa or Fulani or Berri Berri, three difficult and quite separate languages, with equal fluency.

\* Two writers on Africa who deserve special mention are C. W. Hobley of E. Africa and Migeod of W. Africa, both ex-officials of the Colonial Administrative Service of many years' experience and both with the scientific habit of mind. It is significant, I think, that neither secured high promotion, not even a Lieutenant-Governorship or a minor Governorship.

Primitive man seems to have found it easy to evolve language. In Nigeria alone there are perhaps several hundred entirely different languages; in all Africa there must be some thousands.

Many of these languages are doomed to die out and to give way to another, a process indeed which can be observed to-day. Hausa is spreading over Northern Nigeria and even now can be regarded as the *lingua franca*. Hausa, by the way, means language. To speak Hausa is to speak *language*! It has a vocabulary which is very large indeed, drawn partly from Arabic and partly from some original African base, but its grammar is almost entirely non-Arabic. Its main characteristic to a European, perhaps, is that its verbs are conjugated by means not of the verb but of pronouns. In fact, it may be said, broadly speaking, that the verb does not change for indicating tense and voice, only the pronoun, without which a verb cannot be used and does not really exist. Another characteristic is the employment of separate and different words for things which among us would be indicated by combining words. E.g. there is a word for "black," another for "white," another for "horse," but you cannot say a "black and white horse": a horse that is black and white has a separate word of its own which is related neither to the word "black" nor to the word "white" nor to the word "horse." Hence the great size of the vocabulary. Another point is that there are extremely few adjectives: you must use nouns and verbs. Another point, though a trifle, is that they have the true aspirated P—the Greek $\phi$. The word "pussy" may thus be pronounced like "pussy," "fussy," or "hussy." It is a good language for expressing the concrete, but defective where anything (*a*) very exact or (*b*) abstract is to be expressed. It would be impossible to translate a treatise on philosophy into Hausa, and probably much of the Epistles in the New Testament cannot be translated. The Hausa language is an accurate index of the character of the Hausa people. It also abounds in proverbs which are cheerful, worldly-wise, shrewd, and reasonable.

*April 4th*

The heat is an affliction now. The temperature gets up to about 110° in the early afternoon. The nights are so bad that one cannot achieve more than an intermittent dozing, and again and again one is awakened by sheer thirst. The members of the Station are all in a state of exhaustion.

*April 6th*

I have been sent by motor into Misau Emirate for two or three days. I left immediately after breakfast. After two months' confinement between the office walls and the barrages of returns, figures, and memoranda, I felt like a schoolboy released at end of term.

Arrived at Misau about mid-day. The rest-house is good, set in a big compound, planted with shady trees, standing at a reasonable distance from the town, and commanding such view as is available here. The walls and red-coloured rectangular buildings of the town and the tall date palms make a good sight, and all around is the busy happy rooted life of men tilling their own fields and tending their own beasts in their own way.

The Emir of Misau drove up in his car, accompanied by only a small retinue and without drums or trumpets, about five this afternoon. I walked out and met him in the compound, shook hands, and showed him inside. He declined a chair and sat on a rug which one of his servants spread for him. He is young, thirty to thirty-five, I should think. He represents the Fulani aristocrat at its best and most ideal: very good-looking, beautifully dressed, and with a dignity and courtesy so fine and yet so easy that one felt as a Westerner feels in a Japanese home, a shade gauche. What a world of difference there is between his sort and the negro, the man of the forests and the coast; yet all the present bias is in favour of the latter. In his manner and his face there is just the suggestion of melancholy and abstraction. His father ended up insane.* His Emirate, a little monarchy tempered and supervised by us, consisting of about a thousand square miles and of eighty-six thousand subjects, and admirably governed, must be one of the happiest States on the face of the earth. Everyone has all he needs to eat and shelter himself with, there is no serious crime, men and Emirate are without a problem. The Emir himself is familiar with every detail of the administration, down to knowing every Item of every Head in the Votes Service Ledger.

* In the appropriate records at Divisional H.Q. there is an amusing series going back to ten years or so in the past discussing and counter-discussing whether the late Emir was insane. X——, who was in this Division for many years but who recently was singled out for high office, maintained that he was not insane, it was merely his manner, whereas his reliefs maintained the contrary, one competitor playing off another competitor, the poor Emir meanwhile becoming more and more raving until at length there could be no doubt and he had to be confined.

Amongst my instructions is that I am to urge the Emir to induce more children (all boys) to attend the two Government schools in his Emirate. What is the good of sending more boys to the schools? Many, if not the majority, cannot find jobs when they have finished, and, given the African's preoccupation with status, they are not likely to return, except by force, to hoeing and digging when they have been dressed in white gowns for five to ten years. It is not surprising that parents say that it is better not to lose the boy's character and services from the farm from the beginning: if we let him go to the Government school he cannot find a job, we are short of the labour of one producer for five to ten years, and after that he is a liability. What is needed in Education policy in Nigeria is a careful working out of probable demand and then to relate the supply to it. The mere production of literates, or, rather, semi-literates, is as expensive as it is bad socially.

Whether the deadness of mind and imagination has been more pronounced in the control of the Railway or the Education Department is a nice point, but pronounced it is. To enter one of these dreary schoolrooms with its class 3a and so on, is to encounter an atmosphere as finite and arithmetical as that of an American town of the Middle West.

## April 7th

Rose before dawn. Pleasant sipping tea out in the compound enjoying the cool and watching the sun rise like a ball of fire out of the east. The drive in the lorry to Akwiam, a little after sunrise, was also good, the first half of the journey lying through stunted bush, but the latter half through country that was well populated and fairly open. For some miles on either side of the Misau River and around Akwiam is open fallow farm-land, mile upon mile of it, dotted with palms and baobab-trees. The people are Fulani—settled and farming, not nomadic, Fulani—and as usual good-looking. Akwiam itself is, like all the towns in this Division, indeed throughout the Hausa-Fulani country, walled and moated; but twenty-five years or so of neglect—our coming and our régime has put an end to the need of walls—has in this climate and its furious rains washed the walls into the moat so that in general the walls are only a few feet above and the moat a few feet below the level of the ground.

This Akwiam country is good, and, somehow, throws a spell

which makes the discomforts, the bad food, the insects, the malaria, the isolation, and the smells seem a price more than worth it.

*April 8th (Sunday)*

Motored back to Misau this morning, and on to Azare this afternoon. The night was one of the worst, if not the worst, I can remember out here. I had to rise five or six times to drink, my throat was parched, and each time after dozing off I was soon awakened as though in response to being stifled. Throughout the night dogs came in packs scavenging for food and howling around the rest-house compound.

Mohamadu's packing! He has been with me for about three years, and before then he spent at least seven years with other officials, and knows exactly what is required on trek, yet he still makes a long fumbling job of it and has not even begun to have worked out any method or system. The time he can spend untying the knots in the tape holding the mosquito net on to the rods or in packing the crockery is remarkable. Yet this fumbling awkwardness becomes nimbleness itself when he turns to certain other things: thus just before leaving Akwiam to-day, while walking under a tree, I noticed a green snake dangling towards me. I hopped back and called for a stick. Mohamadu came and despatched the creature with the prettiest neatness and rapidity.

*April 10th*

X—— very sound to-day on the theme "What poor critters these Hausa and Fulanis must think us." The only thing they see of us is *aiki, kurdi, sharia*—work, money, and as policemen-cum-magistrates. If we go on trek, it is to worry them into expediting tax collection or by investigating some peculation or with some other disagreeable business; and it is on such occasions that we are always more or less hurrying, scowling, and irascible. They see the worst of us. They rarely see us in a mood of gaiety or repose. The things which they regard as the least important and most tiresome in life we treat as the all-in-all, while what they regard as the end of life—ease and laughter—appears to have no existence among us. We are the enemies of life.

Here is the fatal flaw in any method of Colonial governance which concerns itself merely with the efficient working of an administrative machine; and, so far, no bureaucracy has ever been evolved which concerns itself with more than that. In Africa, not only is that not enough, but it is not even the main task, which is one of human nature and human relations. If we rightly conceived our mission here, it would not be the fussing careerists to whom power and place would be given merely because they had an arithmetical accuracy, or a faultless memorization of laws and regulations, or tracked down more misappropriated half-crowns than their colleagues; we should raise rather the men who can roar with laughter and take things easily.

There was a good fall of rain this morning and early afternoon. About 4 p.m. I went for a stroll, passed the D.O.'s house (the D.O. is away for a few days), and noticed the three garden boys heartily watering his garden though everything was sodden with rain!

*April 14th*

This afternoon I walked out in a north-west direction from Azare, and on return took in Charo Charo. The air was clear and clean after the recent showers, the sun had lost its fury, and the light its glare and the landscape of fields and big trees, with a herd of antelope feeding under them, was full of repose. In and near the hamlets the women were beating out corn in the wooden mortars for the evening meal, singing as they worked; there was a sound of children at their play and laughter, and the contented droning of the men at their gossip; everywhere a sense of tranquillity and beneficence. When I first came to Nigeria and used to trek in the Emirate of Kano it was a delight to camp in the better Hausa villages, with their comfortable huts and great shady trees and man and beast and bird all content and at ease. Of course, our sensitive nostrils and our preoccupation with hygiene spoil it for us; but for those, like the villagers themselves, who are free of such inhibitions, it is a life perfect of its kind.

The first thirty years or so of our régime here has, I should think, been—and is being—the happiest era ever enjoyed or to be enjoyed by these people. They still enjoy all that is good from their past, but are free of its evils—slave-raiding, war, and the capricious treatment of person and property by their rulers and their rulers' hangers-on. They are now, and for the last thirty years have been, at the zenith: they have all they need, and most of what they can want, which is little as our wants go—"they who want least are most like the gods, who want nothing"—and they have security and stability. But this happiness will soon disappear. The apparatus of European life will be adopted more and more, and with greater and greater acceleration; and whether any of the spirit of Europe is or is not adopted with it the old African ideas and rationales will perish; for in order to satisfy his new material wants the native will inevitably transform the economic structure of his society, and it is the economic structure which will determine most of his ideas and habits. The unwitting enemy of his present happiness is the trader who teaches him to desire new clothes and new toys, and the Agricultural Officer who teaches him how to produce new crops, or the Technical Officer who teaches him new crafts that can be turned to producing the money necessary to satisfy his new wants, or the Education Officer with his alphabet. The African is specially prone to their flashy appeal and will quickly throw away his gold for gold-paint, losing a richness that we can never give back to him, for we no longer have it or its equivalent ourselves.

At Charo Charo there is an iron-smelting industry. All the village is engaged in it. They farm in the rainy season, and make iron in the dry. There are about twenty furnaces, six to eight feet in height and about three feet in diameter. There has been a plentiful supply of good laterite in the neighbourhood; in fact Azare and its environs stand on a bed of laterite. As the refuse of the furnaces can be seen in all directions for several miles around Azare, it would seem that in the past the furnaces have moved from point to point as the supply of easily mined ore became exhausted. There is still plenty of ore left, but wood of the kind suitable for charcoal has been exhausted, and what is now used comes from Shira, twenty miles away, on pack-donkeys. The furnaces, in essentials, are constructed on the principles of our own iron furnaces. The iron-makers are strong in physique, intelligent, purposeful, and happy. Their craft is doomed, however: it is only a matter of time before it succumbs as other native crafts are succumbing to the competition of the cheaper mass-produced goods of Europe and U.S.A. and Japan. How did primitive man stumble upon the invention of smelting? It is so complicated: the making of the furnace is a difficult business, let alone the bringing together of the right kind of iron ore and wood that must be charred. Vaccination for smallpox, hit upon before there was any bacteriological knowledge of the disease, may in origin be the sort of hit-and-miss empiricism of which iron smelting is another example.

## April 19th

Flies! In the office this morning one's knees (bare in shorts) were harassed with biting flies, which made a sharp burning sting followed by weals.

Those little black eye-flies are also becoming troublesome now, especially in the afternoon.

But the filth flies, of at least three different species, are here in their millions, so voracious at certain times of the day that you can't scare them away by flicking your hand; you must push them away. Though this is usual in most places before the rains begin, they are rather more numerous here because of the insanitary lay-out of the Station.

The ordinary idea of people at home about the healthiness of the African is mistaken. It is poor—a lower standard than our own. It is not merely that about half of those born die before they reach maturity and that perhaps two-thirds are dead before they reach thirty-five, but the surviving one-third show a heavy proportion of weakness and sickness. Their food is badly cooked, and they eat at irregular times. Colds seem endemic. Tuberculosis is not uncommon. If you camp in a native village, there is not a hut at night-time from which the noise of coughing does not come more or less continuously. Although they have acquired a partial (not complete) immunity or tolerance to special local diseases they are victimized by others, including some which are generally thought to be a product of "civilization"—cancer, pyorrhoea, and perhaps appendicitis. They seem more prone than we to hernia, the incidence of which appears to be very high. Venereal diseases also have a very high incidence. It is thus a mistake to think of primitive man as being healthier than civilized man. The contrary is the truth. Animals in a wild state are also subject to much disease, as anyone who has done any shooting knows.* A domestic dog that is properly cared for is a healthier animal than a wolf. After all this is what one might expect, for civilization implies the more and more expanded application of reason to the process of living, and so the greater control of environment.

But where primitive man is better off than civilized man is that he is incomparably more free from nervous wear and tear. He thus has a greater insensibility to pain, and, more important still, he

---

\* Cf. Mr. Hobley's paper in the *Journal of Society for Preservation of the Fauna of the Empire*, Part xvi, 1932.

does not anticipate or heighten actual ills by imagination. The hernias and wounds, etc., that a native endures almost without notice would kill most Europeans through mere thinking about them.

*April 20th*

To-day is the sixth day since this weather began: dense low clouds, a sunless sky, complete stillness, and humidity. One's body is never dry from perspiration (significantly, all but one in the Station have sore throats). Pyjamas and shirts are wet through within half an hour of putting them on. It is not pleasant, but is less exhausting than the heat of the cloudless glaring weather which alternates with this sultry weather—an alternation that will continue until the rains begin.

*April 22nd (Sunday)*

The D.O. and X—— left this morning *en route* for Jos, Lagos, and leave. Two good men and two good officers, the one the best kind of superior officer and the other the best kind of colleague.

I moved into the house vacated by X—— this afternoon. It will be the eighth house occupied by me since last June, not counting rest-houses. My books, most of which on account of uncertain postings I have not been able to unpack or look at since last August, have, I find, suffered badly from mould and white ants.

My three houseboys and my cook are Moslems, but my horseboy is Pagan (but he is trying to learn his prayers). I noticed this evening that when they were having their meal the Moslems ate together but the Pagan horseboy alone. Women, too, never eat with the men, no matter what their class or rank. The meal is taken squatting on the ground around a bowl, into which each man plunges his hand as required. No spoons or forks are used. The staple of most meals is soup and a thick porridge. Meat is eaten when they can get it.

*April 24th*

During the past week most of my time has been taken up with attempting to explain and translate to the native officials concerned the terms of the new Criminal Code and the other changes—the so-called judicial reforms of the present Governor—which came into operation from April 1st, and the bearing of this on their work.

The code should, of course, have been translated into a standardized technical Hausa version by the linguistic experts of the Translation Bureau, but such foresight as that cannot be expected; instead, each Divisional and sub-Divisional officer, already overworked, must struggle through with his own translation. A pretty medley of versions will thus be produced throughout the country. (One can picture the months, indeed years, of memoranda writing rising out of X—— discovering what he considers to be a wrong translation in this or that Division by his predecessor.) It is difficult to understand in English the nuances of some of the legal offences, let alone translate them into Hausa and to make their reasonableness plain to the native officials. E.g. "official corruption" can be punished by seven years' imprisonment, while "judicial corruption" can be punished by fourteen years, but "extortion by officials" can be punished by only three years, and "an official receiving property to show favour" by six months and the whip, etc. The maximum penalty for child-stealing is seven years—the same as for stealing stock or receiving stolen property!—but for kidnapping (whatever the distinction may be) is ten years.

Then there has been the way of introducing the changes. They came at a time when the Administrative Staff had just been depleted by no less than 15 to 20 per cent, due to the retrenchments judged by the Governor to be essential for the solvency of Nigeria, so that the remaining Staff was already overworked without having a fundamental reorganization of this kind added to their burdens. Then there was a disturbing year or year and a half of uncertainty: it was known that the Governor intended some drastic changes, but it was not known how much would be approved by the Colonial Office: hence a series of circulars giving commands; then modifying commands; then the draft of ordinances; then regulations in Gazette; and all the time a spate of memoranda rising out of the prevailing doubts and confusions.

In some cases (e.g. corporal punishment) the provisions of the ordinances were enforced by special executive orders before the ordinances themselves came into operation.

There was a case for a judicial reorganization, done without any spirit of prejudice or vindictiveness, with a severely selective regard to the excellences of the English Common Law, and after due study and reflection by competent men. It was in no sense an urgent need; at the most it was desirable in some directions. But this in practice will have accomplished little of substance in return for its dislocation. The old courts still exist, though under different names, and with redistributed powers; and the new judges, assistant judges, and magistrates are, in Northern Nigeria at least, men who are Administrative Officers but who, at some time or other, have passed the Bar Examinations; and where, as in the outlying Provinces, special full-time judicial officers cannot be appointed, ordinary Administrative Officers, without Bar qualifications, carry on the judicial work in the old way. Nothing more substantial has been achieved than to reduce the powers of Native Courts, and let in lawyers and legalism where previously both had been kept out, and, of course, to plant several rules and regulations where hitherto only one had flourished.

An example of the last is the rule that the Residents of Sokoto, Adamawa, Bornu, and Bauchi Provinces are to be *ipso facto* Assistant Judges within their Provinces, but that their appointments are to be made by name and in writing for each successive Resident or Acting Resident, with all the ensuing business of new warrants and preparation of Gazette announcements whenever a Resident leaves the Province. Why could it not have been done with at once by saying simply that until further notice the Residents or Acting Residents of those four Provinces will *ipso facto* be Assistant Judges?

*April 25th*

The chief *mallam* at the Divisional Office brought along a scorpion he caught on the road this morning. It was at least four inches long, black in colour, and looked like a crayfish, with its two horny manacle jaws $1\frac{1}{2}$ to 2 inches long and $\frac{3}{4}$ inch wide. Not a friendly beast. And very fast in movement. Natives tell of certain cases of death resulting from scorpion bites; but such reports cannot be trusted. A Southerner cook I once employed was bitten and became ill, but unfortunately not fatally (he was a wicked fellow).

On returning to the compound this evening I found it in an uproar: the cook and his wife were fighting again. He announced that the marriage is at an end. He has repeated three times in her presence the Moslem formula "I divorce you," and that is all there is to it, according to Islam.

But the making of marriage goes on. The Emir, whose unmarried children are still numbered by double figures, had five of his daughters married off to-day! He asked for an advance on his salary in order to meet the expenses.

*April 26th*

The man who was in charge of this Division for some years in the past, and who has been given accelerated promotion, seems to have devoted his activities here mainly to spending N.A. money on white elephants. The Azare workshops are piled high with things bought at his instance: there is a motor road-roller which does three miles (I think three) to the gallon of petrol—a cost so fantastic that it will be many a year, if ever, before the N.A. can afford to use it. The roller is thus rusting unused in a shed. There is also a Guy motor in a similar condition. And a mechanical saw. And a steel lathe. And, most remarkable of all, an entire Decauville Railway complete with locomotive, trucks, and rails—and nothing to use it for. The surprising thing is that the then Resident of Kano (in whose Province this Division used to be) ever sanctioned so much expenditure of N.A. money, not to mention its expenditure on such objects. But those were the good old days.

*April 28th*

The second clerk in the Divisional Office came to my house this afternoon and evening in order to help in checking and arranging the monthly accounts of the Local Treasury. After we had finished the work I gave him some refreshment and had a talk. He is the best kind of educated Lagotian—big and healthy body, quiet, modest and intelligent, and with a touch of genuine intellectual curiosity. Wants to learn French. Asked about the Indian question. Also what we thought of French Colonial policy (e.g. African Deputies in the French Chamber and an African Under-Secretary of State).

This raises the question of nationalism, more particularly African nationalism. One cannot help being sympathetic to it, for although it does and always will attract some of the worst men—the noisy stupid mouthers—it does and must attract some of the best. It is not merely that we sometimes send out unsuitable rulers among and over them, nor that we are very troublesome in bothering them about things which they see in a different light from us (sanitation, vaccination, efficiency, treasury vouchers, etc.), but that there must be an irritation at the sight of a band of aliens giving themselves airs and maintaining a standard of comfort so much higher than that around them. He would be a bold man who essayed to prove that this clerk is inferior either in mind or in character to the average of the Europeans who order his life for him.

Yet, at the same time, he with the rest of the Africans has got his money's worth out of us. There can hardly be two opinions about that. Nor can there be any two opinions as to the necessity, in the general interests of the people, of our continuing here. So long as this necessity continues, a good deal of tact and delicacy will be required on the side of the tiny minority like this clerk and on our side—once again a situation in which the human nature of officials will be more important than their technical efficiency. And it will be a long time before there can be any hopes of self-government, or of even effective nationalism in the African Crown Colonies, let alone in all Africa, because there is so little to build any homogeneity of feeling upon. Africa has never had what Europe or even certain great Asiatic groups have had—the influence extending over centuries of a common corpus of beliefs and loyalties. If you walk from one end of Europe to another, you will find amidst all the diversities the common stamp of Graeco-Roman civilization and Christianity. If you walk along a straight line merely a hundred miles or so in length in Africa, you traverse peoples and cultures which for all their similarities scarcely touch at a single point down at bottom. When will the Munchi feel himself at one with the Yoruba, or the Hausa with the Ibo?

### April 28th

The Hausa expression for the conversion of a Pagan to Islam is *Ya tuba*—"he has repented"; the idea being that to be a Pagan is mere wilful continuing in the dark!

### April 29th (Sunday)

Surnames are a late development in any country. In England it was well towards the end of the Middle Ages before they were in use among the commonalty. In Turkey they are adopting them only now. Africans have no surnames, but in the South as they become Europeanized they assume them, rather in the same way as happened in Sierra Leone or in the ex-slave States of U.S.A. Sometimes the names of the locally eminent are borrowed (in Sierra Leone Macaulay—after the father of the historian, its early Governor—is very common); sometimes pure fancy (Johnson and Cole are high favourites); but mostly by tacking on a *Mr.* to some scriptural name (Mr. Joseph, Mr. Andrew, Mr. Matthew). Hyphenated names are popular and are becoming fairly common.

Names among the Moslem people here in normal use are limited to about a dozen or so, all drawn from the Moslem Hagiology, including Isa (Jesus). There are no surnames.

*April 30th*

I left Azare for Misau by lorry this morning, whence I begin a tour (by horseback) of Misau Emirate. The objects of the tour are (1) to explain the new judicial system and to get it going in the Native Courts of this Emirate, and (2) to study and report on a tribe of Pagans, the Kare Kare, in its south-east corner. In addition there are the usual routine matters.

In the afternoon the Emir of Misau and his Council called on me at the rest-house. I return the call to-morrow.

The heat was fierce again to-day—all around a white yellowish glare.

*May 1st*

Impossible to sleep through the heat last night. Also there were packs of scavenging dogs prowling and howling around the compound. I got up once and emptied my revolver into the air with the hopes of scaring them off; but to frighten them is like trying to frighten away flies.

At 7 a.m., after I had taken a walk, the Treasurer of the Emirate arrived with his books for the monthly check. I got through about half by 9.30, and finished the rest this evening. We have just started him on a Daily Abstract, which, intelligent and keen as he is, he finds a shade mystifying. At 10.30 the Emir's car arrived to take me off to call on him at his "palace." The head of the Dogarai, together with six other mounted Dogarai, met the car at the city gate, and thence escorted us in state to the Emir. On alighting, I shook hands and was conducted by him to his Council Chamber, a fine lofty hall in unburnt brick and mud and of the native architecture so suited to this environment, passing *en route* through devious courtyards and halls, which recalled *The Arabian Nights*.

After a general talk with the Emir, mostly about his coming visit to Kaduna (for a conference of the Emirs and High Chiefs of

Northern Nigeria), he being much concerned about travelling in a train (between Jos and Kaduna) for the first time, we went and inspected (*a*) the Treasury, (*b*) the Emir's office, (*c*) the Prison, (*d*) the Alkali's Court, (*e*) the School, (*f*) the Dispensary. Everything in first-class order, but I was glad to get it over: going about and standing around under this merciless pre-rainy season sun was an ordeal.

Then began the main business of the day, which lasted on into the late afternoon—the difficult business of explaining the Governor's legal reforms, and especially those sections touching on the work of the Emir, or his Council, or his Judges. They were outspoken in their resentment of having their powers reduced, and the Emir hinted that they would like to know in what way they had misused them to bring about the curtailment. I affected not to understand the hint. And they were outspoken in criticizing the virtual abolition of corporal punishment. The Emir and the Chief Alkali asked what punishment could they award in its place: they said that the offenders, especially Cha-Cha players, who were normally given the whip, have no money and therefore cannot be fined, while to imprison them would overcrowd the jails. I had to argue against them and defend the change, though what they say is too true to be withstood. The Emir also protested against the abolition of payment of compensation for wounding, saying that this was a rule laid down in the Qur'an.\* They then questioned me as to the sections dealing with appeals, which are so involved and contradictory that I had to ask them to leave the matter over so that I could get a ruling from the D.O. For example, a litigant can have his case "reviewed" by the Resident free of charge and on demand, or he can "appeal" to the same person officiating as an Assistant Judge for ten shillings. Or, to take another example, an appeal lies from the Chief Alkali's Court, sitting as a Court of Appeal, to the Judicial Court of the Emirate. There is, however, no appeal from the same Courts sitting as Courts of Original Jurisdiction to anything less than the High Court: thus, to take a concrete case from Katagum, if a Gadau man is sentenced by the Alkali of Gadau for theft he can appeal to the Chief Alkali, and thence to the Judicial Council. But at no stage could he appeal to the High Court. Had he, however, walked a few miles southward before committing his theft, he would

---

\* Lugard's promise to the Emirates when they submitted was that their religion would be safeguarded; their law is a part of their religion.

have appeared before the Chief Alkali in the first instance, and herefore would have had an appeal to the High Court; but none to the Judicial Council! Or, yet another example. There is no appeal from any Native Court to a Magistrate's Court, but only to the Court of the Acting Assistant Judge in Bauchi Province. The Divisional Officer may, however, intervene either by reviewing a case under Section 25(1)(A), in which case he might in certain circumstances pass a sentence of imprisonment for life, or he may transfer the case under Section 25(1)(C) to the Magistrate's Court, in which case the Magistrate's powers of imprisonment, being limited to twelve months, are no greater than those possessed by a "B" grade Native Court!

Finally, the new Court Warrants are not yet ready, and are not expected to be ready for another couple of months. And when they come they will all have to be made out just when the tedious business of writing out a new issue under the old ordinance has been finished. Within twelve months all that labour has to be scrapped. And yet they ask how can they reduce office and clerical work!

I noticed that among the Emir's books there is an Official Emir's Diary. A few years ago the D.O. of the day requested him to keep such a record, to be made up by his personal scribe, with entries under such headings as "The Native Courts," "The Dogarai," etc., ending up with "General News," such is the strange passion in certain of this Service for paper and ink. The wretched scribe has nothing to say, as any untoward or significant incident is always reported to the D.O. by letter (there is on an average at least one letter a day from the Emir to the D.O.), and so for month after month he has gone on making perfunctory entries such as "The Courts have been well conducted this month," "The Dogarai have carried out their duties satisfactorily," etc., under their appropriate headings, and ending up with such "general news" as "A hyena ate three goats in —— village," "A hyena killed five sheep in ——," "The Emir took horse exercise on" such and such a date. Once a month this journal is sent to the D.O. for his signature, and he signs it, no doubt, in a trance.

*May 2nd*

Heard a lion roaring last night. One has been known to be in the neighbourhood in the bush south-west from here for some time.

A couple of months ago one near the Kano border, about thirty miles or so from here, killed fifty goats, seven sheep, two cows, and three horses!

Trekked from Misau to Dunkwi, which is the seat of, and where I was met by, the District Head. He is a brother of the Emir, and last year was implicated in intrigues against him even to the extent of being credibly accused of compassing his death. He has a villainous face and is said to be far gone in syphilis. To-day happened to be the weekly market in Dunkwi. A large concourse—not less than four thousand, I should think. The usual animation—unceasing rattle of chatter, laughter, gaiety, disputation, and fighting. What an institution is the African market, and what fun they get out of it. A youth from Misau was here with a bicycle, hiring it out for rides at two-tenths of a penny (*annini biyu*) per course. Those, the large majority, who could not ride could sit on it and be pushed along by one of the owner's assistants, and they were allowed to ring the bell. He lacked no clients. I am told that he has now given up his old occupation and earns his living by going from market to market like this, and is a rising man. He has just acquired a third wife.

Smallpox has been bad throughout the District this dry season—twelve deaths in the village of Sirko alone, and sixty-two cases there at the moment.

The heat has been so persistently bad that I early and wisely resolved not to go to bed at all: one wastes more energy tossing from side to side in a state of semi-asphyxiation (mosquito nets are stifling at this time of year) than from sitting up cheerfully. I called the messenger, Mallam Jibir, gave him a supply of Kola nuts (which they chew and prize highly: the flavour is astringent but a good thirst-quencher and a stimulant—Kola nuts are the base of the American drink Coco-Kola), and got him talking. He is the best of the Messengers in the Division, though they are an exceptionally good lot, a mountain of a man in physique but with gentle and very good-tempered ways and highly intelligent. He is a Kano man, half Hausa and half Fulani, his father being a Village Head (in Gabbasawa), now an old man whose death is expected at any time. Mallam Jibir thinks that his own chances of being selected as his father's successor are strong but that he is hampered by his being absent from the spot (several hundred miles away). He was interesting and well informed on the inner motions of the Emirate of Katagum. The Emir, it seems, is an unhappy, disappointed, and

lonely man. Excepting two or three only, he has found the various
D.O.s who have been in charge of the Division since the war
uncongenial. (There was one celebrated affair when the D.O., a man
who later was retrenched, and the Emir, after a disagreement, both
raced in their cars to the Resident at Bauchi, a hundred and
twenty miles away, to report against each other. The D.O. lost the
race, and apparently his case, as he was removed from the Division.) The Emir's main troubles, however, arise from his family.
The only one of his sons whom he does not dislike is the eldest,
the District Head of Shira, the child of a concubine, and whom
he hopes to have made his successor. He hates and distrusts the
District Head of Azare—the very District in which the Emir
lives and has his H.Q.—who, it seems, is the only one of his sons
born of one of the four Qur'an wives, the rest being born of concubines. He thinks he intrigues against him with the Administrative
Officers. During the Governor's visit a few months back he also
quarrelled bitterly with the Yarima, the ablest of his sons, who is
now in charge of the P.W.D. of the Emirate, as to whether the
Yarima or the District Head of Shira should accompany the
Governor to the border, the Yarima neatly thwarting his father's
wishes that D.H. Shira should have the honour by refusing to supply
the latter with any petrol. Since then he has not spoken to the
Yarima (excepting at official meetings), and he has driven the
Yarima's mother out of the harim. Speaking of the harim, Mallam
Jibir says that over ninety children (he thought a hundred and
thirteen) have been born to the Emir, but that about fifty of them
died young (such is the African infantile mortality rate). The Emir
was only sixteen when we made him Emir, in Lugard's first period,
I think. Speaking of the hordes of women in Emirs' harims, Jibir
said that in the bigger harims, e.g. of the Emir of Kano, the
Emir being reputed to have two hundred or more, there are women
who pass from youth to old age without ever seeing the Emir or any
other man. It is not merely concupiscence that leads to the immuring
of these poor slaves, but also local ideas of *girma* or status. The
condition of mental and physical health among such women can
be imagined. A familiar theme in Hausa story, and not unfamiliar
in fact, is their efforts to smuggle in some *joli garçon*. The limitation
of the number of women in Chiefs' harims and the determination
whether they are there with or against their will is a matter
which Government might well take up.

Polygamy is said to be "natural" to the African or to the tropics. But is it? It can only be natural there (as elsewhere) if a very pronounced majority of women over men exists. Otherwise, if, as is normal in all human groups, the women and men are nearly equal in numbers (the women in a slight preponderance), every man with a wife or wives over and above one wife is depriving some other man or men of partners. This, in fact, happens: in some African communities there are men who cannot come by wives. Hence prostitution, which flourishes to a degree undreamt in Europe. In this connection it is worth remembering that the twelve million negroes in U.S.A. are monogamist. After all, the reason for monogamy is simple arithmetic—men and women are nearly equal in numbers.

*May 3rd*

Left Dunkwi about 4 a.m. and rode to Gaina. Just after arriving two horses broke loose, and, as is the wont of these stallions (no horses are castrated in Nigeria), fell to fighting. A lad who tried to separate them was kicked on the back of the head, receiving a dreadful wound. I did what I could in the way of first aid: for a time it looked as if he must bleed to death. The kick would have killed a European. The African head, fortunately, is made of more durable material. When I was on the Railway Construction there used to be fights now and then between Southerners (Yorubas and Ibos), picks being employed as weapons. The wounded used to be brought to me with pick gashes, some of them serious gashes, over their skulls; but not one man ever succumbed. They normally worked the following day.

Although no more than an average of two hundred yards long by two hundred yards wide, this village has been walled: the wall is still four or five feet high and the moat about twenty feet wide and three feet deep. It shows what life must have been like thirty years ago when such a village required such a wall.

If one gets sufficient of the confidence of the older men to ask them what changes they notice as a result of our coming and taking over Nigeria, their reply invariably includes some such phrase as that we "have swept the land," or we "have mended the land" (*turai sun gyarta kasar nan*); such is the way they think of our pacification.

*May 6th (Sunday)*

Was down with fever yesterday and the previous night. Though feeling feeble (just managed to keep myself on the saddle), I rode from Akwiam to Yanda, over flat ground and through about a dozen miles of low, dense, uninhabited bush; it was like walking on a narrow path between two walls eight to ten feet high.

The pre-rainy weather continues. For seven weeks now it has been like this. In bed one's pyjamas and head are wet with sweat within a quarter of an hour, and balls of sweat keep rolling into one's eyes and trickling down one's back and face. On several occasions during the last month thunder and lightning have come, but only rarely bringing a shower, generally, instead, a terrific windstorm (I thought the rest-house would be blown down two nights ago), and when the wind has blown itself out the sultriness returns.

The horse throughout the three hours' trek this morning was maddened by stinging-flies. They settle on his belly or legs and in places hard to get at. The poor brute kept up a stamping and twisting all the way.

*May 7th*

Arrived at Jalam from Yanda. This is the centre of the Kare Kare Pagans whom I am to study and report on, a two or three weeks' job.

Just about lunch-time, however, a lorry arrived, sent post-haste all the way from Azare, with a letter from the new D.O. telling me to return at once as he had been suddenly transferred to Gombe (where he served last tour) and has to leave at the end of the week! I must be in Azare when the new relief arrives in order to help the latter when he begins. Such are the postings. It is only a fortnight since this D.O. arrived, having come straight from leave in England, and it was known before he arrived that the man at Gombe was leaving. The man who is now to come here was posted to Adamawa, but on arriving had been told to go to Bauchi; now he is re-reposted to Azare. In money alone quite a sum is lost by this chaos. There were two lorries to bring X——'s loads from Gombe to Azare; now there will be two more to take them back, and yet two more to bring the new relief's loads from Jos, the standard price being tenpence per mile, and the total mileage involved something between five hundred and a thousand. There is also the cost of sending this lorry out from Azare to take me back, which represents about another hundred miles at tenpence per mile.

## May 8th

Rain at last! It began with a tornado yesterday afternoon and kept on all last night. The condition of the track will not allow the lorry to leave to-day. I shall have to wait until at least to-morrow.

I walked out around the nearby villages this morning. Nearly the whole community was out in the fields sowing the corn. They planted in trios: one man made a hole with a long-handled hoe, another (or, more accurately, generally a woman) threw the seed into the hole, and a third covered the seed with his feet. All done very quickly.

A spirit of jubilation abroad. Not only was the air clean and the pestiferous weather over at last, but this season is spring to them and life takes on a new lease.

## May 12th

I have been back in Azare three days, but the day after arriving I went down with malaria. The new M.O. (the old one went on leave while I was in Misau) after taking blood tests has prescribed a régime of twenty grains quinine for me for some days, and then a course of the new drug Atebrin. The practice in West Africa is to take five grains of quinine daily, and now and then, e.g. over the week-end, ten grains. There seems to be some scepticism in expert circles as to the efficacy of quinine, especially in India, but experience in West Africa seems to show that quinine is at least a partial prophylactic against the kinds of malaria prevailing here.

## May 17th

The M.O. here served in the Cameroons last tour, and while there acquired this piece of pidgin English. It is the Creation story told by a Crooboy:

> Dem first time, you savvy, nothing to live. No other thing, no ground, no wata for himself, all he be mixed like so so potapota. Then God he begin. He part him, some place he put some ground, some place he put dem wata, but mem he no fit look him, because so so dark. By and by God he say:

"Better I make some lantern." Then he hang him one big one, he call him say "Moon," and after dat he fix plenty small one for up, call him say "Star."

Then he begin to make all thing, he make any kind beef, he make some bush, he make farm too. After that He say: "How I no get some people?" Then he some ground for hand, he mash him. He make him turn up like a man. He call him say he "Crooboy." Before He put him for some big big garden, plenty chop he live for inside, plenty plaintains, plenty makabo, plenty fruits, plenty palm-oil, any kind beef he live, dis be all work no live, so dem place be fine too much. Then he call for dem Crooboy: "I give you this fine place for sit-down, all ting I dash you." So dem Crooboy he sit down for dem garden, he waka there, he waka das all for himself, he waka so t-e-e-e-e-e-e he tired.

One day he come for God, he say, "Massa I come for you, I get some P'lava for tell you, no be you, who make me, no be you, who done put me for dis garden? You no look out for me? Because you be Massa for me? Dem garden you done put me, he fine too much, I like him, plenty chop he day, but all dem chop he live for spoil because I no get woman, for cook him, I better think you dash me one. God he say: "All right, no p'lava, I go give you one, make you sit down, you wait . . ."

## May 18th

The rest-house occupied by the Engineer was burgled last night. Thieves entered his dressing-room and carried off two trunks and various odds and ends, including his camera.

I enjoyed sitting out on the top of my house late this afternoon looking towards the west: open park-like farmland, just touched with green after the early rains, and dotted with big trees (*madachi* and *dorowa* and *baobab*), and the sky open and glowing, and the egrets flying home.

## May 19th

A swarm of locusts flew over Azare this afternoon, about three-quarters of a mile long, half a mile wide, and ten feet from the bottom to the top of the swarm, looking, in the distance, like a brown low-lying cloud. It is the first swarm of any size I have seen since 1931, when I was in the Lake Chad country of Bornu. This locust problem is promising to become the outstanding economic menace of the country.

*May 20th (Sunday)*

A man has been through here who served in the Secretariat (Lagos) for a while. Speaking of the tone and atmosphere there, he said it was so competitive and jealous that they were almost frightened to talk freely to one another, and the minutes or memoranda one wrote were treated as a matter of rivalry. I had rather forgotten some of the elements of the competitive atmosphere. One tends to adapt oneself and accept it as something inevitable, like the climate, which is a danger: for the tendency to a demoralization of the Service and a defective *esprit de corps* are too easily acquiesced in.

Was down at the hospital with the doctor to-day. The District Head of —— was there and wanted some injections of N.A.B. (generally used in cases of syphilis). The arsenic in it makes it an effective tonic (and as such is often used): it is in great demand among the Africans as an aphrodisiac, for which purpose the District Head was wanting it.

*May 21st*

To-morrow I return to the bush *en route* for Jalam and the Kare Kare Pagans.

*May 22nd*

I set out from H.Q. before daylight this morning and reached my first destination (Gambaki) four hours later. In addition to myself and servants were twenty odd porters carrying camp equipment, a representative of the Emir of Katagum (who will go as far as the Misau border, where a representative of the Emir of Misau will take his place), a Government Messenger (I have brought Mallam Jibir again), and two Dogarai. Most of the way lay over level sand and through the typical dense stunted bush; but near Gambaki the country undulates slightly and becomes open. The grass has now shot above the ground and the land wears a spring-green look.

*Durumi* trees, dark green in colour and shaped like an umbrella—much more so than the Umbrella pines on the Riviera—are particularly numerous here. Wherever there is a village in this part of Nigeria you find them, and pleasant they are to see either from the distance or when one is underneath their shade.

There has been as much smallpox in the south-east part of Katagum Emirate as in Misau this year. Numerous deaths. There are two vaccinators, whose duty it is to go up and down the Emirate vaccinating, free of charge, all who want vaccination. In keeping with the usual (and perhaps unavoidable) nepotism, one is a son and the other a cousin of the Emir. I find that they have not been up this way for months, and it appears that when they did come they played the old tricks: they represented themselves as having power to vaccinate all and any who had not been vaccinated, and they levied money. In the latter activity they caught the people either way: if a man did not want to be vaccinated, they accepted a penny from him as "hush-money" and passed by; but if a man wanted to be vaccinated they charged a half-penny. As all but a few are terrified of vaccination, the pennies exceeded the half-pennies collected. Such fraud is practised with the connivance of the District and Village Heads (in any case they could hardly withstand near relations of the Emir) and of the people. If one generalization about the African is true above others, it is his fundamental dishonesty (dishonesty is too strong: it postulates social habits which are yet unknown among him: it is rather a custom of what to us is dishonesty) in money matters: all tribes and all classes within them seem alike in that respect.

This afternoon around four a tornado blew up. Tremendous wind and then rain. I feel certain that, contrary to general belief, both the heat and the tornadoes are severer in the northern than the southern parts of Nigeria: severer in Kano, e.g., than Enugu. The North is worse climatically, but the Administrative work and the natives are more interesting. I wouldn't be a D.O. in some Divisions of the South for a Governor's salary.

## May 23rd

Another raging storm this afternoon. An hour of crashing thunder with mighty flashes of lightning; then wind; then the downpour. After sunset it had all passed over. The suspense of sitting for an hour or so in thunder and lightning like this is considerable, for you never know whether the lightning will or will not strike where you are, and so hurl you into eternity. Natives are killed every year. Two years ago death and havoc were worked by a flash striking Lokojia jail.

I have been asking the representative of the Emir of Misau, who is with me, about himself. He is an ex-slave: the Emir's father acquired him as a slave when he was a boy. He tells me that at present every Dogari in the Emirate is an ex-slave. This is probable. In Katagum, too, many of the minor (and some of the senior) functionaries are ex-slaves of the Emir or the Emir's family. The point to be emphasized is that slave-owning entailed responsibilities and duties on the owner which he never thought of avoiding. Slaves were treated almost as members of the family. To this day the Emirs, in addition to paying them their official wages or salaries, make them special seasonal gifts and interest themselves in their and their families' well-being.

*May 24th*

Left a little after four again this morning. So dark for the first forty-five minutes that at times I could not see the horse and horseman in front of me. In the near distance was the eerie wail of a hyena. The sky lightened, and then came a sunrise in bold, rich colours. The country improved over the second half, the dreary bush opening out and giving place to big trees and palms and grassy vales and meres. In the early light and under the mantle of fresh green grass there were places that looked like England in early summer.

Yayu (my destination to-day) has once had stout walls and moats, but they are now mere mounds and ditches. Our occupation of Nigeria has had the effect in Moslem country of making town and village fortifications unnecessary, and in Pagan country of bringing the people from their hill fastnesses down on to the plains.

The rest-house here is near enough to the town to get all the smells and noises, and just that point of all points of the compass has been chosen which brings all the town drainage towards it.

*May 27th (Sunday)*

Arrived at Jalam this morning, the centre of my Kare Kare enquiries. To-morrow I shall begin again what I began when recalled three weeks ago.

A snake dropped on my shoulder and slid on to the ground as I was passing under the doorway this morning. It wriggled into the thatch, and we could not find it.

## May 29th

Arrived at this hamlet (Garin Chiroma) early this morning in order to talk to the local Elders in their own homes and to see something of the inside of a Kare Kare colony that is off the beaten track. Camped in a leaky hut. There is no local supply of water here, although they have dug a well as deep as two hundred feet (this is a remarkable performance when their appliances are considered. The Kare Kare are famed as well-diggers. In the old days their very survival largely depended upon the talent). Having no well of their own, they have to walk to the well in a place called Janda, about five miles away. Thus every pot of water here costs a walk of ten miles in addition to the labour of drawing it up from a well two hundred feet or more in depth. And it so happens that this well (like many other wells in Kare Kare country) is affected with Guinea Worm. Guinea Worm is a curse over great areas of the Northern Provinces. There are parts where as much as 10 per cent or more of the population is put out of action at any given time you like to enquire. The parasites enter the system with the water drunk, and there get into the bloodstream, develop, and come out through some part of the leg, emitting eggs into any moist place or body (normally a pool of water at the edge of a well) coming in contact with the leg and causing an abscess and acute pain. In large parts of the country it is unusual to see a man or woman whose legs are symmetrical: one leg will be thin, and possibly a little twisted, as a result of an attack of Guinea Worm. The easiest preventive is to drink only boiled water: and though an African knows that no European ever gets Guinea Worm, and has had it explained to him that the reason is that the latter boils his water, he nevertheless takes no heed and still drinks unboiled slimy stuff.

## May 30th

On the way back to Jalam this morning we passed a village (Janda) which is surrounded by a thorn-tree fence ten to fifteen feet in height and as many feet thick—utterly impenetrable.

We continue getting tornadoes every afternoon, and will do so, I suppose, for some weeks yet. They are always plentiful and violent at the beginning of the rainy season. Thunder generally begins to rumble in the east a little after noon, and then goes on steadily increasing; by four or five a wind blows up in gusts; and then it drops, and there is an ominous stillness, and the sky darkens in the east with low clouds and black and white "wool-packs" and sinister-looking smoky-coloured wisps across the edges; and then come crash after crash, working up to a terrific fury of noise and flashes, the earth vibrating to each peal; and at last the downpour.

While sitting in the gloaming after the storm this evening I felt, but on account of the dark could not see, something move across my knee (I was sitting in shorts, a foolish thing at this time of day). I did not move, but called for a light; when it was brought I saw a centipede about seven inches long. Moral: never sit in the dark.

*June 3rd (Sunday)*

I have now had a week amongst this branch of the Kare Kare, and have spent long hours every day in talking to the elders and in trying to learn something of their customs and history, and also, *en passant*, what they think of us. It is hard work getting them to talk: they are suspicious and, like all Africans, tend to give you an answer that has little or no relevance to your question. Getting the truth out of them may not be as hard as getting blood out of a stone, but it is often harder than squeezing moisture out of cheese. The Government Anthropologist (now retired) made a sojourn among them some years ago, but it was brief, confined to a few localities, and apparently unfinished. This present enquiry is being made in consequence of the Governor's stirring up the question of Pagan Administration, his wish being, if I do not misconstrue it, to reorganize such tribes into separate governmental units, each with its own "native administration" based on its own traditional institutions; an idea sound enough in theory and, had the question not been neglected for many years, not too difficult to put into practice in the case of most Pagan tribes. Its main weakness, even in theory, is that a means of making the petty Native Courts effective instruments for distributing justice and righting wrongs has not been sufficiently considered, let alone fully thought out; while, as a matter of practical politics to-day, most of the Pagan tribes in the Moslem country have for a whole generation been rapidly assimilating themselves to Emirate governance, so that to try and force them back to what present-day anthropological investigations picture as their traditional institutions thirty years or more ago is academic. But nevertheless the general discussion on and ventilation of the subject has been entirely for good, and in certain parts of the country such changes as have been made were desirable.

The Kare Kare tribe numbers about forty thousand souls. When we drew boundaries, not only at the inception of our régime in Lugard's day, but also again at the several rectifications which were made in these parts in 1915, 1924, and 1928, we cut the tribe up amongst two Provinces and three different Emirates (Misau, Katagum, and Fika) within those Provinces, sharing them out amongst the Emirates concerned, despite the fact that they had never been subjugated by the Moslems. The boundary-making was done in an arbitrary way and with indifference to the Kare Kare: villages were actually split in halves (Buramu, Kwobkwop, Kobe, Zaura, etc.). Yet it did not turn out a bad arrangement, for the Emirs and their men have (like most of their fellows in the same position) proved tolerant and tactful rulers and have given the Kare Kare better rule than they could give themselves. The policy congenial to high places at the moment of amalgamating them into one administrative unit as a so-called democratic federation of Elders should be resisted as far as the Kare Kare are concerned. Not only will any such scheme involve the enormous labour, cost, and general unsettlement of redrawing both Provincial and Emirate boundaries, but it will also result in some such anarchy as that which now prevails among the Idoma tribe. These people have no traditions of association and no habits of government, living as they did in isolated and practically autonomous households, each under its own absolute patriarch. Moreover, they have and they feel no grievance against the present order, which in fact has treated them well. That is not to say, however, that no changes are desirable: the present Court system, in particular, needs drastic amendment.

The Kare Kare managed to maintain their independence in pre-British days because they lived in a no man's land between the big Emirates, separated from them by miles of waterless bush and living in strongly fortified enclosures, walled and moated and often fenced with dense thorn-trees. Though slave-raiding was their constant lot, it was always costly and risky and never very profitable to their raiders. Not only was the getting to their country so arduous, but they could generally endure longer sieges than the unwatered besiegers. All the Elders can remember those days. One man gave me a vivid account of a raid made thirty-seven (?) years ago by the combined Misau, Katagum, and Darazo (?) forces of two thousand mounted men: the weather was so hot, and both men and horses by the time they reached Jalam were so exhausted with thirst and hunger, that not only did they fail to carry the siege but they were repulsed with heavy losses. As is often the way with old men going back to their memories, the narrator recalled various odd and particular circumstances.

After our régime was established and slave-raiding had ceased the Kare Kare gradually came out from their enclosures and made farms and homes in the bush, spreading further and further afield. The outstanding fact in the history of the country for many miles in all directions from Jalam (except perhaps south) during the last twenty years has been this dispersion and settlement. They now cover an area of more than fifty miles by fifty miles.

The basis of their society is the family (in the extended sense), and authority lay with the father of the family. A father could have capital punishment inflicted on members of his household. Whenever a dispute arose between members of a different family the family heads conferred and arrived at a settlement. The tribe was thus a loose confederation of family heads; and the only time when common unified action was taken by a part of it (they never got to the stage of taking it for all the tribe) was during war or raids, when campaign leaders were appointed. There was never a single Kare Kare chief and never any local chiefs. Families belonged to a specific group of cousinry, each group being exogamous. War was the force that held together the mixed elements of the tribe, but what made them a more or less common physical stock and what gave them their sense of social solidarity was this exogamy. It threw and still throws a network of ties from one end of their country to another. If you take a census of the married women in any given hamlet or compound, you will be astonished to find from how many and how different quarters they come. Such coming and going was (and, alas for Administrative Officers who have to settle the ensuing litigation, still is) heightened by the transient nature of what for want of a better term must be described as their marriages. There are few women who in their old age cannot fall back upon recollections of a long series of husbands. Even within this loose wedlock adultery was so much an institution that it had no moral or criminal status: it was merely a source of action for debt. Not less than five-sixths of Kare Kare lawsuits to-day concern compensation for the usufruct of women. Interest in the actual paternity of children was (and is) not strong: children are wealth and they belong to the husband, the owner of the purchased property who produced them. (A case was recently dealt with, which got as far as the Residents of Bornu and Bauchi Provinces, wherein a Kare Kare had abducted a woman seventeen years ago. After that length of time the woman wearied of him and returned to her rightful husband, taking with her such of her paramour's children borne by herself as were still unmarried. Kare Kare law not only debarred the paramour's claim to the children, but it also recognizes an obligation on his part to return to the rightful husband such bride-price as he may have received on account of his daughters! The paramour has no grievance, the Elders insist, because not only has he had the services of the woman, both as a wife and as a farm labourer, property for which he paid nothing, but he has also had the services of her children.) The status of women is thus very low, being little higher than that of domesticated animals. As the crushing culminating example, in a discussion on how bad the times now are, the Elders tell you of modern Kare Kare women who even contradict their husbands!

Kare Kare institutions are illustrative of the fact that the more primitive man is the more complicated his institutions are. We await to-day a generalization summing up this fact and its deductions with the force of Maine's great phrase (Maine had made his observations for it as an official in India) "from status to contract," surely one of the profoundest generalizations ever made. For enough is known now to show that the march from primitivism to civilization is a process of simplifying and still more simplifying. Civilization is simplification; non-civilization shows a complicated tangle whose complications are due to a confusing of causes and results. Cross-cousin marriage is an example. An odd but minor aspect of this complication among the Kare Kare is provided by the refinements of the differences between paternal and maternal relatives: sons may inherit and marry the widows of their father, and nephews those of their paternal uncles, but only a maternal uncle can order a nephew about, and the nephew enjoys a sort of communism as far as his maternal uncle's property is concerned. Thus too the word "father" is addressed alike to the actual father, the father's brother, the father's male cousins, and so on; and similarly the word "son" is addressed to more than the actual son. Another strange fact is that those separated by two generations—e.g. a man and his grandfather—are equal. Then there are the playmates: there are strict and intricate rules as to who can play with whom. Grandchildren and grandparents are playmates; you can play with your wife's younger brothers (but not her elder!); and so on. The final and baffling mystery is the use of personal names: the Anthropologist* seems to have got some order out of the chaos.

The standard of value was and still is the donkey. All their main transactions are stated in terms of so many donkeys, and all awards in the Native Courts are given in the same currency. It is interesting that the donkey has no other use among them: it is not ridden nor does it carry loads (an occasional exception is met with nowadays, but it is definitely an exception).

Polygamy is practised, the only limit being a man's wealth. Bade, the Assessor of the Court at Dagauda, has eighteen wives, and an Elder died the other day leaving twenty-five.

There are women among them called *dagaya* who claim to be seized with occult powers and after a seizure are able to divine and to cure. They exercise considerable influence and, as far as I can see, for good; they are believed in with absolute trust and not a little fear. A noteworthy fact is that the seizure may occur at any age, even (though not often) before they are married. The whole phenomenon and institution would repay detailed study by anyone with an interest in psychology and the occult.

As with most Pagans, their besetting vice is drunkenness. Most of the Elders are chronically fuddled. An amusing incident happened in 1929 (I think): a predecessor was sent out to redraw the District boundary near here and arranged with the Kare Kare D.H. and his Elders to meet him and the representatives of the other District on the spot at sunrise. Having spent the night joyously, however, they were not able to leave their compounds until some three hours later. The reactions of my predecessor can be imagined, though they were not less than the drunkards deserved. To this day every time an Administrative Officer visits Jalam he is plagued with deputations asking for a rectification of the boundary as then drawn.

To reconstruct Kare Kare Administration in such a way as to make it accord with their traditional institutions would thus be to erect an oligarchy of patriarchs—and drunken senile patriarchs at that. A society based on patriarchy carries the principle of promotion by seniority of service to its last absurdity. Any reorganization of "Pagan Administration" which resurrects rule by Elders is retrogressive.

* Mr. Meek, see *Tribal Studies in Northern Nigeria*, on the Kare Kare.

The rule of the Moslem and within the cadre of District Head and Village Head and Native Court—the defects of which have been greatly exaggerated during the present reaction—is much preferable. Women have a higher status and justice is more certain. In any case the destiny of the Kare Kare, as of most Pagan groups in the Moslem North, is to become Moslem just as their language will become Hausa. I am assured that there is not a Kare Kare living to-day who cannot speak Hausa. This is and will be all to the good: the Moslem-Hausa culture is not too strange for their capacities, but it is also greatly superior to their own culture. To stem a natural movement towards it would be as much a disservice to them as it would be artificial.

This morning we trekked up to Dagauda. For ten to twelve miles south of Dagauda we rode through a continuous stretch of rich farmland dotted with hamlets and big trees. Dagauda itself (though the H.Q. of a District it is only a village) is a pleasant place, unhemmed by bush and well drained. There are two *dorowa* (locust-bean) trees in the rest-house compound which are the biggest of their kind I have seen, one being particularly enormous, the weight of its total timber probably being as great as that of a tree in the Rain Forests. Left to themselves the Africans would destroy these trees: they have got beyond the stage of producing beans, and though they are fairly shady the African prefers the *durumi* for shade.

*June 4th*

On rising this morning and putting my foot into my stocking a sensation of burning and stinging forced me to withdraw it in a hurry. A search revealed a brownish insect about one-third of an inch long but with a business-like stabbing limb nearly the same length in front. My foot swelled up, and (it is now evening) is still stinging.

I did the routine inspection work of the District H.Q. and went into the affairs of the D.H. (who is an uncle to the Emir): the lock-up; the market; roads; water-supply; smallpox; cattle-tax; the coming count of the population for the general tax; and above all the Native Court.

The Native Court consists of an Alkali, who is assisted by two *mallams*, a Kare Kare assessor, a Kare Kare oath-giver, and two Messengers. The personnel is good enough, but the Court works creakily. The litigants are nearly all Kare Kare, and like many

Pagan groups they have an imperfect sense of the necessity of abiding by the Court's decisions and processes. The Court on the other hand, like most Native Courts confronted with similar difficulties, is impotent to execute its rulings because it has not sufficient force at its disposal. There are only two Dogarai here, and not only are they at the disposal of the D.H., as they should be, but they are required to take whatever telegrams arrive from Azare or the Tsetse Investigation H.Q. on to the telegraph office at Potiskum (a half day's ride away), or whatever telegrams arrive from Potiskum on to Dambam (also a half day's ride), their means of transport being the tardy local pony. As telegrams arrive on an average at least once a day, the two Dogarai in practice are excluded from nearly all work but that of telegraph messengers.

*June 5th*

The eldest son of the D.H. turned up yesterday on a short visit to his father. He is in charge of the school at Misau town, has been to Katsina College (an incipient university), and looks capable and has all the handsomeness of the Fulani-Hausa type. I asked him how he liked staying in the village. "It is not pleasant: it is the country," he replied. It is extraordinary how urban the African is at heart even when he comes from and normally lives in the bush. No Frenchman ever delighted more in his Paris than the Hausa in his *birni* (metropolis). He revels in its crowds and noise and colour and smells.

*June 8th*

I have been spending three days in the south-west corner of the Emirate of Katagum, having crossed the border just north of Dagauda, looking into the Kare Kare who live there (in the District of Udubo). The D.H. and the Alkali and his assistants met me. The Alkali is a very old man, slender and refined in appearance and with gentle ways: he suggests the old scholar poring over his books. The D.H., on the other hand, is a robust, vigorous, manly type. He has the reputation of being the best D.H. in the whole Division; not unjustly, from what I have seen of him.

The night I stayed in Zindiwa, nearly on the Bornu border, was memorable for the hyenas. I have never known them to come in such numbers, or to roam about so boldly, and to stay so long. From 9 o'clock in the evening until we left at about four in the morning the wailing (they wail rather than howl) scarcely slackened. I did not dare fire towards them, as I was camping in the town and such shooting would be too risky ... Yesterday a caravan of camels (five) passed the Fulani hut I was camping in, *en route* for Bornu. I was surprised to find them so far south now that the rains have set in.

*June 9th*

At Dambam. I have come here partly in order to explain the legal reforms and partly because Dambam District has a large Kare Kare population. Dambam town itself was once a strong city and the seat of an Emir, but in 1915, following a rising, the Emirate was suppressed and its territory given to the Emirate of Misau. Dambam town and Dambam District of to-day are the kernel of the old Emirate. The present D.H. is not in the direct line of succession to the old Emirs, but he is of the family, and the reduction of his status to a District Headship under a former equal rankles deeply. This was shown to-day when I mentioned that the Kare Kare at Jalam had asked for a rectification of the Jalam-Dambam boundary: his soft low voice and almost feminine manner gave way to a passionate outburst on how his family and his people had been reduced, and how for the last twenty years they had seen one strip after another of the old Emirate carved off and given to former equals or subordinates. I felt sorry for the old man, for he has obviously spent long hours in brooding over the business, and although I cannot pronounce on the rights or wrongs that were done then, it is not impossible that somebody blundered.

There is a small lake three miles from Dambam with two hippos in it, father and son. There used to be a female here too, but she was shot by somebody, deservedly execrated for it.

I have now finished collecting data for the Kare Kare report. There are still many outstanding matters, and especially is it desirable that the investigations be continued among the Kare Kare living in Fika (Bornu): I intend applying for permission to go there. I might also get accelerated promotion out of it as an anthropological investigator! I have seen every Kare Kare Hamlet and Village Head in Katagum and Misau Emirates and all the present N.A. officials who have anything to do with them. I have also questioned dozens of old men and women. Broadly stated, my judgment is that there should be no basic changes in the present way of administering the Kare Kare, though some drastic amendments are needed as regards justice and the courts. All of the Native Courts dealing with Kare Kare cases show the same weaknesses:

(1) Summonses are ignored in the majority of cases, parties declining to come unless brought in by a Dogari. As the Dogarai at both Dambam and Dagauda are generally absent carrying telegrams there arises great delay through disobedience.

(2) Decisions of the Court are ignored or carried out only in part so that month after month may drag on while the Court makes ineffectual attempts to induce a party to observe its decision. This has arisen partly because of a lack of force at the Court's disposal, and partly because as in time all parties grew into this disobedience the Court was afraid to imprison them for contempt.

(3) As the currency in Kare Kare transactions is still the donkey, and as all decisions are made in terms of donkeys, wrangling takes place as to whether the animals brought by the loser are up to standard value, the successful party refusing to accept what is offered, sometimes breaking the peace in the Court-house and sometimes walking to Azare to lodge a complaint at the Divisional Office (the mere threat to do which is generally enough to make the Court try to buy him off, as not only is the Court afraid of a censure for a wrongful decision but it naturally wishes to avoid all the pother and inconvenience of walking there and explaining its activities).

(4) Oath-giving according to Kare Kare rites is done normally by one who inherits the occult prescriptions for inducing truth in the oath-takers. There are two such men in Udubo District, four in Dambam, and four in Dagauda. Each litigant has his own fancy and elects where he will take his oath. As the oath-givers live in widely separated places the formality of swearing might take a week or more in arranging for, and going to, and returning from, and performing the rite. The oath-givers are paid a fee by the swearers, and if successful the party makes him a gift amounting in most cases to about 10 per cent of the value

involved. Such an oath is of course more than an oath: it is really an ordeal. Two men are said to have died recently after a suit in the Dagauda Court, popular opinion holding that they perjured themselves at an oath-taking.

(5) Cases between men living in different Emirates: the present practice is that if a man in Dambam has a complaint against a man in Fika he goes to the D.H. of Dambam, who arranges for his scribe to give him a letter, setting forth the facts alleged, to the Emir; the Emir then gives him a letter addressed to the Emir (or more accurately the Moi) of Fika and sends it to the D.O. at Azare, who in turn sends it on to the D.O. in Fika, who delivers it to the Moi, who passes it on to the relevant D.H. It is not surprising that one sometimes meets with complaints which arose two or three years ago but which are still in process of being settled!

(6) Bride-price is too high. The present price for a woman is seven to nine donkeys plus a varying number of lesser animals like goats and fowls. A Kare Kare bride thus costs about £3 to £4. A Hausa or Fulani bride in this Division rarely costs more than £1 in these days, and often only 10s. or 15s. There are several objections to so high a scale, but the most serious is the difficulty it entails on a young man in acquiring a wife. The general price-level is anything from 50 to 100 per cent lower than it was four years ago, yet the young man has to come by the old unreduced bride-price.

*June 10th (Sunday)*

To-day was almost cloudless, with a gentle breeze, and after last night's rain everything was clean and fresh and green. Yamai, where I am to-day, stands in open country dotted with enormous baobab-trees. I have never seen Africa look better.

Smallpox was particularly virulent around here this dry season. Many deaths. Smallpox is one of the major diseases here. The vast majority of people have had it: those living are those who have survived it. We have native vaccinators, but their vaccinations are relatively few. The total recorded numbers of vaccinations done in the Emirate of Misau last month were only thirteen. This is due not to slackness on the part of the native vaccinators but to the people's fear of the needle. The Fulani have several ways of vaccinating themselves, the one most followed here being to take the watery discharge from a sufferer at a certain stage of his illness and to rub it over a surface of the skin which has been scratched.

The evening has been as perfect as the morning. Sitting out in the cool I have been talking (as I often do) to Mallam Jibir. He has been to the Government School at Kano (Shahuchi), reads his Qur'an in Arabic, is intelligent and observant, has a very sound character, and is altogether a most likable man.

"What are the stars, Mallam Jibir?"

"We have no other name—just stars."

"Yes, but what are they, what sort of things are they?"

"They are in the sky. Some men say they are white and of the size and shape of a pitcher. But the most learned *mallams* say they are living creatures."

"What kind of creatures?"

"They say that the big shiny stars are Chiefs, the middle-sized ones are rich men and men who have had plenty to eat, and the smallest are the common people."

"Are they far from here?"

"Yes, a long way. Perhaps a thousand miles."

"What is the moon?"

"It is a big white hill up in the sky. It is very big. Once some unbelievers said that Mahomet was no prophet, and in order to disprove them he caused a big part of the moon to be lowered to the earth. It was so big that while it was nearing the earth it darkened part of it. Mahomet caused it to settle in a certain place and left it there, where it is to this day."

Whether the above is widely believed by men of Mallam Jibir's class I cannot say, but it is interesting to see how even a man with intelligence and observation above the average has no curiosity about the non-immediate world. The African in general has no concern over or even interest in the future. Hence he is free of apprehension and anxiety—magic that civilized man has lost.

*June 11th*

This evening I tried Umoru on his cosmogony:

"What are the stars?"

"They are men, or sort of men. Each man has his own star.

The bright stars are of men still living, the faint ones are those of men now dead."

"How big are they?"

"I have not got that news."

"As big as this village?"

"Perhaps, but I don't know."

"Haven't you an idea?"

"I am a commoner. Only the *mallams* and the big men know these things."

"But haven't you ever thought about them? Haven't you ever wondered what the stars and moon and sun are?"

"No. I am only a *yaro*."*

I then questioned him about women and religion. Only the old women attend mosque, he says, so that they alone hear the preaching and the lessons. Girls and young women know nothing of God or Heaven or Hell; and they don't pray—they don't know how to. Sometimes a *mallam* or father will teach his womenfolk to pray, but only rarely.

"Why?"

"That's our custom."

### *June 15th*

I have spent the last two days in Misau town explaining and going through in detail again the legal reforms before the Emir and all the Alkalis and assessors and other relevant functionaries of the Emirate. Have also had a meeting of the Kare Kare Elders, who met separately and also with the Emir's Council; I got them to agree to a reduction in bride-price and to certain other matters, though before the changes can be made effective similar action must be taken by the Kare Kares in Fika and Katagum.

### *June 16th*

A trek from Misau through dreary viewless bush terminating in the dreary, viewless village of Kafin Giade. There are dozens of wasps in the rest-house, possibly harmless but menacing in gait and full of buzz. . . . This evening I have had to abandon attempts at writing because swarms of flying insects, attracted by the light, kept getting into my eyes and face. And now a tornado is blowing up, which, as this rest-house has not been repaired for over a year,

* A boy.

thanks to the economy campaign, and the thatch is leaky, will give me and mine a ducking.

*June 17th (Sunday)*

From Kafin Giade to Giade, another twelve miles or so through thick bush, terminating, however, in country more or less open and with a partial view of Shira Hills.

I noticed on the way what I have noticed several times before but what one is inclined to overlook, viz. that termites attack living plant tissue. In a number of cases a large part of the shrub (branches, stem, and leaves) was covered entirely with the white-ant mud. On knocking it off it was seen that the leaves had not yet died, but they were withering. Apparently the creatures cause the plant, or part thereof, to die by so covering it and then they consume it.
. . . I have seen the mud tunnels of termites running up on a living tree to as high as ten to fifteen feet, and then abandoned, they having found, presumably, nothing at the end. I have also seen them build a mud tunnel under a sheet of iron, on which was stacked some boxes, over the edge of it and up on to the top and for four inches along to the boxes. Does the killing of living tissue, and its rarity, argue that their power of self-preservation is still developing? Or have they, as is said, reached the limits of their evolution?

We killed a snake in the rest-house to-day, and just missed another. The latter fell on Mohamadu and struck at his arm, but he shook it off without mishap.

The D.H. here has leprosy. The disease is in the early stages, but its symptoms are evident. Yet such is still their fear or distrust of our medicine that he, educated (in the Moslem way) though he is, will not go to the M.O. and tries to disguise his misfortune.

*June 19th*

At Isawa. I return to Azare to-morrow, having been absent in the bush for four weeks.

Here at Isawa is one of the three rest-houses recently built by X—— in accordance with a new design of his own. Admirable it is, too. One appreciates a hard floor, and thatch that is sun- and rain-proof, and with reasonable huts for one's boys, after a month of sheds and leaky compounds.

*June 21st*

Back at Azare. Despite all the rain in Misau, Azare and most of the country to the north has missed it. The downfalls have been patchy. There has been no rain here for twenty-one days, and if none comes soon the crops will suffer seriously. Hence prayers are being offered, accompanied by drumming and wailing.

*June 22nd*

A command has just come from Kaduna which helps on nicely the now well-consolidated movement for turning Political Officers into clerks and to keep them in offices. On account of the financial situation there is a shortage in the staff of the Post and Telegraph Department and their votes of travelling have been reduced. Since officials of the P. and T. Department will therefore be unable to do the work, Administrative Officers in the future are to inspect (i.e. to check the complicated and finicky) accounts of Post Offices and Postal Agencies.*

*June 24th (Sunday)*

A swarm of locusts arrived this afternoon, more than a mile in width and length. The wretched people betook themselves to their farms and tried to frighten them away by making a noise.

*June 25th*

The subject of officers having tea parties with Emirs is now being discussed by Kaduna, and it looks as though the future will see an addition to our List of Returns—a monthly return of tea parties with Chiefs and Emirs.

*June 26th*

For the last few days we have had good rains at Azare. At nighttime, after the tornadoes have passed, the frogs and crickets, but especially the frogs, raise such a din that if I turn on my gramophone and go outside I cannot hear it.

In my official capacity as (*inter alia*) sub-Treasurer I received the following letter from one of the new M.O.s at the Tsetse H.Q. at Gadau this morning:

* Kaduna, No. 22252/8, June 13, 1934.

THE TREASURY, AZARE.

GADAU.

Dear Sir,
Will you kindly cash the enclosed cheque, and oblige.
Yours faithfully,
——, M.B., B.Ch., D.P.H., D.T.M. & H.

A lover of labels!

## June 27th

A road runs in the front of my house, ten yards or so from the door. Last night about 11 p.m. I was kept awake by the sound of a group of Southerners standing and talking on it just opposite the house. They were clerks or the like from the Tsetse H.Q. at Gadau. I called a boy to send them away, to tell them to talk further along the road. They refused, saying "This is the road," and, of course, legally they were free to stay there all night. No officer, under the present régime, would dare drive such men away.

## June 28th

We are all democrats nowadays. Such is the force of example from Lagos that a very senior official in the Northern Provinces has sent out a circular about how the African is to greet us. The Hausa greeting (to one another, not merely between him and us) is to bend down. The senior concerned now wishes to initiate and encourage another and more equalitarian salutation: he wants a raising of the hand and arm in a sort of Fascist salute. The boys at the local Government school are now being drilled in the new rite.

Two recent interesting books on Africa are those of Major Orde-Browne and of the International Missionary Council's Research Department on *Modern Industry and the African*. They show, amongst other things, the differences between the forces at work in East and in West Africa. There is no compulsion, either economic or administrative in West Africa, on Africans to leave their farms and become labourers. Yet a small class of more or less permanent labourers has arisen, perhaps fifty to sixty thousand in number, which works on the tin mines, in construction camps, and at or around big trading centres like Kano. The labourers choose this life in definite preference to farming their own plots: they like the regularity of receiving hard cash in their hands (the ordinary African, though assured of enough food and clothing and shelter, handles little cash), for which luxury they will gladly risk unemployment, and they like the less law-abiding and less-disciplined life of camps and labourers' quarters. Not knowing East and South-East Africa at first hand I cannot speak, yet I fancy some of the effects of modern wage labour on the Africans, though bad, have been exaggerated. Thus the second book discusses serial wifehood and its commonness in labour camps. Where in Africa, within or without labour camps, is it not common? The phenomenon is no doubt more common in labour camps than elsewhere, but it is certainly common enough elsewhere. Another misconception will probably be produced (or rather reinforced, for it is already widely held) by the passage ascribing the breakdown of tribal customs and sanctions to the sending of the villagers on to the mines. Some weakening, in general a regrettable weakening, of customs and sanctions does follow a sojourn in labour camps; but this weakening would come and is coming in any case, and the main factor is something else. It is the *pax brittanica* (or *pax gallica* or *belgica* or *italiana* as the case may be) which has led to the suppression of slave-raiding and inter-tribal warfare. Before the *pax* tribes were held together not because of the members' common physical stock (this, like their customs, would generally be in flux) but because of their common enemies. Before the *pax* tribes lived in a state of nature, each against the other, so that for very self-preservation the members of a tribe clung to one another: to cease to cling or to be thrown off meant the wilderness, and with it certain death or certain slavery. The *pax* has been the great disintegrator of the tribe. To-day no native has any fear of being turned out, or himself turning out, of the tribe. There is in fact travel and mingling on a scale never dreamed of before. I have had occasion to observe this personally in four different tribal groups. It is, for example, the predominant social fact of Kare Kare life.

*June 29th*

It is a year ago to-day since I returned to Nigeria from leave.

A typical problem has arisen here: the head warder at the prison claims that a box containing £70 and various articles has been stolen from his house in the prison. First, how did such a man ever come to accumulate £70? Second, how could one man carry off such a heavy load by himself (the money is alleged to have been in shillings, sixpences, and pennies)? Third, how did the thief manage to get it through the small hole he is alleged to have dug through the prison wall? Fourth, how did he manage to accomplish so much, with its ensuing noise and clatter, without awakening someone, not to mention the warders who were supposed to be on night duty?

*July 24th**

Word has just arrived that the D.O. has to announce a cut in the salaries of Messengers, to run as from August 8th, a week hence. The maximum salary for Messengers is reduced to a figure that will mean a 30 per cent reduction for Mallam Buwoi, our Senior Messenger, who has been a faithful official for over twenty years. How would the senior official concerned feel if he were called upon to manage, within a week, a 30 per cent cut in his budget? What will Mallam Buwoi think of us?

* This entry is taken from the author's Journal though coming after the termination of the twelve months, as it illustrates a central theme—lack of planning and a hand-to-mouth system of administration.

## Part Two

## A Tract on Colonial Administration

### I
Administration in Nigeria

### II
The Administration of the Colonial Empire

### III
The Problem of Public Administration in the Modern State

# I

## ADMINISTRATION IN NIGERIA

### (1) THE *MILIEU*
*There is death in the air.*

THE environment of the average European in West Africa is of a kind to excuse much. He lives in a climate which for six months or more of the year is like a hot-house, when his skin is never free of sweat and a constant care is with the mould which attacks his boots and hats; and the rest of the year is about equally divided between the *harmattan*, when the air is laden with a fine choking dust blown hundreds of miles from the Sahara, and the months between the *harmattan* and the rains, when the heat and glare of the sun are scarcely endurable. Disease is around him and with him, always, as in the case of malaria, sucking on his vitality, and sometimes it is fatal.

Nor does the landscape often redeem the climate. In general it is flat and shut in with bush or tall grass, giving no view beyond a hundred yards or so. For my own part I found that this absence of a long view, this feeling of being pent up between leaves and stalks with no outlook on the world, was the biggest single demoralizing factor which I have ever encountered.

Further, the food is such that Europeans living away from the coast, and especially those living in the bush, suffer from chronic malnutrition. It is not merely that they subsist for eighteen months straight off on a diet of local fowl (a wonder of toughness and tastelessness) eked out with native vegetables, with African eggs (there is a difference!), and in some places coarse river fish and in some places milk, anything additional thereto being tinned food; but the soil in West Africa is said to be lacking in certain essential dietetic elements like phosphorus, so that all food produced in the country is likewise lacking in them. The African cook, too, who is called upon to prepare food of a kind which he does not himself eat, and is therefore without a personal understanding of it, is rarely good. He often works desolation. A friend of mine, for example, whose cook was prone to over-drinking, was once served at dinner with a custard made of Keating's Insect Powder!

Again, the housing is frequently bad. Officials are supposed to be provided with a furnished house, rent free (or to be compensated adequately where the house is not furnished). In some stations the housing is excellent, especially in the Southern Provinces; but in many of the Stations in the North officials are still required to live in grossly insufficient quarters, junior officers often being accommodated in mud-walled sheds, roofed with poor thatch, where white ants, lizards, snakes, scorpions, insects (of an impressive numerousness, diversity and biting power), birds nesting in the rafters, winds, dust, tornadoes, can enter and do enter and war against the occupant's soul. The young man who comes out from England tries for a time to mitigate the environment by hanging a print or two on the walls and putting up a shelf or two of books; but after three years or so the hopelessness of the struggle overwhelms him and he compromises with his *milieu*, accepting as his normal lot what a few years previously would have disgusted him. In Kano Station, where over £300,000 has been spent on a dubious Water and Electricity Supply Scheme, Political Officers, thirty odd years after our occupation, are (excepting the three or four senior men) still housed in temporary tenements.

Even worse in its effects than the quality of the housing is the sense of insecurity. Why strive to make a home when one might be sent hundreds of miles away to some other post to-morrow, or the next day, or any day? All is flux; and quite unpredictable flux. So many instances have been given in the Journal that it may seem unnecessary to labour the point, but as these are in no way exceptional, a further illustration is offered. The usual experience of an officer departing from the Colony for home leave is something like this: On departure he is instructed as to where he will be posted on his return; during his leave—often towards the end of his leave, when it is then too late for him to make arrangements in the Colony —he receives other instructions posting him somewhere else; and it is quite probable that on arriving at Lagos, or even in the train *en route* to his Station, he will receive a telegram commanding him to go somewhere else. Having at length, after all these tergiversations, reached some Station, he still has no notion how long he will be staying there; it may be for eighteen months or longer, or it may be for only a few days. The taxpayers' money and the officials' energy and spirits are squandered with an equal recklessness. In 1933, referring to eleven colleagues personally known to me and returning to Nigeria about the same time as myself, I made a list with four columns headed (*a*) names of officers, (*b*) where posted prior to departing for leave, (*c*) where they were told they would be posted on returning from leave, and (*d*) where they actually began their tour of service when they returned. Only three of the eleven returned to (*b*), and only four found themselves in (*c*), the rest being sent hither and thither. It is not uncommon for a man to serve in three, four, or even five different Stations, possibly separated by hundreds of miles, in the course of his eighteen months' tour.

It can be admitted that in a country where ill-health and consequent invalidings are common the necessity of moving a man suddenly in order to fill up a post unexpectedly vacated by a sick man will sometimes arise. It can be admitted, too, that the panic of 1931-2, when retrenchment of staff was carried to a point beyond the minimum requirements of the Service, now makes it impossible to maintain that margin of spare men which could and should be used for such relievings. But when all is said, the root of this evil, which goes back long before the Depression, and which is bitterly complained of by the Service in other African Colonies, is that no system of postings and transfers has ever been worked out, either in the Secretariats or in the Provinces. If it is possible to get several hundred trains a day in and out of Paddington Station, it ought to be possible at Kaduna to plan ahead the movements of 170 or so Administrative Officers over a period of eighteen months.*

Not only is health of body and mind thus on a much lower level than one would enjoy at home, but the great tonic of congenial social life is absent. Either men are in solitude, or they are forced to live in constant association with a small group of people who may have little or nothing in common, but who happen to be thrown together and form that particular tiny white island in the sea of black. In this small group, too, there are never any children— apparently children are an essential condition of the healthy human group—and the women are greatly outnumbered by the men, and they seem to stand up to the rigours of the life with even less success than they.

Further, the tour of service is now too long. Till after the war

* In Sokoto, in 1933, an officer of twenty odd years' service, acting as a Resident on his previous tour (and now promoted to a Residentship) took over the Provincial Office from a Cadet!

the tour of service in West Africa was twelve months. It was then lengthened by the not inconsiderable proportion of 50 per cent—to eighteen months. This was an error, as the Warren Fisher Report\* seems to recognize, and it has been placed on record officially that a main reason for the high reputation of the Service in the Sudan is the short tour there. For, under the circumstances of life in the West African Colonies, time seems to stand still. You are compelled to see so much of your immediate environment, and you see nothing of the world beyond, except what your mail brings you once a fortnight (the interest in and the longing for the mail is a significant pathological phenomenon), that the average man has soon exhausted it. He feels like a prisoner between four blank walls, condemned to pass his days in looking at nothing. Or, to change the metaphor, he and his colleagues are like people on a raft in the ocean: they have seen nothing but one another and the waste around them, and that for a long time, all stripped of all covering. The likes and dislikes, the whole man in fact, becomes known to the last detail. It is, of course, not always as harrowing as this. Sometimes the majority is wise enough not to tempt Providence, and instead of foregathering every night they meet only once or twice a week. Sometimes, too, it happens that the small group is congenial. It can then be very pleasant: life at its best.

During the last three or four years most of the Administrative Officers have also been overworked, sometimes grossly overworked. The Colonial Office permitted the Governor to carry through in 1931–2 a drastic retrenchment, reducing the personnel from about 430 to about 350,† i.e. by nearly 20 per cent, and at the same time to reorganize the judicial system and to initiate a new policy for administering the non-Moslems, thereby heaping a great volume of additional work on the shoulders of this depleted personnel. The Governor spoke much and often of his concern for the welfare of the African, but his Administrative Staff waited in vain for a word or sign professing concern for the welfare of the 350 men who were engaged in implementing his policy. Practically every Division in the country can show surprising figures as to the staff shortage. In Katagum Division, to take one instance, there were four

---

\* H.M. Stationery Office, *Report of the Warren Fisher Committee*.

† Address to the Leg. Co. Suppl. to Extraordinary Gazette, March 6, 1933. It should be recognized that from one-quarter to one-third of the staff is at any given time absent on leave.

ADMINISTRATION IN NIGERIA 197

Administrative Officers in 1931, in 1933-4 there were only two, and at times there was only one.

Such then is the *milieu* in which the English official in Nigeria must live. If a visitor should arrive from England and travel the country, even for a couple of months, he would feel that there was nothing very untoward about it, for a visitor can hardly be expected to discover these subtler and more intimate realities. If he comes out and travels, as, for example, the Under-Secretary of State, or indeed as any person with advantages over and above those of a private obscure person, he will and can see little of the Service as it is. He will be like a man who visits a department store and sees only the magnificent shop windows and the magnificent office of the manager. How the shop really works or how the shop assistants spend their lives will be beyond his ken. The point is not that Englishmen do not die off in sensational numbers, as did their precursors in West Africa a century ago, though as a matter of fact their true death-rate, regard being had to the selected physical stock and the age of the personnel, is very high; the point, rather, is to ask "In what condition or as what sort of people do they survive?" The answer to that question is not always palatable, for too often they survive with their Englishry worn and a little tarnished. After even a decade of the life not a little of the representative English character perishes. The very beginning of an understanding, and therefore of a successful conduct, of the responsibilities of our Crown Colony administration, is to recognize that the *milieu* is highly abnormal. A few Europeans are as healthy in body or mind in West Africa as at home, and perhaps not less than one-third are not markedly below par; the majority, however, are subject to a more or less continuous unfitness. Instances of the pathology of West African life have been rigorously excluded from this book, partly because the victims are more sinned against than sinning, but mostly because such instances would throw a lurid ray here and there that would cause him who is unfamiliar with the country as a whole to see it in a false light. There must be few officials, however, even of only a couple of years' experience, who have not seen for themselves disconcerting manifestations of the *Furor Africanus*.

Colonial administration will continue imperfect until it takes full account of the *milieu* in which its officials must live and of the effects of that *milieu* on average human nature. Action should be devised, as it can be devised, but so far has not been devised, for counteracting those effects.*

* Cf. letter, written in the time of Napoleon, from General Sir J. Moore: "It is not the climate alone that kills troops in this country; it is bad management. We seem as ignorant as if we had never before made war in it." Quoted in Gregory, *The Menace of Colour*, p. 173.

## (2) THE PERSONNEL

*"But what went ye out for to see? A man clothed in soft raiment?"*
Luke vii. 24.

A FIRST-RATE personnel would wilt at some point or other if subjected continuously to a *milieu* like this. Nigeria, like other African colonies, has not always been staffed with a first-rate personnel. The Administrative Service there, as in the rest of tropical Africa, originates from a series of improvisations; and in most colonies the origin, after all, is of fairly recent date, so that the senior ranks are now filled with the improvised appointees. Northern Nigeria goes back to 1900–3; Tanganyika only to the post-war period. The improvisations were done with care, but those responsible for them were limited by the conditions under which they worked, especially by the quality of the supply that offered. For some reason or other it is only within the last decade that there has been the offer of a large supply of men for appointment in the Colonial Service who could stand general comparison with the men in the Civil or Defence Services at home or with men in the Imperial Services abroad like the I.C.S.

Let it be emphasized at once that the majority of the men in the Service in Nigeria have been of a character and a capacity not below the average level, and some among them have been of conspicuous ability, and some of exceptional character. At the same time, however, there has undoubtedly been a thread of inferior quality running through the Service larger than was comfortable.

The origin and building up of the personnel is best understood by thinking of it as consisting of five layers. The first layer was brought out mostly just after the Boer War, most of the appointees being Boer War veterans, and most of them too having rather varied, if not chequered, careers behind them. Most of them, however, did good pioneering work, and in this layer was Mr. Hastings, who produced a piece of fine literature on those days.\*
The last of their number retired recently. . . . The second layer dates from between, say, 1908 and 1913. The men composing it were brought out immediately on graduation from Oxford and Cambridge (in a few cases from Provincial or Scottish universities). It would hardly be denied that the men who came out from Oxford or

\* *Nigerian Days.*

Cambridge in those years—those palmy years when there were more jobs going for Oxford or Cambridge men than the number wanting or needing them, and when the Empire provided more attractive posts and on not very difficult terms of entry in India, the Far East, and elsewhere—were not on the average among the most gifted men of their year. Those of them still here are all Residents and in the most senior posts. . . . The third layer is known in Nigeria as the "Fifteeners." They came out in 1915, some of them about a year after the war had been in progress. They attained to Residentships in the very short time of fifteen or sixteen years' service. Men of their age who went from the universities to the war, survived it, and then came out here, are thus four or five years behind them in seniority. . . . The fourth layer came out in the years between 1919 and, say, 1924 or 1925. It was an inundation rather than a layer, numbering, before the retrenchments, not much under two hundred (this in fact is the residue of what was left from the layer: a large number had already left). They consisted of men of a great diversity in age and antecedents though all had this in common, that they had served in the war. Nearly all had gained temporary commissions, and in many cases an M.C. or other decoration. In Benue Province alone in 1933, out of a Provincial staff of about a dozen there were eight captains there at the one time: it was more distinguished locally to be plain "Mr." The effect of this layer has been to overweight the Service with one type. It need not be said that there were very good men in the group; but to admit so many men of the one kind has worked for stabilizing, indeed for intensifying, that drift towards literalism and clerkliness which all along has been the cardinal defect of the Service. So overweighted is it now with these qualities, and so submerged are the qualities of imagination and the sense of proportion which belongs to the man who enjoys standards of comparison, that there appears little probability of rooting out the one and of growing the other for a decade or two. . . . The fifth layer has been in process of being added since 1925—say for the last decade. Since then recruits have been drawn almost entirely from Oxford and Cambridge. They now comprise nearly half the Service, though, of course, the bottom half. The significant and encouraging fact is that the quality has continually improved, and particularly in the last five years. The improvement is no doubt due in part to the growing difficulties these days of such men finding a job—it looks as though even England may have an "intellectual proletariat" in the coming decades—which has given the Colonial Office a large supply of material to choose from, but the main credit is due to the excellent system of selection and to the standards desiderated by those in the Colonial Office responsible for the selections, which guarantee that the best of the material offering will be chosen. These men are now in general quality as good perhaps as anything England can produce.

Thus such shortcomings in the Service as were due to unsatisfactory appointments are passing. The majority of the Service are now up to standard. The irony of the situation, however, is that such unsatisfactory minority as still remains is, and for some time will be, on the upper rungs. They will still, therefore, be a dominant, probably the predominant, influence. It is disconcerting to observe how and to what extent even within two or three years some of the youngsters assimilate themselves to the dominant atmosphere. If the Colonial Office is going to make the excellent work of its Recruitment Division bear fruit, it must now push forward and tackle conditions in the Colonies themselves.

## (3) THE AFRICAN

"*Yet how sober, and peaceably full of their (not excessive) homely toil, is the life of such.* . . . *And doubtless we exceed them in passionate disorders as much as we excel them in arts and learning, and are subject to better laws and the Christian religion.*"—DOUGHTY, "Arabia Deserta."

\*     \*     \*     \*     \*

"*Faithful are the wounds of a friend.*"

AFRICAN tribes vary in body and in character no less widely than Poles differ from Spaniards or Swedes from Albanians. Yet they have certain qualities which are common, or tend to be common, to them as Africans and which differentiate them sharply from Europeans *

> My mother bore me in the Southern wilds and I am black
> But oh! my soul is white.

So wrote William Blake. Perhaps, ultimately, the differences are only skin-deep. On the other hand, they may be deeper, and Africans in general may never, as some observers believe, be able to get beyond a very short range of consciousness.† If the government of human society could be conducted on scientific lines it would be essential to settle this question of the relative importance of race and environment before determining the policy of African administration; but for the present, at least, this is not possible, and government at the best can be conducted only on lines of intelligent empiricism. The first need in any case is to recognize, and to act on, the basic fact that the African *at the moment* is different. Difference is not the same as inferiority; but difference there is, and to ignore it—to treat the African as a black white-man with rather simpler notions of things than the white white-man—is against the best interests of the African himself.

The first sensation of a European coming into contact with the African is that of smell. This, so the biologists say, is due to a

---

\* Judging from what I have seen of the following thirteen different peoples:—Hausa, Fulani, Berri Berri, Gwari, Munchi, Jukon, Idoma, Shuwa Arabs, Kare Kare, Ibos, Yorubas, Bauchi Pagans, Bauchi Habe.

† Cf. on this point regarding range of consciousness the experiment recently tried by American psychologists of bringing up a baby gorilla side by side with a child. Up to a certain point the gorilla was more intelligent than the child, but it had no idea of experimenting in a disinterested way, like the child, and was much less stable emotionally.

different organization of sweat glands, a specialization born of the African's climate. It marks him off at once, and to the normal European it is repugnant. The shape of the head, the markedly everted lips (an African tends to point with his lips as we use a finger), the colour and movement of the eyes, the sound of his snoring or yawning, the sight of his women spitting, all remind us of something nearer the animal than we feel ourselves to be, animal enough though we know we are at times. Further, he is often very strong physically, but rarely shapely: a well-made symmetrical body, which is fairly common among Europeans, is uncommon among Africans. Again, the reproductive impulses are active enough among all peoples, but among none do they monopolize interests and energies to the degree they do among the African. This also is a natural outcome of his struggle with Nature as represented by the climate and the numerous parasites which create so many deadly diseases there; but it will make association between Europeans and Africans on equal terms difficult and delicate. Hundreds of thousands of Africans possess and exercise a sense of sexual responsibility, and there are many Africans characterized by restraint just as there are many Europeans who are not; but the general drift, born of the general natural differences, is not affected by these qualifications.

Improvidence is as much a part of him as his legs. He cannot postpone a present satisfaction for a larger future satisfaction. There is much to be said for a philosophy of *carpe diem* in his condition of life where the future is more than ordinarily uncertain. That is its justification. It is not the whole of its reason. A large part of its reason is his inability to foresee or to imagine. This accounts, too, for much of his apparent recklessness in danger: travellers have long been astonished at the way natives will frequent water infested with crocodiles when already some of their number have been destroyed there, or at the way they will walk barefoot in the dark over ground infested with snakes.

Whether his mind, as some men think, is of a different calibre from that of the European, cannot be decided in our present state of knowledge. Nor is mere personal experience in itself (*pace* the gentlemen who shout at you angrily that they have been living amongst him for twenty years: living amongst is not the same as observing) enough to form a reliable estimate. For my own part, for whatever my observations may be worth, I am impressed with what I have seen of the African's capacity for mental effort and incline to an optimistic view; where misgiving enters is in considering what, for want of a better word, might be called his moral qualities.

If one overhears a group of men talking the discussion will usually concern one or both of two subjects—women and money. He tends to be greedy even above the rather high average of European greediness. And he is shameless in pursuing the course of possession. He will ask for anything, will approach anybody, and no snub or showing up represses him. Servants and dependents in general are insatiable. Likewise there is little sense of honour. There is probably no branch of mankind which is so little touched by the sense of honour. To appeal to it is, in general, as efficacious as appealing to a wall. Thus, to generalize about the majority, admittedly dangerous, he does not pay a debt or fulfil his half of a contract if he can avoid doing so—wherein lies the root cause of his litigiousness. Amongst Europeans it is probable that no more than 1 per cent of all contracts entered into become the subject of litigation; amongst Africans it is probable that 75 per cent, it is certain that over 50 per cent, of all contracts (not merely formal or legal contracts) entered into are disputed informally if not formally. The records of embezzlements by native employees in the big trading corporations, like the Niger Company, have not been made public, but they must be on a gargantuan scale. An embezzling employee is the unusual, not the usual, figure in European commercial houses; in African commercial houses he is the expected figure. So, too, in the Government it is axiomatic that an African cannot be trusted with a sixpence of Government money. In Kano alone in 1931-2 at about the same time there were cases substantiating that notwithstanding all precautions taken the Transport Clerk in the Magistrates' Office had embezzled something under a hundred pounds, that clerks in the accountant's office at the waterworks had embezzled several hundred pounds, and the Treasurer of the Emirate (who was paid a salary of £720 a year) had embezzled uncertain but large sums.

The European in Africa can thus rarely avoid a sense of the African's untrustworthiness. He feels that he cannot rely on him. Above all, he cannot believe him. Nothing can excel the excellence of his campaign of deceit. After *kurdi* (money) and *mata* (woman) no word is so often on the tongue of the Hausa-speaking African as *rikichi*, which means trickery, double-dealing, cheating.

Another defective quality is that of quarrelsomeness, and it too seems to spring from a lack of inward dignity.

Has he affection? or gratitude? or disinterestedness? Most men of experience would answer negatively. They may be right, though considerable exceptions could be proven.

Then there is his cruelty, and his lack of "an instinctive recoil from injustice." He is cruel to animals. A dog with a broken leg which prevents its moving will be left to lie in pain and to die of starvation; bits are habitually used which make the horse's mouth bleed, and raw neglected wounds on horses' backs are common sights. They show the same insensibility in dealing with one another, providing they are unhampered by family or tribal obligations. I have known of an old woman to be struck down by a train at night-time and to be left, untended, by passers-by. As for the second and more serious quality, "one looks in vain for an instinctive recoil from injustice. . . . A mean, blackguardly act produces no indignation in the African," are words that have been written by Miss Miller,* a missionary of more than a quarter of a century of devoted service, whose great experience and whose popularity among the Africans gives her words authority above the average.

It would be a great injustice to numerous individuals not to emphasize that there are many and conspicuous exceptions to the above generalizations. It would be wrong, too, not to emphasize that qualities which are repugnant to us may go with good qualities, like the African's instinct for manners, and his sense of family and tribal obligation (which might, conceivably, evolve into a social conscience of the highest value). The average European, who has any interest in the native, except as raw material for careerism, generally feels something akin to affection for him, especially for peoples like the Munchi and Hausa, whom it is impossible to dislike, and he is himself often the object, if not of affection, then of something very near affection, from them. Of course it is possible to like people and yet to know that they cannot be relied upon.

But above all would it be wrong if we lose sight of the fact that what now strikes us as indicating a defective moral sense is due to (1) the African's suddenly being brought up against a set of new social conditions for which his old moralities are at the same time inadequate and unprepared; and (2) the fact that everything in his

* In the *West African Review*, June 1934.

struggle to live makes him the realist and materialist *par excellence.**

Indeed, the fairest approach to the African is to realize that his great achievement has been to survive his environment, on the whole the most inimical of any known to mankind. He has evolved a body which can survive not only that climate but malaria, and yellow fever, and bilharzia, and a score of other deadly diseases. The struggle has been so acute that there has been little energy left over after winning this physical victory. He therefore remains the nearest to the animal (using animal in no derogatory sense) of any of the great branches of mankind.† Perhaps he has evolved from a different kind of ape than the rest of mankind.‡ To live has been enough. He has made his peace with life: he does not torment himself with ideas and ideals, he knows no sorrow of the spirit: his wants are satisfied with a full belly and a body at ease. This is not to say his wants will always be so satisfied or that he will never know a travail of the soul. As Mr. Arnold Toynbee has pointed out, the time-gap separating the modern civilized European and the modern African is small when compared with the long stretch of time that man, black or white, has been on earth.§

But for the time being, and as he is now, the African man is deeply different from the white man, and it is he who will suffer most by any line of policy which ignores or makes light of this cardinal fact. If isolated individuals like Aggrey and the rest arise let them be treated as the exceptions they are. The great danger to-day is that of reaction—the left-wing reaction, which "because our forefathers put him in chains . . . feels obliged to put him in our drawing-rooms."‖ It is as unjust to the African to give him powers and responsibilities which postulate a range of consciousness clearly not his *at the moment* and *on the average* as it is to give a child the powers and responsibilities of an adult.

This reminds us that a particular need called for to-day in the

---

\* It is therefore odd to read an article in the *West African Review*, op. cit., by an African denouncing European materialism and urging Africans not to become materialist, to retain their native idealism—a fair illustration of a literate's having memorized formulae without understanding them.

† Cf. Sir Charles Eliot's opinion, quoted *Dual Mandate*.

‡ Cf. Haddon, *Races of Mankind*.

§ *Survey of International Affairs*, 1931.

‖ Miss Miller, loc. cit.

administration of African colonies is a wise discipline. The old disciplines of African life are rapidly breaking down. In their place is being taken over the furniture and apparatus—so far rarely the spirit—of European civilization, something that has been achieved at the cost of centuries of effort on the part of Europeans and something therefore that has resulted in an implicit acceptance of certain disciplines. The African takes this over (or such of it as he can) ready made, without undergoing the long struggle of creative effort and without evolving at the same time an implicit pattern of restraints.

The extreme or the logical effects of "Europeanization" are not yet shown over Africa as a whole. Among the villagers and the tribesmen life for the vast majority is still subjected to much of the old discipline and life is still essentially and wholesomely African. But among the literates, mostly found in the towns of recent growth on, or not far from, the coast, the pattern of life has been broken by "Europeanization." This class (known as Wogs in West African slang) comprises a handful of doctors and lawyers and many thousands of men who can read and write English and who, in West Africa at least, are lumped together under the generic term of "clerks." Among the doctors and lawyers are men as able as they are honourable and they should be (and to the great honour of West African tradition are) treated as Europeans.\* Their rarity, however, must be emphasized again, especially as Exeter Hall enthusiasts tend to regard them as typical of all literate Africans. They forget that the doctors and lawyers represent the final process of fine tooth-combing in African schools. The best of the clerks, too, who are generally to be found in the Government Service, are admirable men. Beneath these two groups—the professional man and the authentic clerk—is a hoard of quasi-literates, parasitic, litigious, showy, noisy, insolent, and as irresponsible as they are untrustworthy. They wear the white man's clothing, speak pidgin English, and, by writing petitions or anonymous charges, can create an activity in Government circles that is as mischievous as it is ridiculous. The vicious point in the policy of the Education Department is that once a youth has learnt his three R's he regards it as beneath him to continue the life of a farmer, cultivating the fields

---

\* An interesting and admirable feature of British imperialism in West Africa is that there is virtually no race prejudice of the kind that prevails in Asia.

and living in the village. In a country that is and must always be predominantly agricultural the bulk of the population must follow agriculture for its livelihood—or become parasitic. Any town of any size in Nigeria, and every settlement along the Railway, contains its colony of "clerks": a handful of legitimate clerks and pidgin-speaking artisans, the rest professional letter-writers, non-workers, or applicants for jobs as store-keepers, toll-collectors, confidential agents(!), motor drivers, and traders, jobs which can never exist in numbers equal to the numbers of applicants. They are always from Southern Nigeria: the Moslem in the North shows a magnificent superiority in character and worth to the negroes and negroid peoples of the South in this respect, just as he does in declining to ape European clothes and habits: he has a culture of his own of the worth of which he is conscious.

The author had occasion to see much of the class when serving as Political Officer to Railway Construction. The Engineers were required to give the bulk of the contracts to Africans, who were naturally drawn from the literate class. For a time, in 1931-2, most of the contracts were given to a body which called itself the Nigerian Co-operative Labour Company. The so-called Company had no capital, many debts, and a very large Directorate recruited from men most of whom had been dismissed, for good reasons, from the Government or from trading companies. Special stationery was printed, and a full set of executive officers appointed including a General Manager, a Chief Consulting Engineer, a Chief Secretary, and so on, the organization of the Company apparently having been modelled on the Standard Oil Corporation. For some miles one could not walk a hundred yards without meeting one of the "Company's" officials, resplendent in duck drill suitings, and fortified by sun glasses, solar topees or double-felt hats, green-lined umbrellas, and other prophylactic elaborations against heat stroke. This fantastic concern continued in being for months, when at length it collapsed by the flight of the major Directors from angry unpaid labourers. But not before a few square miles of Nigeria had been turned into a Liberia. It had entered into arrangements with local Chiefs whereby the latter conscripted tribesmen and sent them to work as forced labour on the line, the bulk of such money as was paid for the labour (being only a moiety of what was due) being handed over to the Chiefs personally. Debtors' pawns, mostly girls, were brought up in contingents from the South and put to

## ADMINISTRATION IN NIGERIA

work. Fraudulent arrangements were also made between the Company and their brother clerks in the Railway Department whereby they used the telegraph and the trains without paying. To this day there are several hundred simple Pagan villagers in Niger Province who have not been paid for their labour. Nearly a year after the disappearance of the Nigerian Co-operative Labour Company I had to go through the books of a man who had been a member of the "Company," and in them I found an account of some money which had been distributed (of course without practical effect) as gifts to senior clerks in various Government offices, including the chief clerks in three Magistrates' Offices, a senior clerk in the Lagos Secretariat, and several senior Railway Department clerks.

A mischievous drift in Nigerian Administration in recent years has been the virtual encouragement of the bad traits of this class by the virtual encouragement of written complaints and petitions, a game predominantly and characteristically played by the semi-literates. If the Administration is not to be clogged up with them one of the chief needs to-day is to lay down stringent limitations on the right of petitioning and appealing. *Prima facie* such a limitation would be repugnant to English opinion at home as savouring of a *droit administratif*; but English opinion at home is uninformed of the true facts and makes assumptions based upon its own way of life. Few people in England petition anyone; and appeals are limited both by common sense, and, failing that, by expense. Petty personal interests and petty personal grievances are permitted in Nigeria to run up the whole length of the hierarchy from Assistant-District Officer to the supreme functionary at Lagos. It is not argued that the right of petition or of appeal should be extinguished; but it should be limited; and it can without difficulty be limited. An administrative personnel, which, allowing for those on leave and in the three Secretariats, is only about two hundred, has to serve a population of over twenty millions—one hundred thousand to each officer. It needs no demonstration to show that it is impossible to attend individually to the petty personal complaints of everyone. Yet in practice, no less than in theory, if a complaint or petition is pushed above the heads of the Administrative personnel, the latter is assumed to have made a complete investigation and to have kept a complete written record. The result, naturally, is that Administrative Officers unlucky enough to be stationed in those parts of the country infested with petition writers and complaint makers, attend in detail only to complainants who are potential appellants to His Excellency; this, in practice, means the literates. In the province of Ijebu Ode (just north of Lagos, the tribe being extremely intelligent: it is the home of the counterfeiters), so the writer has been informed by a member of the Central Secretariat, the bulk of the time of the Administrative personnel is taken up with petitions and petitioners. A foreman responsible for part of the permanent-way of the railway traversing Ibo country told me that he had been so harassed by justifying his conduct and in answering false charges after dismissing Ibo navvies, that for sheer peace he now refrained from dismissing them. A case like this—of a European foreman or engineer dismissing a navvy, or of an Administrative Officer giving a certain decision on a dispute involving a few shillings between Southern traders—might result in petitions being sent simultaneously to the King, the Prince of Wales, the Secretary of State for the Colonies, the Governor, and the Resident. The professional letter-writer (his letters are normally endorsed "written free of charge") foments the nuisance, though he is an occasion rather than a cause, the cause being the disproportionate gravity that the highest authority, especially a recent Governor, demands, or was believed to demand, in the treatment of such letters. More serious still is the reception that is given to anonymous or forged letters of complaint. I recollect a case at Minna in 1932 where a series of charges were written against a Scotch engineer of unimpeachable character, on official Railway paper (and therefore by a subordinate Railway employé or by someone in close touch with one), which was signed with a spurious name. Weeks of heartburning were taken up with the affair.* It is said that a certain very highly placed personage was not above reading, and calling for action on, even anonymous letters. The baseness of such conduct cannot be sufficiently reprobated.

As the "Wogs" have memorized all the *clichés* ("British justice," "an insult to decent Africans," "liberty of the person," "bloody nigger"), and have a natural instinct for oratory, they can make effective play, as they now well know, on English liberalism at home, and especially with that section of the Nonconformist

---

* A comparable and not uncommon trick is to send anonymous or forged letters to England to the wife of an official warning her as to her husband's private life.

Conscience which battens on Armenian atrocities, Oriental slavery, and all the other motes in the neighbours' eyes.

A recent example of how much ado can be made about nothing is the noise made by a handful of people on the Gold Coast to the sections (admittedly not all well drafted) of the Gold Coast Criminal Code Amendment Act, a noise that was swollen by certain newspapers in England referring to the Act as a Sedition Bill. In July 1934 an expensive delegation was sent to England; and, at the moment of writing, the *Manchester Guardian*\* reports that there are again representatives of the natives of the Gold Coast (*sic*. That is the real danger—a noisy voluble unrepresentative handful posturing among people at home who do not and cannot know the true facts, as spokesmen of the majority) in England meeting members of the Liberal and Labour Parties, their chief complaint being that the so-called Gold Coast Aborigines' Rights Society is not treated by the Government as "the mouthpiece of the natives!"

Not only is the literate class a tiny fraction of the Nigerian population, and unrepresentative of the interests of the Nigerian population as a whole, but their bluff can be called easily now. But give a continuation of the policy—especially of the Education policy—that now exists and insist on the same attention to their demands and cries for another decade or two and the Government will find that it has, like Frankenstein, raised up a monster which will consume it.

A strong reason (amongst other strong reasons) for removing the headquarters of the Nigerian Government from Lagos is that so long as it remains there it will be surrounded by an unrepresentative but insistent population which colours the attitude of the Government and at the worst deflects it. It is not argued that the genuinely educated and responsible African should not be accommodated. He should be, and he can be: a chance was lost recently in not filling a vacancy in the Supreme Court by the appointment of one of the Lagos barristers. Nor is it any reflection on the genuinely educated and responsible African to curb the troublesomeness of the quasi-literate insurgent. Rather it is a disservice to the former to associate him or his interests with the latter.

The only governing principle to our Administration, after all, should be that we treat the African as an end in himself and not

\* *Manchester Guardian Weekly*, March 15, 1935.

as a means to any ends of our own. That is the meaning of the paramountcy of African interests. And so long as we can justify our being in control of African colonies at all it is our duty and our responsibility to determine how those ends are to be achieved. Our danger is of eluding them and of turning a minority of Africans into spoilt children at the cost of the rest.

(4) INDIRECT RULE

"*Parturiunt montes, nascetur ridiculus mus.*"
HORACE, A. P. 139.

\* \* \* \* \*

"*Refined policy ever has been the parent of confusion and will ever be so as long as the world endures. Plain good intention, which is as easily discovered at the first view as fraud is surely detected at the last, is, let me say, of no mean force in the government of mankind.*"—BURKE.

NIGERIA, more particularly Northern Nigeria, enjoys considerable fame in connection with what is called Indirect Rule, or, as the latest refinement has it, Indirect Administration. A large and somewhat intricate exegesis has grown up around what in origin and in content is quite a simple matter.

What happened was this: In 1900 Sir Frederick Lugard (as he then was) was appointed High Commissioner of Northern Nigeria, a country he was to pacify and bring under British control. Control was established by 1903. Sir Frederick found that he was called upon to govern a population of many millions (though, as it turned out, not as many millions as was estimated at the time) scattered over an area nearly twice the size of the United Kingdom. He had to improvise an administrative personnel and there were no hopes of getting out officers to the number required for governing the new conquest directly. Further, most of the country was already under the control of the Fulani Emirates which were there as a going concern and which impressed Sir Frederick by the quality of their administrative machinery and administrative ability. He did the obvious, indeed the inevitable, thing: he left the Emirates to continue in being, subject only to certain broad limitations.\*
That was all there was to it. Sir Frederick was not the first Colonial Governor to resort to such an expedient. British rule in India can provide examples from as far back as the eighteenth century; the French were already doing the same thing in parts of their East Indian Empire; and the Dutch were embarked upon it in the Dutch East Indies; though Lugard showed his administrative genius in

\* See Lugard's annual reports to Chamberlain, 1900-1, p. 26; 1902, pp. 84 and 92.

the technique and the details he worked out for running the system.*

On this expedient was gradually built up an imposing superstructure of ideology. It is only fair to say that it was early observed that an ideal might be extracted from or be associated with the expedient, and, further, that the ideal itself was a good one. The ideal, briefly expressed, was that it is a good thing for primitive man to evolve along his own lines instead of being made to follow the lines of an alien culture. But it is also fair to emphasize that in actual origin, as also in actual practice, the system of utilizing chiefdoms already in existence as going concerns for governing a subject people, and the ideal of the autonomous non-alien evolution of that people, are two separate things and have no necessary connection. It was another of Lord Lugard's merits that he managed to join an ideal to the expedient.

Lugard left Nigeria on his retirement from the Colonial Service in 1919. In 1923 *The Dual Mandate in Tropical Africa* was published, a book that for its effect on the minds of those interested in colonial policy can be compared only with such a work as Durham's Report on Canada of a century earlier or Burke's speeches on the Warren Hastings trial. Any book written on his craft in the reflective evening of his life by a man of such epic experience of the Empire, of such singleness, integrity, and dignity of character, and of an outlook and a background so much wider than that of the usual Imperial functionary, was bound to contain much of very great value. To praise it would be an impertinence. There is nothing else quite like it in all the literature of British imperialism. Further experience has suggested, and no doubt will continue to suggest, modifications here and there, and as an expression of the adventurousness and gallantry of the author's life the present writer prefers Lord Lugard's *Rise of Our East African Empire* (a book in the authentic line of descent of the classics of the English explorers and pioneers); but the essential substance of the *Dual Mandate* is beyond question.

The *Dual Mandate* owed its immediate reception to the fact that it was the first reasoned case for our "dependent" Empire, and that

* Their quality may be best appreciated by reading *Political Memoranda*, compiled in a book in 1918, which he issued to his officers, still the indispensable handbook of the Administrator.

it gave a moral basis to that case. Africa, so the argument ran, could not be left shut up merely for the benefit of the African; the outside world also had an interest in and a claim to share its great and special kind of wealth;* but the outside world, in exercising its legitimate claim, must heed the legitimate interests of the African and must therefore comport itself as his trustee. Obligations, like interests, were dual. And as an example of how the outside world should exercise its trusteeship, details were set out of the system of administration that had been built up in Northern Nigeria, which was described as Indirect Rule. The book came at an opportune time. Not only was the administration of all the non-Indian part of the "dependent" Empire a closed book at that day so that authoritative information was sought for its own sake, but the British conscience was becoming more and more sensitive about the Empire. *The Dual Mandate* was a comforting as well as a highly informative book.

Lord Lugard's fame and the success of his book put Nigeria on the map, and the men who had been officers in the Service there from the early days now saw themselves as the makers of history. They were then in the saddle and were not slow to appreciate their old merits or their new opportunities. The simple and healthy linking on of an ideal to an expedient was elaborated into an occult science. Indirect Rule became a formula as hieratic and as dead of creative development as an outworn theology. In fact a theocratic oligarchy closed the canon, refusing any addition to their scriptures, "the interpretation of which was their own monopoly"; and Indirect Rule degenerated firstly into a systematic glorification of a number of able but unscrupulous careerists, secondly into the practice of preserving at all costs the status and power of the families of the hereditary Emirs and chiefs, and thirdly into an undue preoccupation with Islam and the Emirates to the neglect of the Pagan peoples. From time to time a Lieutenant-Governor (until 1931 the Lieutenant-Governors of the Northern Provinces were little interfered with by Lagos, being *de facto* Governors of Northern Nigeria) would speak *ex cathedra*, his utterance being transmitted within sealed confidential envelopes to the administrative personnel, thus giving birth to a corpus of *hadiths*. The principle of Indirect Rule, indeed, was saved from

* A dangerous argument, as it cuts both ways: what of the White Australia policy?

being openly discredited only because most of the simple elementary government required there, notably away from the various headquarters, went on without overdue attention to the externals of the principle and because the Land Policy (dating from Lugard's time),\* and the impossibility of European settlement being undertaken in such climate, had preserved the economic independence of the people. It is not possible to put one's finger on a single contribution or new idea or new development in the administration of the policy of Indirect Rule in Nigeria since Lugard's time.† Numerous innovations there have been; but they either were of trifles (though always loudly advertised trifles) or of sheer perversions. Lord Lugard's own sense of loyalty would probably force him to deny this strongly, but nevertheless the verdict of the future historian, no doubt, will be that Lugard was not well served by his successors (most of whom were his promoted subordinates).

It is not easy to make clear to men outside the Service to what a size and to what a pitch of absurdity this bubble had been blown. As a reference for the future student one might direct him to consult the instructions and circulars issued to officers, especially those from Kaduna, and especially those issued between 1926 and 1930. Indirect Rule and its originators (then construed to be the same as the men at the top in Northern Nigeria at that day) was praised with ecstatic fervour. It was also made clear that the mystery was so profound that it was practically beyond the understanding of junior officers, not to mention persons outside the Service, and, excepting an odd man here and there of quite unusual ability and of at least twelve years' seniority, it could never really be understood by those who had not been in the Service in the pre-war years when the principle was being worked out. It was freely admitted that this was a disturbing situation, but if only junior officers would appreciate their advantage and follow unswervingly the directions of their seniors, the worst might yet be avoided. Very awkward cases sometimes arose. For example, when Cadets and quite junior A.D.O.s asked how are you going to develop these Emirates, which you have turned into medieval monarchies, into modern states, or communities? or how can most tribal societies

\* Broadly speaking, land cannot be alienated in Nigeria: it is owned by the Government in trust for the natives. See relevant Ordinances; also good general account in Buell's *The African Native Problem*.

† Some would claim the establishment of the Native Treasuries to be a contribution. The case against them has been argued in the Journal supra.

by developing along their own lines grow into a society equal to modern life? Such men were quickly marked down as temperamentally unsuited for life in Nigeria. No more damning remark could be made in the annual secret report on an officer than that he was "direct" or not sufficiently imbued with the spirit of Indirect Rule.

A deplorable feature of this perverted form of Indirect Rule was its pretence. Officers were continuously exhorted to be "indirect" in this highly formal sense, when not only did they see that occasions in the interests of justice often called for "direct" activity, but they saw daily the very men exacting this standard of "indirectness" from them acting (and generally rightly acting) in the most "direct" way.

Another regrettable feature was the manner in which the system worked to bolster up effete and corrupt chiefs at the expense of their people. As late as 1932, thirty years after our subjugation of the country, it was found amongst the Gwari chiefdoms that forcible seizure of girls for the harims of chiefs (Kuta and Guni), continuous and heavy exactions of both goods and money from the commoners, embezzlement of tax, arbitrary imprisonment and other persecutions, forced labour on a scale whereby in some cases half the able-bodied male population were conscripted to work in construction camps for the benefit of the chief and against the will of the conscripted, and possibly even "palace" murders, were the order in some of the Gwari chiefdoms. Some of these things, as at Kuta, had been going on, unbeknown to the D.O.s, for nine years, at a distance of only a few hundred yards from the Divisional Headquarters.

At about the same time serious scandals were brought to light in the Bida Emirate, and a year or so previously they were brought to light in the Sultanate of Sokoto. The tenacity shown by those in power in Northern Nigeria in refusing to remove higher chiefs was remarkable. It required spectacular criminality to induce Kaduna to move against them, to such a degree had Indirect Rule been perverted into a policy for conserving these petty autocracies, the argument running that a native would sooner suffer injustice from a native authority than justice from an alien.

The cardinal weakness of Indirect Rule as practised in Nigeria after Lugard's departure has been the tendency to build up autocracies and to ignore the villages. Perhaps the author may be permitted to quote here what he had occasion to write towards the end of 1931: "Indirect Rule will become a mischievous policy unless steps are taken within the next few years to build up a strong village administration. All that is good in native rule and economics and culture is from and in the villages. This bolstering up of chiefs (who now enjoy a security that was unknown before our coming) can be safe only if a 'democracy,' or some such equivalent to an effective restraining public opinion, can be built up in the villages. A concentrated drive in this direction is (as I see it) the first need in native policy here to-day." It is only fair to recognize that it was not merely natural, but also to some extent unavoidable, that the Government during the first decade or so of our occupation should concentrate on the various native *central* governments; but that excuse had long disappeared.

Perhaps the best, certainly a surprising, example of the mentality of those then in charge was the proposal to make Europeans resident in Northern Nigeria subject to Native Courts. It is hard to believe that men in their sanity and knowing in their day-to-day work the exact nature of the Native Courts, their efficiency, reliability, and so on, could have gone so far as to put such a measure down in a Bill. Yet that is what happened. We have the succeeding Governor's testimony for it, the more impressive because he was obliged to state his justifiable amazement in "Parliamentary language." Speaking in the Legislative Council in February 1933, he said, " . . . I have not proceeded with the proposal incorporated in a Bill which was discussed in this Council in February 1931 . . . to subject all persons automatically to the jurisdiction of the native authority within whose area they might happen to find themselves. . . . I confess that I have never been able to understand the provisions of the Bill. . . . It is difficult to believe that it was intended that the Administrative Officers, for instance, should in fact be subjected to the jurisdiction of the native authorities, even in the organized Emirates, and if this was the case (as almost certainly it was) then we reach again the realm of pretence in administration of which I am so, unashamedly, afraid. Moreover, some of the native authorities are of the most primitive, almost nebulous, character."*

The new Governor arrived in Nigeria in the second half of 1931.

* Governor's speech to the Legislative Council, printed in Supplement to Extraordinary Gazette, dated March 6, 1933, p. 18.

As his immediate task was to deal with a deficit it was some time before his ideas on native policy were made known. A Governor controls the fountain of promotion, however, and can therefore make his ideas felt very swiftly. His Excellently indicated some animosity to the old Northern Nigerian regime, inveighing against the semi-monarchism that had been allowed to grow up in the Emirates and against the neglect of the Pagans. He circulated a thesis of his to the effect that the traditional basis of native institutions was not autocratic but conciliar, and that what was needed in Nigeria (amongst other reforms) was a search for the particular form of conciliar basis suited to this or that tribe or group, and then a reorganization of the native authority in accordance therewith. This worked like magic. The beliefs of years were jettisoned and a spate of anthropological reports flowed in from all parts of the country (the springs of which had shown no signs of drying up towards the end of 1934) proving, with an impressive unanimity, that the traditional basis of the tribal institutions investigated was, in fact, as His Excellency suggested, conciliar; and the neglect of the Pagans under previous régimes did not go unnoticed. So good were they that His Excellency himself had occasion to commend the reports, especially those from South-East Nigeria; and he sent one report, by a certain Resident, accompanied by a memorandum from another official, to the Secretary of State, as being probably the most important that had been issued officially for a long number of years in the Northern Provinces.

The two documents referred to have an interest additional to their immediate subject matter because one of them showed a conversion, following more than twenty years' experience of the country and its administration, the extent of which can be measured by a document from the same hand only five years previously, when the pro-Emirate régime was at its height and the mode of interpreting and practising Indirect Rule was just that which the later Governor was reacting against.

At that time the writer of the document referred to was Resident of a certain Province, and, as was then the fashion, produced a circular on Indirect Rule for his staff and then transmitted a copy of it to the Lieutenant-Governor of the day. The Lieutenant-Governor, who was described in it as one of the founders of Indirect Rule and received much subtle praise, had it printed and circulated to all the Administrative staff; indeed, until the later Governor came copies of it used to be given to Cadets on their first entry into Northern Nigeria as the official statement of Indirect Rule!

The present author, who received such a copy on entering the Service, and later, with the passage of time and its turn in the wheel of fortune, received a copy of the two documents referred to above, applied to the Colonial Office for permission to publish extracts from them in his study of Indirect Rule; permission, however, was refused. It is regretted that several amusing and instructive essays must therefore continue to blush unseen. By taking sentence by sentence and comparing them one with another, and then with the very important policy speech made by the Governor to the Legislative Council in March 1933, it is possible not only to show the doctrine of Indirect Rule as a somewhat varying quantity, both as regards its substance and as regards the interpretation of its history, according to what happens to be the school of thought of the Governor of the day (who is also, it must be repeated, the controller of the fountain of promotion), but also to throw an essential light on the morale and tone of the upper rungs of the Service.

Hence, not unintelligibly, though regrettably (for no other system can take its place), there has grown up a reaction against Indirect Rule, both within the Service and outside it. Years of observing a practice which departs and must depart widely from the theory, which theory nevertheless is extravagantly belauded and its more or less unimportant externals insisted upon, breed a disquieting kind of cynicism which shrugs its shoulders and asks, "What else can you expect? . . . *c'est la vie* . . . and see how it brings or fails to bring promotion." Here is some of the "pretence" to which a Governor himself has made reference.

As for the outside critics, odd ones, like Mr. Murray,* had ventured to demur to the claims of Indirect Rule at an earlier date, but the incident which mobilized an impressive volume of criticism was Tshekedi's case. Tshekedi, it will be recalled, was the acting Chief in Bechuanaland, who, in 1933, had a white criminal flogged, and whom Vice-Admiral Evans, temporarily officiating as High Commissioner of the South African Protectorates, then arrested, following a descent into Bechuanaland with howitzers and two

---

* A. Victor Murray, *The School in the Bush*. Also cf. *Western Civilization and the Natives of S. Africa*, ed. I. Schapera, 1934, for discussion as to value of retaining native customs.

hundred marines. The subsequent correspondence in the Press,* which included letters from ex-Colonial officials, showed that there was a body of opinion that more than demurred to, indeed that was actively hostile to, Indirect Rule.

The Tshekedi case, nevertheless, is not really relevant to the question of Indirect Rule because the conditions it brought to light were the product not of Indirect Rule, but of no rule.

In any case the principle of Indirect Rule is not in danger. It rests not on immutable laws but on immutable poverty. No other system of administration which would conform to the standards required by England can be afforded in British Africa. The impossibility of directly ruling millions of Africans makes a temporary delegation of power to native authority inevitable; thus in Kano over two million are ruled by nine Europeans. This, in general, and if adequate supervision be forthcoming, need be no bad thing. In general, indeed, it is a good thing. But it is not the most important aspect of government. Land tenure; weight of taxation; the presence or absence of a compulsion to work for the white man; education;† in short, the question of the economic independence of the African is much more important than what particular administrative machinery is used for carrying out the will of the Suzerain. For, let it not be forgotten, the Suzerain does not and cannot abdicate its will, and clashes are frequent and are bound to be frequent between that will and the desires of the native authority.

That then, in origin, as in present substance, is what Indirect Rule is. Whether a series of quasi-autonomous and quasi-autocratic states of paramount Chiefs, as in Nigeria, can evolve into a single Central Government or into non-autocratic or non-oligarchic communities is for the future; for the present the question is not of any great consequence. It is enough that they now work, and work with commendable efficiency (on the whole), and that, through financial necessity, for the time being they are secure. As for the ideology that has become associated with the expedient, that is a different matter. In so far as it is practicable, and excepting certain tribes where the customs are not worth preserving or are incapable of development (the responsibility for the decision is our own), it

* Cf. *Manchester Guardian*, from September 23 to October 2, 1933.

† All these important subjects received Lord Lugard's attention, notably taxation and land tenure, and in such a way that neither of the latter constitutes a real problem in Nigeria to-day. It is unfair to Lord Lugard to associate his administrative work solely with what is called Indirect Rule.

is, to my judgment, of the utmost importance to enable the African to develop along his own lines and to develop naturally as an African instead of artificially as a pseudo-European. It is of importance, but for much, perhaps for most, of Africa, unfortunately, it is impossible. The game even now is nearly lost. Education—even the bare literacy, and its results, given by the elementary schools—and the effect of the missionaries' evangelization and of the adoption of English law and of modern commerce are new wine which the old bottles of African culture cannot always hold. The most, probably, that can be made of Indirect Rule will be to develop African self-government in local areas (which, of course, is no small thing), and to do that means concentrating more and more on the villages. The great merit of Sir Donald Cameron is that he has sought this widening of the policy. It is still not too late in Africa to avoid some errors of our Indian venture. As for the rest of the elaborate façade of Indirect Rule, it is much ado about nothing—cardboard and plaster packed up by the careerists.*

* The best account of Indirect Rule for to-day will be found in Miss Margery Perham's study in *Africa*, though in the present writer's opinion she tends here and there to see it rather too theoretically and not sufficiently as only one element in the whole corpus of administrative practice; this, however, does not seriously affect the unusual excellence and insight of her study.

## (5) MISSIONS AND MISSIONARIES

*"We live in times of such obvious transition, decline, poverty of deep creative conviction, of such excess of analysis over synthesis ... when ... to produce reality, to adore and to will, and to see things in the large and upon the whole and at their best is what we all require."*—BARON VON HÜGEL.

SHOULD missions be encouraged or disallowed? The answer to the question will vary according to the temperament and the preferences of the responder. If he feels that the African will get more satisfaction from life undisturbed by the penetration of ideas and habits from the outside world his response will be for discouraging or disallowing missions. But to pose the question in this way is irrelevant. The penetration has already gone too far to be withstood, and, still more, the African himself wants and, if only for love of mere novelty, will insist on getting as much of the outside world as he can; a fact that should be recollected when discussing Indirect Rule. The African is showing on all sides a preference for alien as against his indigenous institutions.

There is thus no general issue of African religion *versus* Deism. The issue, rather, is Christianity *versus* Islam.

The desirability or otherwise of Islam as the new religion of the African has been much canvassed. Perhaps the strongest point made against Islam is that it has already exhausted its possibilities, and that as a consequence it is just perpetuating a static ethic and rationale derived from sixth-century Arabia. There is something in the point; but it is surely not the whole truth, for there have been modernist and reformist movements in Islam, especially in Egypt and India (e.g. the Ahmadiyyah). Then there is the prophet Mohammed: he certainly does seem incomplete as the perfect and eternal exemplar. Another objection is that Islam lowers, or at least keeps at a low level, the status of women. From the present writer's experience and observation in Africa, for what it is worth, this is not true. The status of Pagan women is lower than that of Moslem women. Indeed, the treatment of modern women in Africa is liberal in most directions, especially as regards divorce. Be that as it may, the great merit of Islam is that it offers the African an explanation of the Universe and a code of ethics superior to his own and yet not too difficult or too different from his own, especially in sexual matters. The more completely Christianity is apprehended, on the other hand, the more completely does it separate the African from his old natural way of life and from his natural environment. Again, Islam is definite and defined, while the essence of Christianity, being mystical, is vague. Even the propagators of Islam are men of his own race, often of his own village, and rarely (if ever) professional proselytes. From every point of view Islam is not alien. Thus it spreads silently: one villager is impressed: he observes and tries to learn the ritual and at length enters the brotherhood; and so it grows.

His taste is surely not at fault in being impressed by the ritual of Islam. To hear the muezzin make the prayer call in the half light of early dawn or late evening or at the still hour of the afternoon heat, is to behold the beauty of austerity, and to feel that all is dust and vanity and nothing imports but Allah, the one, the undivided, and the eternal. The ritual of Islam has the economy and therefore the immediate force of great prose: nothing distracts from the central point—Allah and the individual.

Mary Kingsley wrote that "the Moslem is the gentleman of West Africa." It is not merely that his religion is free of the vulgarity of most Christian converts with their execrable Moody and Sankey hymn tunes and crude texts, but the Moslem has a poise and a stability and a code which the Christian convert generally (by no means always) lacks; probably because the Moslem can practise something he can understand, while the Christian convert cannot. Thus, as I see it, Islam is a religion better suited to Africa. Yet, it seems certain, Islam will gain few converts in comparison with Christianity.

A point that is often made against Christian missions is that they give rise to competition between various Christian sects. The point has been overdone. Competition is in the African's blood, and strife between religious sects may become a sublimated outlet for the competition that formerly led to head-hunting. Also it involves some kind of energy of mind and spirit, and it sets up a rallying point around which the sense of loyalty to a community can be fostered.* Nor, again, is it a defect that the Christian religion is

* An interesting development is taking place in some of the south-east communities of Nigeria, where the native church elders and the village court elders are the same now.

propagated by men who often are of small intellectual stature, preaching crudities and disproportions.* The African is now in a state where a message delivered with faith and conviction, and where the example of disinterested living makes an appeal that no intellectual gifts can equal. Nor must it be forgotten that there are some remarkable examples of mission effort—missionaries like Dr. Nassau of the Congo, Kemp of the Gold Coast, and above all Mary Slessor, the Dundee mill hand and a female personality not a whit less forceful than Florence Nightingale. On the other hand, these appear to be exceptional cases. The most successful missions have been those which concerned themselves more with general humanitarian and "uplift" work—healing, teaching, etc.—than with Christianity as such. Up to a point this is all right, but, after all, Government provides a medical service; and, again, the mere teaching of the three R's, also a Government function, is more a curse than a blessing.

The grand counts against Christian missionary effort are two. Firstly, it comes at a time when, for good or for evil, a basic movement in European thought and practice is abandoning, or at least whittling down, the Christian ethic and explanation. Secondly, Christianity, because it is so spiritual, is vague. The logical development of Christianity appears to be a mysticism like Quakerism, the central tenet of which is "the inner light" and that "the kingdom of God is within you," a tenet that some thinkers, e.g. Dr. Johnson, held to be incompatible with organized society. If genuinely held it is, as history has shown, compatible; but significantly only a fraction of professing Christians have ever attempted to achieve anything so fine. It is too much to ask an animist African, whose life is full of taboos, inhibitions, and regulations, to achieve it. It is anarchy for him. And Protestant Christianity must *tend* to produce an inward anarchy unless a crude fundamentalism is offered as props in place of the old taboos. Just as Islam appears to be a better religion for the African than Christianity, so Roman Catholicism appears to be better than Protestantism. It makes more allowance for his human nature, and, there being no right of private judgment, it lays down exact rules. Of the several million of professing converts in Nigeria there can be but a handful who have really arrived at an elementary understanding of Christianity, and whose lives

* For an example of bad mission effort see Maudslay's *Life in the Pacific Fifty Years Ago*, London, 1930; account of Tonga.

are genuinely and deeply affected by it. The Dutch Reformed Church (of South Africa) has been working among the Munchis for a generation now and has been fortunate in having a band of missionaries outstanding for devotion and common sense. Have they got one hundred indubitable converts? What, too, of the s.u.m. among the Gwaris? And has the devoted and gifted lady who has worked among the Hausas for more than a quarter of a century yet gained a dozen Christian adherents? The chief of a Methodist Mission in the Southern part of North Nigeria, a man of outstanding disinterestedness and manliness, whose mere presence among the natives is a beneficence, told the writer that if he (the missionary) succeeds in teaching the boys manners and hygiene he is pulling his weight and his efforts are justified. That would not be denied. But it is not Christianity. Of course, he might reply that the children of these first converts would advance several steps farther and eventually Christianity itself would be apprehended. Finally, there are the African Churches themselves. Many are polygamous. A raw sectarianism flourishes. There are three hundred different African Christian denominations in South Africa alone.*

Missionaries of authority have defined their task to the African. According to one it is to "dissociate the Christian way of life from his own culture and to help the African to make it his very own"; and to another "to translate Christianity into the idiom of the African's soul." The definitions are cloudy. And how are the missionaries to accomplish this? The supreme danger of Christian Missions is that of breaking down the old sanctions and of offering in their place something which the African in general—whatever may happen with a few exceptions—is unable really to assimilate and which therefore will lead to a simulating of something he has not got and so to a moral poison. This, I believe, is the reason for the superiority of Moslem over Christian Africans and for the bad reputation of mission boys.

Yet nothing very much can be done about it. There is an African demand for the missions. His snobbery naturally attracts him to it as being the white man's juju and therefore probably of an

---

* Vide *Modern Industry and the African*, appendix. Among them are the following: African Christian Catholic Baptist, African Seventh Day Zulu Chaka Church of Christ, Mount of Olives Baptist Church, Unto the Church of God, Apostolic Jerusalem in Zion.

efficacy superior to his own. Also it supplies free, or very cheap, reading and writing lessons. Again the hymns and services appeal to his love of community singing and ritual, and (in Southern Nigeria—not the North) the membership of a Church group replaces the membership of a tribal group that is no longer what it was.

## (6) ENGLISH LAW: LEGALISM AND LAWYERS

*"And they had hair as the hair of women, but their teeth were as the teeth of lions."*—Revelation ix. 8.

As the facts are, and as the facts have been, the question of the administration of justice is incomparably more important to the vast majority of natives than the question of Chiefs and councils and the territorial limitations of Chiefs and councils—that is to say, than what the practice of Indirect Rule is ordinarily concerned with. The ordinary native is not greatly interested in or greatly affected by the particular person who collects his tax (the amount of which is decided in any case by Government), and who receives the emoluments of office and who is the mouthpiece of governmental decisions. The rose under any other name is just as sweet to him. His land is secure, and his intimate day-to-day life (family, religion, and ordinary habits) is also secure. His chief concern outside his village circle is how and by what persons and according to what customs his disputes and grievances are settled.

The system that has been built up in Northern Nigeria and was later reproduced more or less in Southern Nigeria (excepting the narrow strip known as the Colony) for administering justice among the natives may be broadly summarized as comprising two main elements: (1) as far as possible justice should be administered by native judges and according to native law and custom; and (2) as far as possible English law and legalism, above all lawyers, should be kept out of it. Three kinds of courts were therefore evolved: (*a*) The *Native Courts*, in which native judges, adjudicated in accordance with native law, were to deal with all ordinary suits and crimes. Their powers, naturally, varied in proportion to their status and efficiency. In the organized Emirates they were omnicompetent, even up to awarding the death penalty, while on the other hand the inchoate Village Courts of certain Pagan tribes might be limited to powers of three months' imprisonment. (*b*) The *Provincial Courts*, which were, in fact, Administrative Officers acting for the time being as Trial Officers, and in which certain special cases—e.g. a dispute between a European and an African, or a difficult suit transferred from a Native Court—were settled. And

(c) the *Supreme Court*, which had jurisdiction over all causes in certain places (e.g. in Lagos) and over all persons (e.g. Europeans other than in (*b*)) in a certain category. Lawyers were not permitted to appear in the Native Courts, or, as of right, in the Provincial Courts. Under such a system lawyers and English law were used to a minimum. The overwhelming bulk of native suits were settled in Native Courts and exceptional cases which were too difficult for them or, for some other reason, were not suitable for their jurisdiction, were settled by Administrative Officers. The judicial powers and activities of Administrative Officers who did not necessarily have what are now called legal qualifications (though actually many Administrative Officers have passed their Bar Examinations, and all have passed examinations in the laws of Torts, Contracts, Crimes, and Evidence and Procedure, in addition to examinations in the local ordinances and statutes) were justified on the ground that their special intimate knowledge of the local people and their customs and their own common sense and instinct for fair play would be more likely to result in rough justice (and no one pretends that any system in this world can provide more than rough justice) than the forms and methods of English law.

The system is one that had been warmly commended both for its principle and its practice by various competent observers.* It has also had its critics, among them, apparently, but not unexpectedly, a professional Law Society in England who, it is said, made representations, at the instance of some West African lawyers, to the Colonial Office on the point. At any rate, the Colonial Office sent its legal adviser out both to East and to West Africa on a tour of inspection. What precisely happened is not fully known publicly, except that the legal adviser reported recommending changes. The conduct of the Colonial Office in this matter would appear to be requiring explanation. What relevance can there be between a proficiency in a knowledge of English law and the qualifications for saying what should be the judicial system among this or that African people? A great jurist like Maine might have given valuable advice (though not because he was a legal technician); but the jurists concerned would not claim to be Maines.

The Governor of Nigeria of the day was also among the critics, and by April 1934 he succeeded in imposing on the country what

* E.g. Buell in *The African Native Problem*.

have been described as his Judicial Reforms. To summarize them very broadly they have resulted in, (1) a limitation of the powers of Native Courts, (2) the abolition of the Provincial Courts, (3) the extension throughout Nigeria of the jurisdiction of the Supreme Court (the name of which, except in the Colony, has been changed into the High Court), to which appeals may lie from certain Native Courts, and (4) the admission of legal practitioners to practise before the inferior and superior branches of the High Court. The Ordinances enacting these changes are highly complicated, for the attempt to impose one broad system over a heterogeneous area, which is not yet susceptible of any such unification, has resulted in various exceptions and special provisions that in parts nullify the effort to create one single system and in any case will demand many official interpretations before definiteness can be attained on every point. This matter will not be noticed further here as it concerns a defect in administrative practice. The points of immediate interest are firstly the changes in (indeed, in theory, the revolutionary break with) the old system, and secondly the motives behind the changes.

The Governor never took the Service into his confidence, and an air of mystery surrounded the business all along, but in so far as any coherent explanation was ever given his speech to the Council in 1933 might be quoted.

He then said:* "If the judgment of the Court is to be the judgment of an officer experienced in the art of sifting and weighing evidence and is to be based solely on the evidence which has been laid before him in the case, it does not matter a great deal to me what he is called.... But if the decision of the Court may properly be swayed by ... non-judicial considerations within the knowledge of the administrative officer, and is therefore not to be based solely on the evidence which has been led, then ... the Court has ceased to be a judicial tribunal and the officer has ceased to be a judicial officer. Change the system of law, if you will, and punish the people by administrative measures, by administrative officers exercising a kind of parental correction because the people are primitive; but remember always, pray, if you do so you will thereby be depriving the natives of the protection of any judicial court and any judicial system of law." This, as will be observed later, is not quite a fair statement of the issue. The basic motive behind His Excellency's attitude was made clearer a little further on: "One last word on

* Address to Legislative Council, March 1933.

the subject. I have been inspired in framing these judicial reforms ... with the conviction that in many cases persons are being punished who ought not to be punished, or are being punished excessively."*

Although this Governor had had no experience of actual personal contact with the native either as an administrative or as a trial officer, his experience being entirely secretariat, it is not easy to understand, especially in a man of exceptional ability and character as he was, how he should have been able to ignore so completely the other side of the argument and to jettison what had been a promising experiment of the greatest social import, namely, the resisting to the utmost point practicable the penetration of legalism and lawyers into the administration of justice. For the time being the actual effects of the "reforms" are not very great over most of Nigeria. A new multitude of vexatious rules has been let loose, but the new judges and magistrates are drawn from the Administrative staff; financial reasons have prevented the recruitment of lawyers from home for all the new judicial posts. But though the present men are largely the same as formerly the machine is a new one and the thin end of the wedge of legalism and lawyers has been inserted; and legalism and lawyers, once there, have a way of gaining a momentum which is not easily withstood. April 1934 is the watershed between the old and the new.

The magic of a phrase will be enough to convince most people of the soundness and the necessity of the changes. "Judicial Reforms," "the evils of a *droit administratif*" or "the rule of law" are formidable *clichés* with which effective play can be made. Too much has been heard of "that excellent mystery, the Common Law," as Clarendon called it, and not enough of the effects of its workings.† It is probable that the next generation or two will see some profound changes in the administration of justice among Englishmen in England. It is only now that a scientific as contrasted with a theological attitude of mind is being brought to bear upon the subject of justice. The pressure will come not only from sociologists and scientists and students of the State, but from the forward-looking members of

* Op. cit.
† Apart from its delays and expenses, cf. decisions like Buckle *v.* Holmes; Saloman *v.* Saloman; Redmond *v.* Dainton; Heath *v.* Hedges, etc. Mr. Gladstone had no undue admiration for the Law. Cf. *Personal Papers of Lord Rendel.*

the legal profession itself. The Lord Chancellor's Committee, or the phenomenon of a judge like Sir Henry McCardie, is illustrative of the drift.

For what is the effect of English legalism in Africa? The question is quickest answered by traversing certain characteristic positions of English law. Firstly, a fundamental tenet of our law, above all of our Law of Evidence, is to give the maximum benefit of doubt to a criminal. The onus of establishing sure and unquestionable guilt lies upon the prosecution, and an intricate body of extremely severe and extremely rigid rules has been built up in order to safeguard that principle. Thus, it is notorious that someone whom everybody knows to have committed murder may get off.* This is good in principle; and it causes no harm in practice in England because wrongdoers (in the criminal sense) constitute a tiny fraction of the total population, and if a few escape now and then the cement of society is not loosened; and because, in fact, wrongdoers do not normally escape, a system of police and detectives and universal and rapid means of communication like roads, quick traffic, newspapers, telegraph, etc., make it possible to track in minute detail the movements and doings of almost any given individual over almost any period of time and thereby establish whatever case there may be against a suspect. Thus the maximum benefit of doubt can be given to a criminal because there also exists the maximum chance of establishing his criminality. Contrast this with conditions in Africa: primitive, or even no communications, no detectives, a handful of native police, no finger-print experts, and so on. In most parts of Nigeria it is impossible to keep track of a man's movements. Secondly, the law is administered by hedge barristers, men whose only legal qualification is a passing of the not onerous Bar Examinations, whose findings are subject to review and whose promotion depends on their having as few reversals to their count as possible; they therefore naturally tend to follow the dotted line of the letter of the law with an abandon unknown in its administration at home. If ever the rule of law is followed it is by these men, unsure of themselves and chronically and inevitably concerned with promo-

* Cf. Lord Lugard, *Journal of the African Society*, p. 8: "Even the methods of British justice, with its rigid rules of evidence by which a murderer may escape, though known by all to be guilty . . . are puzzling to the native mind. 'Why,' asked an intelligent African, 'does the white man allow two professional liars to argue on opposite sides and try to confuse the mind of the judge?' "

tion. I once drew the attention of a Master in Chancery to the decision of a magistrate in Nigeria which had been made on grounds of the Hearsay Rule in Evidence. He expressed amazement and said that even in England it would have been regarded as an unsound decision, whereas, given the conditions prevailing in West Africa, it must have been quite inapplicable.

Even the Governor was obliged to allow that certain disputes would have to "be settled administratively by the Resident or a senior District Officer . . . and the decision will be final, subject only to the ordinary right of appeal to the Governor possessed by everyone." In short, some *droit administratif*.

No discussion will be entered into here of the effects of a legal attitude to arrangements so fluid as "contracts" between natives, nor to its effects, once pressure of population on land becomes operative, in creating a landless proletariat and in concentrating wealth. The emphasis is confined to the central point, which is that whatever the merits of English law may be in England its effects when imposed on an alien environment are to work for injustice. Legal accuracy, literalness, and formality flourish at the expense of justice.

Here is an example: In 1931 during the construction of the new railway between Kaduna and Minna (a stretch of a hundred miles, completed in 1933), a contract for making earthworks was given to a European who described himself as an Irishman but was said (with what truth I do not know) to be a Roumanian Jew. His record was well known to the responsible authorities, including a blackmail case of a peculiarly cruel and sordid nature. Nevertheless he was given a contract and put in a position of employing several hundred illiterate labourers. His treatment of them was such that they eventually rioted and he just escaped with his life in July 1931. A series of civil cases were opened against him by (or rather on behalf of) the labourers both in the Supreme Court (the Magistrate's Court at Kaduna), and in the old Provincial Court, but in every case he produced lists of the labourers' names with amounts against them purporting to have been paid on certain dates, and, in testimony of the payment, a thumb print (an ink smudge), to determine the authenticity of which there was no means at the disposal of the Court. The "evidence led," which the Governor says must be the only consideration in judicial causes, was such that he always won. As far as I know this man lost not a single case. Officials, even the Kaduna Secretariat, became frightened of him. For eighteen months after the riot cases cropped up, and I myself spent a considerable amount of spare time in trying to work up a case for this or that group of labourers, but never with success. The European escaped, the labourers lost their money, and the only positive action on the part of Government was a ferocious censure of several pages in length addressed to the District Officer in charge of Kuta Division for having let the riot occur or having been unaware of its impending outbreak—a censure that had later to be withdrawn on its being shown that the District Officer was ill in the Lagos hospital at the time, and, also, that the labourers and the construction happened to be outside the territory of this officer!

This is what is and must always be the effect of legalism (which so far has always been inseparable from the law) in these communities. The wrongdoer is at an advantage over the decent citizen,* the strong over the weak, the literate over the illiterate, the babu over the bushman.

It is conceivable that experience would have shown that a definite cut-and-dried system like English law was, for all its defects, inescapable in the long run. It is undeniable that many Administrative Officers have had to spend undue time in judicial work, and that a specialization of administrative and judicial functions has certain advantages. The complaint, however, is that an experiment of great originality and significance and one that on the whole was justifying itself was abandoned at the instance of one Governor, a law officer in England, and a handful of officials in the Colonial Office, and it was abandoned without discussion.

* Cf. *Nigerian Daily Times*, July 28, 1934, for report of criminal case and the nominal sentences passed, clearly in response to the Governor's "fear that persons were being over-punished."

(7) INFERIORITIES IN THE QUALITY OF
ADMINISTRATION

"*He that seeketh to be eminent amongst able men hath a great task; but that is ever good for the public; but he that plots to be the only figure amongst ciphers is the decay of an whole age.*"—
BACON.

THE business of running the Government machine in Nigeria is unusually simple and uncomplicated. The country has fewer problems than any other governing unit of the same population in the world. There is no problem of racial antagonism; there are no economic problems, the economy still being based on a self-subsistent husbandry and exempt from population pressure; there is no conflict between white capital and coloured labour, there being no white settlers and only a slight amount of capitalist exploitation; and there are no political problems, internal or external, of any kind. Social problems like caste, economic problems like agricultural indebtedness, political problems like nationalism, as in India, are all non-existent. All that is required is to maintain law and order, to administer justice, and to collect the taxes required for paying for these services and certain minor services—fairly sparsely distributed—like education, hygiene, etc.; and, given the system of Indirect Rule and the paucity of European staff that prevails, most of this work is done by the natives themselves. The running of the bigger local government units in England is much more intricate and demands a very different order of administrative ability.

Yet, simple as are the demands thus made, the administrative machine has stalled at several points and has shown a tendency to get out of control. A short cut for, say, a Parliamentary Commission, investigating the way our Colonial Governments are run, to see defects in the quality of administration, would be to study the financial history (budget by budget, item by item) of the country during the last decade, and especially the parts referring to the activities of the P.W.D. and the Railway Department. Another illustration would be provided from the way the retrenchments of 1931–2 were carried through. Another, the "reorganizations" (especially their cost and their *raison d'être*) of provincial and divisional boundaries made from time to time. Another, the whole process of bringing into action the "judicial reforms" of 1933–4.

Another, the water shortage in various parts of the country (cf. Beebey Thompson Report), contrasting this with the £300,000 scheme for Kano town. The Commission might then enquire into the fact that, though handling hundreds of thousands of pounds in a year, the accounts of native treasuries (really run by Administrative Officers) were not audited before 1931–2, following a certain case; and it might then go on to things like the non-funding of the Widows and Orphans Pensions Scheme and the Public Officers' Guarantee Fund. A fruitful minor approach would also be to study the biography of a report: e.g. an A.D.O. on trek in the bush sends in a memorandum to his D.O., who sends it on to his Resident, who sends it on to his Chief Commissioner, and the last sends it on to Lagos; then its return through all these channels; after which it may well make the full circuit again. But examples need not be multiplied. The point is, why does the machine show this tendency to get out of control?

A main reason, no doubt, is what for want of a better term might be called the demoralization of the personnel, which will be observed presently. The other main reasons would appear to be four-fold: (a) a lack of continuity, in personnel and in policy; (b) over-centralization and non-delegation; (c) the Administrative staff being required to spend too much of its energy and time in mechanical clerical routine work; and (d) at all points and in all things too much ado about nothing. Only slight reference can be made to these here.

As for lack of continuity, many examples have been given in previous pages of the rapidity and unexpectedness with which Administrative Officers are circulated. The Division which sees the same D.O. for three years following is rare. Katagum Division, for example, has had nine different officers in charge within five years. Even Residents are moved from Province to Province.* Governors themselves come and go. From the end of the war up to now Nigeria has had five different Governors. In 1934, within a few months, the Chief Secretary, the Deputy Chief Secretary, and the Principal Assistant—i.e. the three senior men after the Governor—all left the country and the Governor himself left the following year; and this was after a drastic change in policy and

---

* In the North, cf. e.g. Adamawa, Kabba, Zaria, Sokoto, in the last four to five years. With this state of affairs, cf. Lugard's dictum that Residents should practically never be changed.

machinery, left to be worked by men who in general did not believe in the change.*

As for over-centralization and non-delegation, one of many possible examples is given hereunder. It must be admitted that in order to exercise an adequate control some degree of centralization is not only desirable, but inevitable; administrative capacity, however, consists in deciding what power should be centralized and what should be delegated.

In the latter part of 1932 it was decided in Niger Province to retire a Messenger (couriers whose wages range from £18 to £40 per annum) on the ground of his age and long service. The question which arises in such a case (it is not an infrequent question) is whether the retired man should be given a small pension or a lump sum gratuity and, in either case, how much. The procedure, and, indeed, everything that requires being done, is laid down in official regulations. Yet, despite this, the Resident of the Province had to write to the Secretary of the Northern Provinces telling him the facts of the case, suggesting a settlement, and asking for instructions. After a while the Secretary of the Northern Provinces wrote back to him asking for certain further information; the Resident sent it; the Secretary of the Northern Provinces then wrote saying that he is in correspondence with Lagos. Eventually His Excellency the Governor authorizes that the messenger is to have a gratuity of such-and-such, the instruction wending its slow way back through the Central Secretariat, then the Northern Secretariat, and finally the Resident of the Province, to the Provincial Office where the Messenger was employed.

As for the Administrative staff as a whole being required to spend too much energy and time at mechanical work; more than half the work done by Administrative Officers is of the kind that in the Home Civil Service would be done by the writing assistants or the clerical service. The ratio of clerks to Administrative Officers suggests the condition of things. Thus in Idoma Division there are four (sometimes five) Administrative Officers and only one clerk.

As for much ado about nothing, the author had intended to cite an actual case by quoting a certain memorandum which was sent

* Cf. the remarkably inept practice prevailing in the New Zealand Administration of Samoa. The N.Z. Civil Service Committee proposed that officials should be seconded from the N.Z. Civil Service and remain in Samoa for not longer than two years. F. M. Keesing, *Modern Samoa*, 1934, pp. 113-4.

out to the staff in the Northern Provinces in 1931 containing a remark of the Lieutenant-Governor of the day on arranging officers' leave. The expression was as indefinite as the subject was trite, yet the document was made confidential. The Colonial Office, however, refused him permission to publish it, doubtless because it was appreciative of the fact that the document provided a perfect example of the game of turning out paper which means exactly nothing.

Being a "confidential" this precious document could be handled only by the European personnel, from the typing and roneo-graphing to the final delivery. Its every movement—from the Secretariat to Provincial Offices, and from them to individual officers—had to be made within a sealed enclosure (waxed at both ends, marked with red ink, and the whole then put into a second outer envelope), the sealing and enclosing being the handiwork of Administrative Officers only!*

The combined effect of these characteristics is to turn government into an elaborate business of paper and ink and with rules so numerous and complicated that even their makers cannot always understand them, let alone carry them in their head.† It erects a great artificial barrier, rising higher and ever higher between the rulers and the ruled; and, because it gives the men at the top so much to decide upon that they can decide only hastily or upon only the more pressing matters, while their subordinates are reduced to spending days not in making decisions, but in preparing memoranda and returns to provide the men at the top with data for the decisions which they have not the time to make or make in a hurry, government thus becomes a process without thought or imagination behind it, a hurried hand-to-mouth routinism. And so the machine stalls and tends to get out of control.

* Another example was the Instruction in 1933 that officers should serve in a Provincial Office for only three months, and only if not having previously served in a Provincial Office or in a Secretariat—an instruction quite impossible to execute, as ought to have been self-evident before it was issued.

† I.e. Crown Colony administration is slipping into just those defects which are agreed to have disfigured Indian administration, for which, as seen by an ex-Governor, cf. *Some Personal Experiences*, by Bampfylde Fuller, e.g. pp. 27, 32, 34, 92, 107–8.

## (8) DEMORALIZING A SERVICE

*"The code which must guide the administrator in the tropics is to be found in no book of regulations. It demands that in every circumstance and under all conditions he shall act in accordance with the traditions of an English gentleman."*—SECRETARY OF STATE at Corona Club, 1923.

THE basic point is the tone of the Service. The average officer is good enough but he is victimized by the system so that he does not always act in accordance with these traditions.*

Given a climate and a pressure of day-to-day work like that prevailing in Nigeria it is not to be expected that mental energy will be a distinction of life there. Mental atrophy, and its child parochialism, however, go to lengths which are hardly compatible with the qualities expected of British public officials. It is unusual to find any curiosity in, let alone knowledge on, current social or economic or political questions. Too many Administrative Officers (excepting those who have been appointed within the last five years or so) are ignorant of even the neighbouring West African colonies, and would be quite unable to pass an elementary examination on the history or the political problems of the British Empire as a whole or in part. Even senior officers of twenty years' service, like Residents, have no notion of the organization and working of the Colonial Office. It is doubtful whether 2 per cent of the First Division personnel in West Africa are aware of the existence of the Warren Fisher Report, although copies were circulated to every Provincial Office. Outside of routine work one sticks faithfully to the *Tatler* and *Bystander* and ephemeral fiction. All this tends to produce a type that has no standards of comparison, and that is therefore prone to see things out of proportion and to view passing local trifles as permanent landmarks, and above all is susceptible to the defects in the system.

A graver defect is the poor *esprit de corps*. Officers in general have no sense of being brothers in the one craft; the ruling feeling, rather, is competition: what matters most is not to let a colleague make a better impression than you. The feeling is like being in a queue before a box-office window where the majority is struggling to elbow its way to the top. An unpleasant but not uncommon manifestation is when one officer "takes over" from another: he

---

* Reference is specifically to the Administrative Service, but similar or comparable observations are applicable to the Technical Services.

criticizes, makes "exposures," "re-organizes," and plays the part of the new broom—the sweeper out and cleaner up of Augean stables left by his predecessor. So impregnated is the tone of the Service with this bad spirit that engineers or doctors, men normally with rigid standards of professional loyalty, are victimized by it.

Another and related defect is the way senior rank is perverted into bossiness and self-ends. The shelter of official position is often used for perpetrating on those within the power of the senior rudeness, inconsiderateness, bullying, and at times sheer blackguardism, which would never be tolerated in normal private life, but which must be tolerated when mere continuance, let alone progress, in the Service depends upon the word of superior officers. The abuse of rank is no doubt a phenomenon well enough known in other hierarchies, either at home or in the colonies, either in the public service or in business; but in Nigeria, where conditions break down restraint and exacerbate vanity to pathological lengths, and where, above all, there is none of the cold wind of public opinion and free criticism to keep the ego-maniac sane, a base man in power can indulge his animosities to dangerous limits.

Why has the Service not a better tone? There are three main reasons: (1) for a considerable time there was a disproportionate amount of inferior quality on the upper rungs of the hiererachy; (2) the system of promotion turns brother officers into economic rivals; and (3) above all, the institution of the Annual Secret Report. To take these factors in turn:

(1) It has been shown that the total conditions of climate, landscape, food, work, and people are such that unless consciously and continually resisted they tend to produce what a famous tropical administrator called "a subtle moral deterioration," and it has also been shown that the improvisations which have built up the Service until a decade or so ago have brought in too great a proportion of men who would be susceptible to its temptations; and these tend to get into the senior posts.* The inferiority takes various forms.

---

* It should be remembered that apart from losses by death there has been an enormous "labour turnover" in the Service. Again and again one is astonished when going through files less than a decade old to observe how large a proportion of the men signing documents then are no longer in the Service. There has been a marked tendency for those who can possibly find another job of comparable emoluments to resign after a few years' experience of the life, which again consolidated a tendency to keep the least able.

The using of native servants or messengers for spying on—including spying on the private lives of—subordinates has been not unknown. Megalomania and ego-mania, however, are the most common manifestations. They may take comparatively harmless forms such as resenting being beaten at tennis or bumped at polo; or more mischievous forms as when an irresponsible vanity is linked to a measure of real power. The machinery of office may then be used to gratify personal animosities. It is this, too, which has led, *inter alia*, to the perversion of Indirect Rule in Nigeria and to what a recent Governor has stigmatized as "pretence in administration." The alleged danger of a Mahdist movement and the length to which that theme was pushed may be instanced. A favourite officer of the day was sent across Africa on a tour of investigation; a Bureau was created for "detecting" the movements of the Mahdists; and reports on Mahdists were as *à la mode* as reports on Pagan tribes are to-day. How much substance there might have been in the "danger" is indicated in the recent words of Professor Coupland of Oxford: ". . . nearly thirty years ago. There has been little, if any, evidence of deep religious antagonism since; and some who know the North maintain that 'Mahdism' was never a real danger in Nigeria and only survives to-day in the files of the Secretariat."* It was all a portentous trifle; but if any official had hinted as much before 1931 he would have been retrenched as "temperamentally unsuited to the Service."

(2) But it is the system of promotion which encourages all the weaker qualities of the personnel and which tends to bring the wrong men to the top. The theory in the Colonial Service is that up to a certain point—up to D.O.—promotion is by seniority of service and after that by merit. The grades of Cadet, A.D.O., and D.O. are attained by effluxion of service (subject to passing certain examinations and efficiency bars), and after that—broadly speaking after twelve years—the D.O. goes on collecting increments until he reaches £960 plus £72 plus allowances. Unless he receives promotion to Resident grade which (unjustifiably) is now subdivided into three sub-grades: Deputy Resident, Resident, Senior Resident, a promotion that, in theory, may come any time after a dozen years of service and not necessarily after he has reached his maximum, he ends up on £960 plus £72. Promotion to Resident grade, and

* *The Times*, February 14, 1934, p. 13.

after that to Lieutenant-Governorships (or Chief Commissionerships as they are now called), and Governorships, is, in theory, by merit alone. In the past it has been usual not to get promotion to Resident grade before at least fifteen years' service, though the age composition of the personnel suggests that it will be much longer in the future. The point is that every officer has an interest, not only in passing his efficiency bars but in possible promotion by merit in the future, and therefore in accumulating a record of merits. About half the D.O.s can, as a matter of arithmetic, count on getting a Residentship; and some Residents can count on higher things. Nigeria, in fact, has provided quite a number of Governors within the last decade or so. As a D.O., then, any officer will end up on about £1,000 a year, and, when he comes to retire, on a pension of about half that figure. If he manages to get a Residentship he will end up on £1,250 a year plus allowances, and later a pension of over £600; or, if he rises to a Senior Residentship, to £1,450 plus allowances and later a pension in proportion; to a Chief Commissionership £3,000; to the Governorship of Nigeria itself to £8,250, both again with pensions in proportion. Hence the strongest economic motive to struggle for promotion. Every hurdle adds at the least £250 a year now and half that figure to the pension, and after the first two or three hurdles the jump is by several hundred per cent. To these rich prizes must be added those of prestige and of command over your fellows: Senior Residentship brings C.M.G.s and big houses; Governorships, even minor island Governorships, bring visits to Buckingham Palace and knighthoods. Nor is the struggle without hope. In recent years Nigeria has seen some dramatic promotions: e.g. there was the man who was a mere D.O. in Bornu in 1926, while by 1933, seven years later, he had become a full Governor, and after only about twenty years' total service. He had been an authority on Mahdism. This futurity, this vicious futurity, makes a successful career in the Service a continuous wriggle to put oneself in the light and to keep oneself there, including the gaining of the approval of whoever for the time being has the power of recommending for promotion. Every Province can boast its covey of "able men" and their window-dressings and other antics.

It is not argued that economic competitiveness is peculiar to the Colonial Service. It is not unknown in organized churches, and is rampant in the academic world.* It is distinguished in the Colonial Service, however, by being related to no measurable standards of productivity as, e.g., in the business world where the test is knowing how to make money, or in the academic world where a fool, though not a scoundrel, has little chance in the long run; and it is distinguished, secondly, by being conducted in an atmosphere (unlike Parliamentary success) free from public examination and comparison. It is a hole-and-corner game in which pronouncements for or against, entirely protected from any contradiction or question, are delivered by men not necessarily wise or good, and with no fixed criteria to base their verdicts on.

An example of how the system may work was provided not long ago by the ascent of a certain officer above his fellows. Always distinguished by a splendid isolation, he was given direct accelerated promotion to a full Residentship. For some years he had been singled out as a prodigy of ability. He was allowed to spend all his service in a certain favourite Province, with occasional spells in the Secretariat, though only spells as his presence in the Province was held to be essential to its functioning. Men who had served with or under him could never understand how he had managed to build up his reputation. He had a big face and a big voice and, from natural gaucherie rather than from malice, was rude and short-tempered, which no doubt accounted for his standing as a forceful personality. A noted disciplinarian, too, where others chastised with whips he chastised with scorpions. And he had the further advantage of being unhampered by either a sense of modesty or a sense of humour. But his arresting quality was his industriousness. This was superb, a plodding mindless assiduity rarely to be encountered outside the world of the white ant. The files of the office concerned were unforgettable. No detail was too trivial, no platitude too exhausted. Obviousness rose on obviousness in his timeless universe. Junior officers would spend twenty minutes in being instructed as to how a mat should be spread for a District Head and how a dog should be tied up (he was especially authoritative about tying up dogs), each single physical action gone through

---

\* Cf. the struggle for priority in publication of results amongst scientific researchers. There was recently a case of three articles forming a single piece of research in cytology appearing in three different journals and in different countries, so intent was the researcher to spread his publicity,

step by step. . . . Not that he was a bad man. But his qualities, some of which would have been valuable in a subordinate clerk and others in a Sergeant-Major, were at their best not germane to what is desiderated in an Administrative Officer, and at their worst were quite harmful. What are the standards of a régime which accord such a person such a treatment?

There is the case of a certain recipient of accelerated promotion who was so disliked and feared by the natives, that when he was promoted and left the scene of his old triumphs they gave *sadaka*\* to one another.

(3) The deciding as to who will be promoted (and also who will be retrenched) rests with the seniors, and the instrument through which the word of a Resident or Lieutenant-Governor for or against his subordinates is carried is the Secret Report written at the end of every year, a document the contents of which are unknown to the officer reported on. There are certain advantages in maintaining a system of secret reporting; but, as the facts are, the disadvantages heavily outweigh them. If you could assume a clear and accepted understanding as to what type of officer was best, and an assured standard of honour and capacity on the part of the reporting officer for truthfully estimating and reporting the qualities of their subordinates, it would be tolerable. Incident after incident in Nigeria has made it clear that no such assumption can be made. The secret personal report is the most vicious single factor behind the demoralization of the Service. Even the official requirement, that, when an officer has been adversely reported on he should be notified in order to give him a chance of rectifying his shortcomings, is not observed, and as will be shown from specific instances, when the failure to observe the rule is brought to the notice of the authorities in the Colony nothing is done about it. Even the Army, which scarcely represents the left wing of administrative practice, now requires that officers must see and initial their personal reports. It is the Secret Report which forms the keystone to the undue power of a senior over his juniors. Their careers are in his hands. Not only does their promotion depend on his good word, but an unfavourable report—and only one unfavourable report—may be enough to determine their retrenchment in times of financial stringency, as was painfully impressed upon men in 1931-2. In

---

\* I.e. presents, as thankofferings. Normally given during religious thanksgiving festivals.

such an atmosphere the winds of freedom must cease to blow, for here is a power of making secret accusations, the very existence of which the accused may never know, let alone his being given an opportunity to defend himself against them. Every officer is thus on guard all the time to please or placate his senior—and all the time, too, he feels insecure about it.

It will be sufficient to illustrate this very great evil by two concrete examples.*

In the first the Resident, the Acting Secretary of Northern Nigeria, and the Acting Lieutenant-Governor—i.e. all the three senior officials concerned—are no longer in the country.

(a) In 1932, a Cadet, who had previously served in the country for six years in another official capacity, broke his journey at Kaduna before proceeding to the boat for England in order to supplicate for permission to bring his wife out with him on his following tour. He saw the man who was then acting as Secretary (i.e. the second man in Northern Nigeria), who, with some impatience, told the Cadet that he would be well advised to make no importunities as his retrenchment was under consideration. Confronted with this unexpected and alarming news (the retrenching was at its height then) he demanded an immediate interview with the official acting as Lieutenant-Governor. On presenting himself before the latter, he, the Lieutenant-Governor, sought to mollify his anxiety, but added that his last report was adverse. He then produced it: what it contained was the *cliché* that he lacked initiative! For anyone knowing the conditions and the men involved it would be judged remarkable that any verdict of the Resident concerned could have been taken seriously, and when that verdict was a hackneyed commonplace, unsupported by instances, it would be judged incredible. Also, of course, the officer condemned was quite ignorant of his sentence. No complaint had ever been made to him. The motive of the Resident, it appeared, was personal enmity over a polo incident.

(b) The second example belongs to two years later. It should be remarked at this point that the first three years in the Service are probationary, on the conclusion of which confirmation is given to (or withheld from) the appointment. Refusal to confirm rarely, if ever, happens. Less than three weeks before his confirmation

* The author is in a position to give exact references to both these cases in the event of a Commission desiring to investigate.

was due, the officer concerned received a confidential document entitled "Warning." In this were given quotations from three secret reports on him. One quotation stated that he was "Not entirely suited to the Service," and the other that "He comes within the category of misfits." The third quotation was in his favour. He was informed that in view of these adverse reports his appointment could not be confirmed unless or until more favourable reports had been received. This meant that in any case his confirmation was not going to be made at the end of his three years' probationary service, and the probability was dismissal. As this was the first intimation that he had received during the three years that his work was inadequate, and as he had been led to believe that it was adequate, he opened a determined campaign which ultimately went to the highest official in the Colony. In the correspondence which ensued, the following facts emerged:

> (1) The two adverse reports had been written about the same time, about four months previously, and from the same provincial headquarters, the one by the Resident's assistant under whom the officer had worked for about a month, during most of which time he had been out in the bush touring, and the other by the Resident himself who had set eyes on the officer on one occasion only, and then for less than five minutes. Neither of the writers of the adverse reports, therefore, was in a position to pronounce decisively on so serious an issue as his fitness or otherwise for the Service;
> (2) Even if these two men thought that they had evidence justifying their verdict they should, as General Order 501 lays down, have informed the officer of it in order that he should be provided with a chance of trying to rectify his shortcomings. Not only was General Order 501 thus disobeyed, but he was led to believe, while working for them, positively by written comment on his work, and negatively by the absence of written or spoken adverse criticism, that they were pleased with his work. Indeed, he was able to produce a note from the Resident's assistant, referring to a report which was later brought forward as an example of his unfitness, that said "Thanks for your report. Just what we want";
> (3) No instances were cited in either case in favour of the adverse judgment—just the bare verdict itself;

(4) This was the first criticism that had been made of his work during the three years of his service. Never had a hint or sign been given that he would ever be judged unsuited (as a matter of fact, his other confidential reports appear to have been favourable); and this criticism arrived three weeks before his confirmation was due.

All these facts emerged, but instead of the authorities at Kaduna doing anything to rectify what was an obvious abuse of the institution of the Secret Report and a flagrant breach of General Order 501, they attempted to snub him into silence.*

Until a better tone is restored to the Service it must remain but a reed shaken in the wind—in any wind.

* It is only fair to the Colonial Office to add that had the officer concerned appealed to the Secretary of State, this grievance would no doubt have been righted; but there are very few officers, especially junior officers, who are prepared to go to the extreme lengths of appealing over the heads of their local Government to the Colonial Office. The game is judged not worth the candle.

### (9) OUR TASK IN AFRICA: THE ESSENTIALS

*"Whatever the world thinks, he who has not much meditated upon God, the human mind, and the* summum bonum, *may possibly make a thriving earthworm but will most indubitably make a sorry patriot and a sorry statesman."*—BISHOP BERKELEY.

To maintain law and order is so elementary and obvious a function of any government of any sort that it need not be discussed here.

In any case it calls and for many a year will call for no difficulties in Nigeria. To maintain the economic independence of the native —a task of a different category—is essential. Throughout British West Africa (allowing for certain small local exceptions), and throughout much of British Africa, this again will be easy, as the land already belongs to the natives and, in general, there is no undue pressure of population on it. In a country that must be primarily agricultural, and its people, therefore, farmers, a social system of free peasantry should remain our constant care. We can easily avoid in Africa the immense evils of Indian peasant life and still more of European proletarian life. The grand achievement of our régime in Nigeria, in fact, far eclipsing Indirect Rule, is that the land is still unalienated, and that every man can till his own plot of he wants to and dispose of his time as a free man in his own way. But this, too, will make no great call on the efficiency of government. The lines have already long been drawn in Lugard's land laws, so that all that will be required will be to follow them with such adaptations as may be called for from time to time. The supreme tasks of government in Nigeria are of another order, and they are twofold.

The first basic task will be, indeed already is, to manage the juxtaposition, and the effects of the juxtaposition, of two cultures so far apart as that of Europe and that of Africa. For, willy nilly, Africans will attempt to assimilate parts of European culture; and the resulting reaction will be disturbing. It is therefore highly important that those in power should be conscious of what exactly is involved, and should consciously control (as far as possible) the process and the reaction to the process by providing buffers and shock-absorbers. Education, the censorship (especially of the cinema), changes in the status of women, the age of marriage, criminal law, travel, are examples of the kind of question which will have to be dealt with. To manage the reaction would be difficult at any time, but unfortunately for the African (and for us) he meets with European culture at a period when it is in chaos, perhaps in decay, where all is doubted, divided, jaded, uprooted, and where religion, morality, and taste are falling before the advance of the vulgarian and the machine.

The second basic task is that the Europeans in Africa—in most places and cases they will be officials—show the African the example of the best way of European life. This may sound trite; actually it is paramount. It comes before all systems and programmes. Our supreme contribution to Africa, and the ultimate test of the worth and service of our régime, is not so much what we do as what we are. To evaluate ourselves by the number of sanitary markets or concrete bridges or hospitals we build or the hours of work we put in in a day at this or that useful routine is to use a false measuring rod. It would be false among all primitive people; it is particularly false among the Africans. In all creation there is nothing which evokes his admiration less than these things. Hence a very first plank in colonial policy should be to appoint and encourage administrators with the relevant qualities. While it may be too much to expect that the administrators should have meditated upon God and human nature, as Berkeley postulated in his ideal man of government, it is not too much to ask that they should be men who do more than fuss with nothing to say to the African but matters of work, or, worse, careerists of transparent dishonesty. The Public Schools come in for much criticism these days, but there can be little doubt that the qualities which are characteristic of the better "Public School type"—qualities that may be found in men who have not been to a Public School; something more than the sweepings of Eton are in mind—are best suited to the needs of the Service: a sense of fun, good humour, a code which forbids haggling with natives over threepence, self-discipline, and a temperate proportionate attitude towards routine and work. The European in Africa must above all things be an ambassador of European civilization.

## (10) OUR FAILURE

*"Mache da takobi abin tsoro."*\*—Hausa proverb.

ALTHOUGH the government is of the simplest structure and processes the machine has often been driven unintelligently and at certain points has got out of control. Moreover, with the problem of managing the contact, and the effects of the contact, between European culture and the African, nothing has been done; indeed those in control seem scarcely conscious of the existence of the problem. As to what may be the developments in the future, including the near future, there is not the slightest notion, nor the slightest concern. The routine of the day fills the entire horizon.

But graver than these shortcomings is the way we, the ambassadors of English civilization, have acquitted ourselves before the African, the closest and shrewdest of spectators. Most individuals have acquitted themselves sufficiently as individuals; but when organized as, and working in, the Administration, many have not acquitted themselves sufficiently. Natives, especially clerks and messengers, see colleagues intriguing against or belittling each other; or there are the personal activities of certain very senior officials; and so on. "In China," Mr. Lionel Curtis has written of Europeans there, "our standing danger is a subtle tendency to adopt a Chinese habit of mind," as *mutatis mutandis* it has been in India.† This is also our standing danger in Africa: to lose our Englishry in compromising with the standards around us. Is our prestige among the Africans in Northern Nigeria what it was thirty years ago in Lugard's day? Or even what it was fifteen years ago? How do we now strike the African?‡

\* I.e. "a woman with a sword is a fearful thing."
† Lionel Curtis, *Capital Question of China*, p. 262.
‡ Specific instances of bad behaviour have not been cited, as they refer to only a minority and would be unfair to the large majority who are guiltless of such inadequacies.

## (11) WE CAN DO THE JOB

*"This happy breed of men, this little world . . .*
*This land of such dear souls, this dear, dear land,*
*This blessed plot, this earth, this realm, this England."*
                                              SHAKESPEARE.

THERE is too much self-complacency at home about our capacity for building and running empires and about our talent for statecraft. We should remind ourselves of our management of the Irish Question since Gladstone's day, a monument to political blundering and stupidity. Nor are we alone in being successful colonial administrators. The French have some fine successes to their credit; so, too, have the Germans, both in Samoa and in parts of Africa; while the Dutch administration of their East Indies need fear no comparisons.

Nevertheless, whether we have or have not administered colonies better than this or that foreign Power we can do the job at least as well as any other: we can draw upon reserves of aptitude that can accomplish all that the situation may demand of it.

Exactly why or how the little world of England sent her sons beyond the seas to all parts of the world and at length acquired an Empire bestraddling the whole globe may be left to the historians. In our view there is one reason: just as England had produced several times as many poets as any other country so, too, she has produced several times as many explorers and colonizers, and the strain is one and the same: the English wayfarer in strange places and the English poet is of the one stuff compounded. Hence the phenomenon of a man like Charles Doughty, or Scott of the South Pole.

The strain is still there. It still sends men out to the colonies, and though some (too many), at length disappointed, throw it up, others stay on. The very encouraging thing about Nigeria, as no doubt of other colonies, is that notwithstanding a group of sly careerists and continuous poor quality in the higher places and a system which sets a premium on both, there are scores of District Officers and Assistant District Officers who go on quietly and decently doing the best they can. It is still not too late to make full use of them and of the good material now being sent out by the Colonial Office for accomplishing our task in Africa. More attention to the amenities, more English common sense, a spice of humility, and eliminate certain defects in the system, and the job can be done

## (12) RECONSTRUCTION

"... *With the current trifles of the day, notes, letters, personal applications, every man's business of more consequence than any others, complainants from every quarter of the Province hallowing me by hundreds for justice . . . and what is worse than all, a mind discomposed and a temper almost fermented to vinegar by everlasting teasing.*"—WARREN HASTINGS.

\* \* \* \* \*

"*Those who always labour can have no true judgment. You never give yourselves time to cool. . . . You can never plan the future.*"—BURKE.

THE author does not pretend to have a set of solutions ready made for the deficiencies outlined in the preceding chapters. The solutions probably will not be uniform, but will vary from case to case, and, further, will demand much thought and possibly experimentation before they are found.

As a starting point to a discussion he would indicate a number of matters requiring and, in his opinion, capable of receiving more or less immediate reformation. The two basic needs—a change in the system of promotion and the abolition of the secret report—are reserved for the end.

*Power of Governors*, and the effectiveness of Colonial Office control. This is discussed in the next section, on the administration of the Colonial Empire.

*Create a Real Staff Grade.*—In administrative work speed is of the essence. The administrator goes to his office in the morning to find a stack of files awaiting the action that he must decide upon —and in general must decide upon during that day—so that in the course of his work he has no time to reflect upon any subject and when evening comes he is too jaded to begin reflecting then. This truth applies (more or less) to all rungs of the hierarchy from A.D.O. to Governor. Whence arises the need for some group which will be freed from daily administrative routine and which will have the training and the aptitude for doing the thinking and the reflecting which the administrators cannot do. It is idle to argue that such a separation of action and thought is a false dichotomy or is contrary to the English way. The issue is not between a separation of thought and action, but between action with thought or action without thought. There is scarcely any thought now. What happens now is that administrators go on plodding through their files and the issues of the day until suddenly they run their heads into something unforeseen and unprepared for, like a collapse in the oil-seed market or a scandal in N.A. finances or a more or less obvious stalling of this or that department; and thereupon hasty solutions are improvised like suddenly retrenching 20 per cent of the personnel, or calling in "experts" like Mr. Hammond to reorganize the railway, or like Mr. Hoey to tell them what they should do about their Public Works Department. These, in general, are remedies which, as in the case of the reorganization of the Nigerian Railway, generally turn out unsatisfactory, as well as expensive, and later have to be dropped because they, too, are hasty improvisations. Recently in Kenya a Land Commission, after two investigations, reported and made various recommendations. It should not be necessary to wait for things to come to a crisis and then to call in such a body. There should be a group on the spot always acting as the eyes and ears of the Administration and so preparing it for future contingencies.

At the moment there is hardly a soul in the Service who has the slightest notion of what is likely to be the situation in Nigeria even four or five years hence. Its economic situation, which cannot be understood without a background of knowledge of world economic affairs, is not reassuring. The world over-production of fats and oils is bound to have profound effects on the ground nut, benniseed, and palm kernel exports from Nigeria,* and therefore on the country's income. There seems to be a surplus of tropical products as a whole: the tropical world is producing more than the rest of the world wants. The structure of Government services in Nigeria has been based on prospects seen from the boom years so that the country probably already has social and other Government services which it cannot continue or at least develop. It is not argued, of course, that these services are undesirable; quite the contrary. Baby crêches in all railway sidings would be admirable. The point is can Nigeria afford them? And to answer that question requires looking into the future and looking into it with an equipment of specialized

---

* The Kano trade in 1933–4 amounted to about 220,000 tons of ground nuts sold at about £3 per ton. The price a few years before was £12. The reaction to the decline in prices has been an increase not a reduction in production.

knowledge that is not at the disposal of the Government to-day. Not only would such a Staff Grade be concerned with observing the economic future so as to plan Government action safely and ahead, but with such a subject as Education policy, and the policies of other technical departments, and with scrutinizing and checking the functioning of the Government machine as a whole.

The appointment should be entirely in the hands of the Colonial Office and should be unhampered by any fixed rules except fitness of the appointee for the functions in view. Thus no age limit and not necessarily any of the conventional qualifications (e.g. he need not be a University man) should be set and his personality and manner, which are of supreme importance in the active administrator, should be quite subordinate to his capacity to think. The Staff Group will necessarily consist of men who are or can become genuine experts, and only with very rare and indubitably justifiable exceptions will members of the Administrative Service be appointed to it. Amongst them there might be an economist, a jurist, and somebody with a background knowledge of history, all in any case being men who can do research and can draw political conclusions from their research. The academic fact-grubber, it need not be said, should be decisively avoided. In order to stifle at birth any possibility of the Staff Group being vitiated by economic competition and preoccupations with status the emoluments should be the same as those of the ordinary administrative personnel (but as in general they will be men of at least thirty when they enter they should of course start on a higher salary than the Cadet). If these ugly vices rear their heads it might be advisable to pay lower emoluments than in the Administrative Service, for the men needed—and they can be found—will find the creative interest of their work sufficient reward. It should be made clear that their work is not more important than that of the plain D.O. out in the bush; it is merely different; a mere matter of the division of labour. All are interdependent units in a whole.

It scarcely need be said that the only connection between the Staff Grade suggested here and the present Staff Grade will be the name. The present Staff Grade, which is merely those Residents given an extra £250 per annum for the last three years or so of their Service, without a single function to differentiate them from the rest of the Residents, is an anomaly for which nothing can be said.

The next reconstruction of the administrative machine needed is to *create a real secretariat*. The present Secretariats consist of Administrative Officers temporarily seconded thereto (the two or three most senior men being an exception) who generally stay for only a tour or two, so that here again there is lack of continuity and lack of expertism—too much again of the roving jacks-of-all-trades and masters of none. Moreover, the bulk of the work in the Secretariat is actually secretarial, and once the ropes are learned essentially routine. It is indefensible that a D.O. or senior A.D.O., for example, should spend his time on such matters as getting Leave Papers ready. What is needed therefore is a Secretariat staffed with permanent European clerks who can become expert in this or that branch of work. The "Writing Assistant" work could be left, as now, to African clerks; most of the remaining work should be handed over to officials of the training and quality of the few confidential clerks (Europeans) now in the Service; and over them would be a group of senior Administrative Officers, including, in addition to the Chief Secretary and the Deputy Chief Secretary, such numbers of the rank of Resident as may be necessary. Thus a staff would be provided which was suited for the particular work required and thus, too, would the efficiency that comes from continuity and specialization be assured. The Secretariat could be subdivided into sections—e.g. one dealing with technical departments, etc., and above all one dealing with all affairs concerning the personal, like postings, leave, annual reports. It is extraordinary that even in Nigeria, where self-congratulation has been carried to extreme lengths, the present haphazard, amateurish, discontinuous Secretariat should have been tolerated without a murmur from those in power.

The next step will be to proceed with the changes that will enable *Administrative Officers to administer*. There must be a relentless frontal attack on the steady and increasing degradation of the administrative personnel into clerks. If the Government is unable to see the question from any other point of view it might recognize that its duty to the taxpayer obliges it to staff the Service with clerks who can be paid clerks' salaries. The present position is that men who are paid salaries for supra-clerical work and who in general adopted the career in order to escape a life of clerical routine, for which, therefore, they have neither taste nor aptitude, are steadily sinking into routine clerical grind. Some measure of clerical and office grind will be inseparable from the Administrative Officer's work; but nevertheless a great deal can be done to lessen the present position. One obvious and practicable step is to increase the ratio of clerks (African) to Administrative Officers. What justification can be offered for such a position as, e.g., in Idoma Division where there is one clerk to four Administrative Officers? Another step is to reform and to mechanize the whole office system. Great strides have been made in office practice and are now being adopted in big commercial houses at home but appear to be unknown to the Service. It would pay the Government to engage a group of "Office Efficiency Experts" to examine and reform the office system. Correspondence, returns, and reports, files and records, accounting and book-keeping: in short the whole technique of one side of the Government needs reforms urgently and drastically. To take a detail: much dreary and mentally destructive work could be eliminated by the installing of a calculating machine in every Provincial Office and in "local treasuries." I doubt if there is such a thing as a calculating machine in the Secretariat at Kaduna: as a consequence the senior officer there who supervises the finances of Native Administrations probably spends not less than three hours a day in adding up and checking figures.

Another step in this connection is to *delegate power and responsibility*. A great deal of time and energy now consumed in sending in reports and asking for action could be saved. In fact the long chain between the man on the spot and the Governor—A.D.O. in the bush, D.O. at Divisional Headquarters, Resident at Provincial Headquarters, Lieutenant-Governor at Kaduna or Enugu, and finally the Governor at Lagos—could be shortened. In general Residents are and, recently, Lieutenant-Governors have become post office men for transmitting communications between D.O.s and the top. There is a strong case for eliminating Residents, and a case for eliminating Lieutenant-Governors. There is an overwhelming case for giving the D.O., the most important unit in the whole machine, more responsibility, and for saving him from dancing attendance on Residents who notoriously dodge responsibility. It would no doubt be pleaded that many D.O.s cannot be trusted with greater responsibility. The reply to that is, firstly, if they cannot be trusted the blame lies with those who appointed or retained them; but, secondly, and still more important, the benefits to be gained are such that it is worth risking the possibility of occasional abuse.

## ADMINISTRATION IN NIGERIA

Another point in favour of taking out much of the superfluous middle of the bottle-neck hierarchy is that men work more efficiently if they can work in their own way and run their own concern. For this reason the institution of Touring Areas for A.D.O.s is worth extending as far as practicable, especially as the age composition of the Service is such that within a few years there will be many more D.O.s than Divisions.

For Administrative Officers actually administering there is the converse need: that technical officials devote their time to their particular technique. Far too big a proportion of the time of far too many forestry and agriculture and education and even medical officials is taken up with doing administrative work, the bulk of which is purely clerical. I recollect cases of the Head of the Veterinary Department having to sign vouchers for paying the wages of porters engaged by a foreman in his department working some hundreds of miles from the Head's headquarters; and another case of a doctor on £660 plus per year acting as a medical store-keeper. In India some of the technical departments are normally under men drawn from the Administrative Service, an outcome, no doubt, of experience proving its desirability.

*Continuity*—The need for this is so obvious and has been proclaimed so often that it might be expected to be accepted in practice to-day.* From top to bottom, however, it is still unrealized. A Governor can reverse the policy of his predecessor and orientate the working of the whole machine in a different direction, as has been seen above. When policy is never really thought out and settled the scope for this nuisance is dangerously great, simply because there is no real policy, only a series of expedients. Just as Governors like to reform, so do their subordinates. Hence the spectacle of D.O.s playing the part of the new broom, and hence that mania for reversing mere details, to the enormous bewilderment of the natives. The root of the evil, as concerns subordinate officers

* Cf. Lugard in *Political Memoranda*, p. 15. This is one of the many passages written by Lord Lugard when in the saddle about thirty years ago, which show that his ideas have not been carried out and, often, the reverse of them is being practised.

R

at least, is the frequency with which officers are moved about. This leads to the question of Postings.

*Postings.*—The present lack of system, the casualness, the changeableness, and the unpredictability, with which officers are moved, and the evil effects thereof both on the natives and on the spirit of the officers themselves, are, it is hoped, made clear from the preceding pages. Senior D.O.s are sometimes moved two, three, or more times in the course of one tour (eighteen months). The Division that can show a list of names of officers who have been in charge for a period of, say, as long as five years, is very rare. Thus Katagum, my last Division, in the five years ending in 1934 had eight or nine different D.O.s. In Katsina Ala in 1933 the officers in charge were changed six times within ten months. One could multiply illustration after illustration. To turn to Provinces, Zaria or Kabba or Sokoto or Adamawa can show a comparable turnover in Residents.

The way to deal with the evil is, as already mentioned, to create a Bureau of Personnel within the reconstructed Secretariat and to entrust it with the duty of working out postings over a series of years ahead. Sickness and other unforeseen events will, of course, necessitate modifications, but they will be nothing in comparison with the present anarchy. Also, officers should be allowed to submit to the Bureau a list of their preferences so that men who have a taste for the forest country might go there, and men with a taste for Bornu there, and so on. At the present time if a man applies for a transfer to a certain place—it is significant that such applications are uncommon—he is snubbed with the formula that His Honour cannot arrange officers' postings to suit their desires, and that they are made according to the exigencies of the Service. Further, much can be done to prevent Stations (i.e. small Stations) being a fortuitous concourse of persons, where temperaments and tastes are ignored and every risk is incurred of producing a strained and jarring ensemble. Especially should some attempt be made to associate D.O.s and A.D.O.s of not too dissimilar temperaments. It is not pretended that all or even most officers can be sent where they would like to go or that every or even many Stations can be made abodes of love and happy laughter. All that is suggested is that it would pay to treat officers as human beings. It pays so much better if men are contented or are free of rankling grievances. The formidable amount of discontent and of bitterness now rampant throughout the Service to-day is a drain on its efficiency and vitality.*

*Training of Cadets.*—At present Cadets are rarely given any training. On their arrival from England they are soon pushed in to fill whatever gap happens to be on the Resident's hands at the moment, and they pick up what they can as they go along, including not a few censures. This again is illustrative of the lack of planning and of adequate conscious control. Cadets should be given an organized and systematized practical training in the elements of administration, which could easily be covered in the three years of their probation, passing through all the major phases of administration step by step. Especially should they be given proper time and opportunities for learning the compulsory languages. Too many senior officers, looking down from their twenty years' experience, expect Cadets to be as familiar with details as themselves. Residents are entitled to expect much of their Cadets, but they are not entitled to expect the gift of second-sight.

*Housing.*—In order to enable and to encourage officials to live as Englishman they should be housed in something that can be made a home of. It need not be a mansion; it need not even be a bungalow. A weather-proof hut, placed on a good site and in some ground of its own, would meet the bill. If the officer has to spend a considerable amount of his time on tour he should nevertheless be able to retain his house and to leave his goods there instead of, as now, having to pack up and store everything he possesses every time he moves. The "deplorable conditions of housing which existed in 1898," of which Lord Lugard has written in one of his books, are far from having disappeared as far as A.D.O.s are concerned in some of the Emirates.

*Shorter Tours.*—A return should be made to the twelve months' (or at least fifteen months') tour of service. It has been seen under what sort of conditions the official is living. For twelve months

* A question was recently put to the Under-Secretary by Lord Portsea as to the condition of and feeling among officials in Nigeria. The Under-Secretary (Lord Plymouth) gave a reply which denied that there was any discontent and made a series of other statements which were equally misleading. *The Times*, May 22 and 23, 1935.

he can keep it up; eighteen months of it kills the spirit. He ceases to fight: it looks too hopeless. The vision of home and England can be kept alive for twelve months, but lengthen the absence by 50 per cent and it withers away. The quality of work suffers equally. If a man were to work continuously without a break at any kind of comparable work even in England itself he would grow stale. And since the retrenchments many men have been required to stay out longer than eighteen months.

*More Staff.*—Staff is now under-strength. When the retrenchments reduced it by nearly 20 per cent, work, instead of being decreased, was increased. A large number of men are working overtime continuously. In the long run—and it is not too long —this is the economy of diminishing returns. Officials become jaded, short-tempered, and shorter-sighted.

But, important as all these reforms would be, they are far eclipsed by the subjects of Promotion and the Secret Report, the two subjects which account for most of the characteristic defects of the Service and of the administration.

*Promotion.*—In every discussion on the Service the question of promotion is pre-eminent. It is pre-eminent partly because of the status and the power that it brings, but mostly because of its economic value. The struggle for promotion is primarily economic. There appears to be no absolutely reliable way of estimating "merit"; even able and honourable men may be misled in their valuation of other men; nor does there appear to be any possibility of entirely eliminating a structure of the personnel whereby a few will be "heads" over the majority, the few the givers and the many the receivers of orders. By delegation of responsibility, the degree of "headship" can be reduced; but the fundamental need is to reduce the gaps between salaries, for only thus can the fury of the economic motive be mitigated. At present the gaps are too wide: a D.O. ends up on about £1,000; a Resident, the next step on, gets £1,250 plus (Senior Resident, or so-called Staff Grade, £1,450 plus); the next step, Lieutenant-Governor or Chief Commissioner gets £3,000 plus; while the Governor gets £8,250. It is a matter of simple arithmetic to show that there will normally be no exact correlation between merit (even assuming that it is real merit) and promotion: if, e.g., there are three senior posts and thirteen men from whom the promotees will be drawn, it is normal that among the thirteen there will be either more or less than three who have the requisite merit for it; it will be rare that there will be three and only three. It is better to recognize that for any given vacancy there will normally be more (or less) than the successful appointee who are worthy of filling it, and that the element of chance in promotion cannot be denied or eliminated. Hence, instead of a gap like that between the £1,000 of the D.O. and the £3,000 of the Lieutenant-Governor, or still more the £8,250 of the Governor, the emoluments should be nearly equal—a difference of a few per cent instead of, as now, a difference of several hundred or even several thousand per cent. This most important point is relevant to all hierarchies, and, in fact, is a main element in the problem of public administration to-day.

*Personnel Reports.*—Above all other sources of demoralization is the present system of secret reporting. In order to eliminate it all reports should be signed by the officer on whom the report is written, the signature to be on the same line as that on which the Resident finishes the report, so as to obviate the possibility of the latter adding something after the officer has signed. In the case of seriously adverse comment the officer should have the right of commenting thereon, and the onus of proving the stricture should rest with the reporter, which, if the stricture were justified, would not be difficult. This would obviate any possibility of an officer's career being wrecked or chequered (and without his knowing it) by some such *cliché* as "lacking in initiative," "temperamentally unsuited," or "not imbued with the spirit of Indirect Rule." Similarly, the onus of justifying a censure passed on an officer by a senior should rest on the passer. Of course, if an officer appeals against a censure or an adverse report and his appeal is found to be trivial or unjustified it should be treated as a serious offence on his part; for discipline must be maintained. The present irresponsibility, meanness, and bullying exercised in censures by seniors who cannot be touched or got at, could be curbed, perhaps in time eliminated, without destroying discipline.

All reconstruction must keep in end our essential mission in Africa, and the fact that what matters for fulfilling that end is the men and the spirit of the men. Everything else is subordinate to this primary need.

## II

## THE ADMINISTRATION OF THE COLONIAL EMPIRE

> " 'Would you tell me, please,' said Alice, 'which way I ought to go from here?'
> " 'That depends a good deal on where you want to go to,' said the cat."
> "Alice in Wonderland."

THIS tract is not concerned with what is generally spoken of as Colonial Policy. The author believes that it is not feasible to lay down any one single Colonial Policy. Only the broadest generalities, like "paramountcy of African interests," can have more than a local application. The rest, including even the details of this generality, must be worked out to suit the local conditions of the Colony concerned. Hence there is little value in such discussions as were made during the Tshekedi affair, as to whether there should be Indirect or Direct Rule. The real issue, rather, is whether the machinery and the men are such that whatever calls may be made on either, or whatever adaptations may be needed, will be forthcoming. Colonial administration, not Colonial policy, is the question for to-day.

We have seen in Nigeria that although much good work has been done, and although the African is better off than ever before, administration has not only been conducted without vision, or any adequate conception of the true nature of our imperial task, but even from the lower view of mere day-to-day mechanical efficiency it has been undistinguished, and shows a tendency for the governmental machine to get out of control. The Nigerian postage stamp symbolizes the quality of the Nigerian Government. Further, and what is of more consequence where personal relations and attitudes are all-important, the tone of the personnel leaves something to be desired. It leaves something to be desired partly through a system of promotion which, for the economic prizes it involves, kills disinterestedness and encourages a persistent concern with the ulterior motive; and partly by a system of secret reporting whereby officers live under the power of their Residents and Lieutenant-Governors to make accusations against them, the existence of which they may not know and normally never do know.

## ADMINISTRATION OF THE COLONIAL EMPIRE 263

Nigeria, it may be assumed, is not worse than the other colonies. It can, in these respects, be taken as an example of the whole Colonial Empire. The author has friends in the Service in Malaya, Ceylon, British Honduras, Sierra Leone, the Gold Coast, Uganda, Tanganyika, and Northern Rhodesia, and has made a point of ascertaining their views. What they complain of in their colonies, and especially in the African colonies, is substantially the same as what is complained of in Nigeria, even some of the very phrases used being identical.

That part of the British Empire which is dependent and which is not under the control of the Foreign Office (as, e.g., the Sudan) or of the India Office covers many hundreds of thousands of square miles and numbers many millions of souls, comprising all varieties of race and culture, and it is subdivided among nearly fifty different Governments.*

Who controls this Empire? What is its ultimate authority? Its ultimate authority is the Parliament of Great Britain. But Parliament delegates its authority to the committee of its majority party, the Cabinet of the day; and the Cabinet in turn delegates its authority to the Secretary (and Under-Secretary) of State for the Colonies. Further, the Secretary of State, as one of several party leaders, cannot avoid giving part of his time to general party business; and as a member of the Cabinet he cannot avoid giving part of his time to the business of general Government policy. The actual amount of time that he can devote to pure administration is thus strictly limited, and it so happens that during the last decade he has been required to devote a disproportionately large part of that time to a series of special crises like those which the names of Palestine, Kenya, Cyprus, Ireland, and Malta will recall to readers. The actual knowledge which a Minister could acquire of the day-to-day administration in much of the dependent Empire for which he is answerable to Parliament and the English people must therefore, at the best, be fragmentary. It is not likely that he will have known even the names of some of the Governors, let alone their characters and personalities. Nor must it be overlooked that according to Lord Lugard† a tradition has existed in the

* The *Colonial Office List*, p. liii, gives thirty-six different Governors. Some of the Governors, however, have more than one Government under them. Moreover, certain special territories which come within the purview of the Colonial Office, like North Borneo or Sarawak or Trans-Jordania, are not included in the list. † *The Dual Mandate*, p. 161

Colonial Office for keeping as much of the business as possible out of the hands of the Minister and in the hands of its own senior functionaries. To which must be added the further fact that until recently the tenure of Secretaries of State has averaged only two and a half years and that of Under-Secretaries less than two years.*

In practice, then, whatever the theory may be, the ultimate authority is the Colonial Office.

The permanent head of the Colonial Office is the Under-Secretary of State (i.e. the permanent, as distinguished from the Parliamentary Under-Secretary); next to him come four Assistant Under-Secretaries; and next to them a varying number of Principal Clerks. Until 1925, what is now the Dominions Office formed part of the Colonial Office, and until 1930 both Offices were under the one Minister who had to attend to Dominions as well as to Colonial affairs. Despite the separation of the two Ministries the volume of business handled by the Colonial Office has grown and continues to grow at a great pace. It is probable that the amount of correspondence handled—a fair measure of its business—is not less than four or five times what it was at the opening of the century. Whether the Colonial Office uses its great power with wisdom or not is beyond the scope of our present enquiry, though there seems no reason for questioning either its general excellence (within the limits to be noted later) or its general integrity. The point to be made here is, in the first place, that in practice a dozen or so senior officials in the Colonial Office exercise the ultimate control over the Colonial Empire, and, in the second place, that given the extent and the variety and the ever-widening development of the two score odd separate Colonial Administrations, even the control of the Colonial Office must be fragmentary and incomplete. Indeed, a Secretary of State himself has said that "it would not be possible to govern the British Empire from Downing Street, and we do not try." It is illustrative of the thesis of this tract, viz. that there is something inherent in the functioning of bureaucracies that leads to confusing means and ends, that in this restricted field of control the Colonial Office should (by the testimony of Lord Lugard) be inflexible in "such matters as the incremental pay of a foreman of works . . . the engagement of a mechanic on some small increase of pay in special circumstances, the writing off of small sums of public money after full investigation by a committee and revision

* *The Dual Mandate*, p. 162.

by the Council, the amount of baggage which an officer may carry free by local rail,"* and similar trifles which might safely be entrusted to the local Governor; yet while it is inflexible in vetoing the few pounds proposed for a foreman's increment it failed to block nearly a decade of extravagance in the colony concerned.

An attempt has been made in recent years to correct a position whereby the men at the Colonial Office have known nothing personally of conditions abroad in the colonies, while the men in charge of the colonies on the other hand have lost touch with England, by seconding officials from the Colonial Office to service in the colonies and by seconding officials from the colonies to service in the Colonial Office. This is a change which follows the fusion of the Foreign Office and the Diplomatic Service made at the end of the war, a change that was hoped to break down the separation of Foreign Office officials from actual affairs abroad and the separation of English diplomats abroad from life and thought in England, a separation (especially when the Minister was untravelled) shown in Gooch and Temperley's *British Documents* to have been so disastrous as to be reckoned as nothing less than one of the causes of the war.† This is a good move. But it does not touch the root of the matter.

For the root of the matter is that the actual control of a colony is normally, after all, in the hands of the Government of the colony itself; that is to say, the position and power of the Governor being what they are, in the hands of the Governor.

Governors are appointed by the King on the recommendation of the Secretary of State (it appears that in practice they are appointed by the senior officials at the Colonial Office; hence, no doubt, the custom of rising colonial officials cultivating suitable acquaintances at the Colonial Office). They receive a Commission and Instructions which include the constitution of their Colony. They are the supreme military and civil head, though of course responsible to the Minister for every exercise of their headship excepting the prerogative of mercy. The Minister's authority is enforced primarily through the budget of the colony, which must be sanctioned by him, and, further, reports and despatches must be sent regularly on which orders may be issued.

\* Quoted *Dual Mandate*, p. 163.
† Cf. *Foreign Policy from a Back Bench, 1904–1918. A Study based on the Papers of Lord Noel-Buxton*, by T. P. Conwell-Evans, Oxford, 1932.

That is *de jure*. In practice a Governor's power may be largely exempt from interruption. Indeed, now that a revolution has displaced the King of Siam, the only constitutional autocracies left in the world are colonial governorships. A strange anachronism in the English polity. A Governor in his crown colony has more *de facto* power than the Prime Minister has in England, and much more status. He is to be compared with kings before the rebellions of the seventeenth century, the era, in fact, when Governors were first appointed. One well-known ex-Governor in discussing his functions writes that "the prosperity of a colony and the welfare of its people depend largely upon its Governor," a passage that recalls a speech by Charles I identifying the State with its head. His trappings in the colony are nearly regal. The story is told of a member of the Royal Family, after an interview with a certain High Commissioner, exclaiming, "Now I know what it feels like to meet Royalty." Nor, given the scale of emoluments usual in the public services as a whole, is he poorly paid: the Governor of Nigeria receives £8,250 (£6,500 plus £1,750) a year; the Governor of Ceylon £8,000; of Malaya £7,000, to all of which must be added allowances and proportionate pensions.

How real in practice is the Governor's power is indicated by the re-modelling of the entire judicial system of Nigeria which the Governor of the day carried through against the disapproval of the Service as a whole. Apparently he was also free to alter tariff duties at his will, for, notwithstanding the theory of Colonial Office control of colonial budgets, he promised a meeting of business men in England to allow cocoa products to be imported free into the country. If an announcement which recently appeared in the *West African Review*\* is correct, there is a probability, in deference to the wishes of the same man, of Enugu, the capital of Southern Nigeria, being closed down and the administrative headquarters removed to Lagos: a sufficient sidelight on the power of a Governor and the incompleteness of Colonial Office control. It is only five years ago that the Southern capital was transferred thither from Lagos, and many hundreds of thousands of pounds have been spent on its construction.

If we could always, or even normally, count on the appointment of Governors who are gifted with energy and wisdom and disinterestedness equal to their powers, there would be less cause for

\* January 1935.

concern. The present autocracy, however, is unsound in principle for the same reason that dictatorship as a system of the State is unsound in principle. You cannot be sure of getting an occupant at the top with the necessary energy and wisdom.

Indeed, the quality of Colonial Governors, regard being had to what England can offer, has, on the whole, been very poor. On what principle are Colonial Governors appointed? On no principle other than success in getting to the top, a process normally requiring the gaining, in their colony or colonies, of accelerated promotion, and requiring, when on leave in England, the making of the requisite acquaintances in Whitehall. On what principle should they be selected? They should have the force of character needed for disciplining the Service and controlling the administration under them, and such a knowledge of the past and present as will give them standards of comparison and a sense of proportion, but above all they should have that personality and culture which will make them representatives of English civilization to our colonial trustees. In general such men will not be found in the Administrative Service. The worst possible appointments are of those who, by the mean arts of the careerist, have, like scum, at length risen to the top, providing the all too familiar figure of clerical hacks mishandling tasks of magnitude, or of sly fellows strutting in big places. It need scarcely be said that among those who have gained governorships some have acquitted themselves well; some with marked fitness; but that does not invalidate the proposition that as a rule Governors should be appointed from outside, unless there is indubitable reason for a Service appointment. That truth appears to be recognized in the Indian Service, where the Presidency governorships are not given to promotees from within the I.C.S.

An outstanding effect of the present situation, in any case, is that the Ministers have more routine work than they can do, the officials in power at the Colonial Office have more than they can do, and the Governor of a colony has more than he can do. The governing is thus carried on by a few men who are all in a hurry and who can never finish what their office sets for them. Reflection, meditation, planning ahead, are, and must be, non-existent. Hence the inefficiency or insufficiency which is to be noted at so many stages. Perhaps the dreariest illustration comes from the long story of ineptitude in education policy throughout the Empire\* which

\* Cf. H. A. Wyndham, *Native Education*, 1933.

still provides different but similar follies as that which led a Dutch Governor of Ceylon two centuries ago to express his delight on visiting a school to hear "the little black fellows chatter in Latin and construe Greek."

Another and graver effect is that the management of England's trusteeship to her millions is carried on without discussion. Great questions are not, as in home affairs, thrashed out to some synthesis on the anvil of thesis and antithesis. Decisions are arrived at by a handful of senior and therefore elderly officials. An article in the *Round Table* in September 1934 instanced three changes involving important principles in colonial trusteeship which had recently been made without public discussion, almost without public recognition: (*a*) The extension of the Ottawa preferences system to Crown colonies, (*b*) the tariffs imposed in certain colonies against Japanese goods, and (*c*) the contribution by East African colonies to a part of the £246,000 subsidy paid to Imperial Airways.

The only discussion ever made now comes from four very imperfect sources. Firstly, there may be an articulate group, perhaps of planters or of other local European interests, or perhaps of literate natives, with special interests in the colony itself, neither in any case being representative of the colony as a whole or without an axe of their own to grind. Secondly, the Opposition or an individual member of the English Parliament—especially a Labour or Liberal member—and especially for reasons of political capital, may take up a grievance. Good is sometimes done this way, but partly because of the great ignorance among all sections of Parliament of colonial details, partly because of a suspicion of non-disinterestedness which attaches to some such questioners, but mostly because of its desultoriness and fragmentariness, such a check on colonial administration is ineffective and sometimes harmful (cf. the Bukuru "beating" incident). Thirdly, there are the professional philanthropists. Good work has been done by them, but also harm. Their motives tend to be as high as their understanding is low, so that though they may make a noise here and there over a slavery incident in Hong Kong, or the Tshekedi affair in Bechuanaland, their influence does not amount to that scrutiny or ventilation which is brought to bear on Government measures at home. The man in the street, when listening to them, cannot avoid a feeling that they do not quite know what they are talking about and that their hearts are larger than their heads. Even when the investigator is of another calibre he is bound to miss much and to make misconceptions, as was demonstrated in an article by Mr. C. R. Buxton recently.* Fourthly, there are the few newspapers, also professionally advanced, of which the *Manchester Guardian* is the best type. Good work is also done by them again, but too often their comment and criticism are based on comfortable ignorance, as the passages published by that journal on the Gold Coast deputation show.

So England's millions of colonial subjects are governed by a bottle-neck bureaucracy, and in no field of the public service is the bureaucracy more unhampered. The governing is characterized by three traits: (1) lack of adequate thought and planning by those in power, whether as Minister, Colonial Office seniors, or Governors; (2) no criticism of or public discussion on the governing; and (3) no effective supervision or checking of the governing. And, exactly what has marred our good work in India is being allowed to repeat itself in the Crown Colonies, and administration is slipping into becoming what it became there, "systematized and formalized to such a degree that the executive officers are the slaves of clerical routine and the judicial officers of legal technicalities, and both alike have lost their old touch with the people."†

Can England be content lazily and carelessly so to delegate its responsibilities? That raises the further question, "Is the British Empire worth the trouble?" The common belief, especially among conventional-minded radicals and certain Continental peoples, is that England derives great material riches from her Empire. This is a mistake. Imperialism in the bad sense has more often taken another form—that of making investments and getting in return a dishonest lien over a country's finances.‡ England as a whole gains little wealth from the possession of her colonies. The raw materials she obtains from them have to be paid for just as though they came from anywhere else, and the manipulation of colonial tariffs in favour of English export industries cannot be carried far, indeed is definitely prohibited in some cases.§ Again, account must be taken of the millions of pounds spent at some time or other

* Charles Roden Buxton in the *Manchester Guardian Weekly*, January 11–18, 1935.
† *The Times*, November 13, 1901, quoted in *Dual Mandate*, p. 127.
‡ In Mr. H. N. Brailsford's memorable phrase one does not take Naboth's vineyard, one invests in it.
§ Cf. *The Open Door* in the Congo Basin Treaties.

on grants-in-aid to the colonies—and the era of grants-in-aid is not yet at an end. Apart from the few individuals concerned, like the finders of gold or tin mines, and perhaps the receivers of contracts, the only other beneficiaries are that section of the middle and upper middle classes which finds careers in the colonial services. An economist, indeed, might argue that, given the unrealized productivity of the economic system of England, this is no great advantage. In any case, it is interesting to note that in France there is now some questioning as to whether the colonies are really worth it.* It is conceivable that the future historian will reckon the possession of our dependent Empire the tragedy of our race because England devoted political energy to Imperial matters which, had it been devoted to the welfare of ordinary Englishmen at home, might have ameliorated the tremendous social problem of millions of our own poor.

Though while necessary to emphasize the mistakenness of the notion that we derive great material advantages from the Empire, it is, of course, academic to argue for its retention or its abandonment on this ground. If the Empire was not ours, some other Power or Powers would possess themselves of it. It will be ours for as long as colonial empires continue to exist. We may as well, then, concern ourselves with the question how best to run it.

The present position calls for two measures. Firstly, as soon as the tension in foreign and Indian affairs has slackened, a Parliamentary commission of enquiry should be established to traverse and ventilate the whole field of the administration of our Colonial Empire. Secondly, a permanent standing committee of Parliament should be appointed on colonial affairs, to which suitable members might be co-opted from outside, for ensuring that England's colonial responsibilities are acquitted in the way England wants.†

* Cf. *L'agriculture du Centre*, October 28, 1934, "En pleine absurdité."

† The suggestion recently adumbrated for an Inspectorate is, in the author's opinion, unsound and should be strongly resisted. There are many practical objections to it which seem invincible, but these are outweighed by its incompatibility with the best English traditions and the present needs of a healthy decentralization. Efforts rather should be directed to providing and keeping the right kind of personnel and of maintaining the right spirit in it. That is the central need. Both the commission and the standing committee should concern themselves primarily with this, which is as fundamental as hitherto it has been overlooked.

## III

## THE PROBLEM OF PUBLIC ADMINISTRATION

"*You do not know, my son, with what little wisdom the world is governed.*"—OXENSTIERN.

\* \* \* \* \*

"*Pray avoid in your official telegrams expressions which can be laid hold of.*"—Lord Granville's instructions to Cromer.

\* \* \* \* \*

THE CIVIL SERVANT
"*In general it would appear
The situation's such
'Twere better not to be too clear
Or give away too much.*"
HAMILTON, "Epigrams."

NIGERIA and the administration of the Colonial Empire raise issues far wider than themselves—they raise the problem of public administration in the modern state.

A man need not be a student to realize that that complex of ways and institutions which makes up modern society is out of joint. Few have escaped intimate personal consequences of the economic depression during the last four years, and few to-day are unaware that war, that final breakdown in the rational control of society, is an imminent probability.

Modern society is based on foundations and reared on a structure entirely different from anything known or even thought of a century ago; and the essence of the difference is that modern society has to be run: it cannot run itself. Among primitive people, and indeed among Europeans (with a few exceptions) until a generation or so ago, if, to take a concrete instance, a farmer worked hard enough and efficiently enough he was assured of at least enough to eat and shelter himself with. A farmer to-day, no matter how hard and how efficiently he works, and how abundantly he produces, is not assured of freedom from starvation, so all-pervasive is the inter-dependence of the units of modern society, so true it is that we have become members one of another.

The units of modern society must be so managed as to run harmoniously and interproductively; a process requiring conscious and unrelenting co-ordination, direction, and control. Indeedd,so complicated is the functioning of any one branch of society that relatively few individuals arrive at an exact understanding of its process. The financial mechanism illustrates this fact, for there we have something that just happens, but as to exactly how it happens the full-time experts themselves are not agreed. The war provided another example: if it showed one thing with certainty it was that the intellectual equipment required for waging a war like that between 1914 and 1918 did not exist amongst the military and naval leaders—the men on whom a misled world later loaded wealth and honours—though they somehow blundered into victory through sheer exhaustion on the other side.*

The partial breakdown in the functioning of the economic processes of society which is so evident to-day has taken place because either we have not yet evolved enough intelligence to understand their functioning, or, if we have evolved it, we have not yet succeeded in putting that intelligence at the top and in charge. If this can result in a breakdown to-day, how much greater will become in future years our need for evolving the requisite intelligence (it probably already exists), or for evolving means for putting it in charge. The whole drift of modern society is towards what used to be called socialization and is now often called planning, but what in truth is just the unescapable necessity of managing a society which grows ever more and more complex and ever more and more inter-dependent, and which can no longer manage itself. State intervention, and with it the extension of the numbers and the activities of civil servants, must therefore be looked for more and more. It is this that makes an understanding of the problem of public administration and of securing disinterested intelligence in control one of the most vital needs of our day.†

It is a remarkable fact that while the scientific mind and the scientific method should have demonstrated their utility so unanswerably in various fields the State still continues to be run by means compounded of empiricism, mass emotion, and the arts of the careerist politician and the careerist bureaucrat. What purports to be the will of the community is often unknown to the community, or is some oblique reaction of a volatile, slogan-fed populace.

---

\* Cf. Mr. Lloyd George's *Memoirs*, vol. iii on the naval, and vol. iv on the military, leaders.

† Great Britain already spends about £88 millions on her home Civil Service annually. Cf. Report of Tomlin *Commission on the Civil Service*.

Parliaments tend to be distinguished by open mouths rather than open minds, bawling out expedients for papering up the cracks. It is significant that there is not even seating accommodation for about a quarter or a third of the members of the House of Commons. And the Cabinet has so much that is immediate and insistent to attend to that it can rarely take the long and wide point of view.*
The system survives to-day only because Parliament and its committee, the Government, control but a mere fragment of the business of running the State, the bulk of which lies in the hands of the permanent officials.

This is another illustration of the fundamental difference in kind between the nature of modern and of previous societies that the power, like the great numbers, of the bureaucracy is an entirely new phenomenon in the English state. Odd officials throughout history from the times of certain medieval Exchequer and Chancery clerks down to Mr. Pepys and onwards have acquired certain special powers in certain special fields; but they were always an exception to the general rule. In the Foreign Office, for example, until the beginning of this century permanent officials were practically confined to mechanical tasks like copying and sealing confidential documents, the Secretary of State himself managing all matters of policy, and, indeed, rarely asking for the views of even high officials.† Now, however, "the corporate influence upon the conduct of foreign affairs" which has been acquired by the permanent officials of the Foreign Office is "of more importance than the personality of individual Secretaries of State." The permanent expert is dominant—a development, as Professor Smith comments, which is more or less true of the whole range of government to-day.‡ Indeed, so far has this been carried in the Foreign Office that, since Curzon's time, an arrangement has existed whereby, in order that the Secretary of State should be left free to deal with European and American problems, Far Eastern affairs, which, for a decade have been turbulent and grave, remain entirely in the hands of permanent officials, and the very statements that the Secretary of State has been obliged to make on them from time to time during crises were uttered by him as a mouthpiece of the bureau-

* Cf. Lord Cecil on "Prime Minister's disease"; and Mr. Amery has said that to attempt a general discussion at a Cabinet meeting is "to brand oneself as Public Enemy No. 1."
† Cf. *The Foreign Office*, by Sir J. Tilley and S. Gaselee, London, 1933.
‡ H. A. Smith, *International Affairs*, 1933.

crats.* With what wisdom the permanent officials exercised this sovereignty has been suggested in the case brought forward by an authority of the standing of Mr. Lionel Curtis.† A surprising gesture of independence was recently provided by the official who at the time was our Ambassador in Japan: when passing through Canada he ventured to make a highly controversial statement to the Press, and one contrary to the public opinion of England on the question concerned. Whether his thesis was sound or unsound is not the point; the point is that a permanent official should take so much upon himself. A Governor of Nigeria developed the habit of speaking in the Royal possessive: "My people."

The power of bureaucracy, moreover, is a power without responsibility, a condition due to the retention of the outworn principle (dating from the days when permanent officials were only clerks) that a Minister take the responsibility for everything done by his Department, and that he defend even its mistakes and derelictions against Parliamentary enquiry to the utmost of his capacity. An example of its operation received some notoriety in the case of Mr. Fitzpatrick, the Air Force officer who was wrongfully arrested by the Metropolitan Police in 1933. The Home Secretary, for as long as a fortnight after the incident, continued to exonerate the officials concerned, apparently without having acquainted himself with the facts of the case, and it was due to the accident of the senior permanent official himself, Lord Trenchard, becoming interested in Mr. Fitzpatrick's grievance that this was redressed and his reputation cleared.‡ Had the permanent official, either through self-interest or a desire to avoid trouble, utilized the opportunity presented by the Minister's attitude, no redress would have been made and the officials at fault could not have been touched.

No one, of course, would impugn the general integrity or the general efficiency of the English Public Service, for both are very high. No other country has such a Civil Service. But this is not to deny (a) that the Civil Service exercises a quasi-sovereignty over large fields, and (b) that it works with certain characteristic shortcomings.

As for the quasi-sovereignty, each branch within the bureaucracy

---

\* Cf. *The Capital Question of China*, by Lionel Curtis, London, 1933, p. 274.
† Op cit., specially concerning leaving legation at Peking.
‡ *Manchester Guardian*, August 18, 1933.

# THE PROBLEM OF PUBLIC ADMINISTRATION 275

tends to treat itself as a sovereign entity. One aspect of this fact is the jealousy between department and department. The relations of the Colonial Office and the Foreign Office, especially in Far Eastern matters, may be cited. . . . The author has been informed by a person in a position to know that at the end of the war, during the disturbances in the Near and Middle East, one English Department of State backed one side and another English Department of State backed the other side, both Departments subsidizing their respective protégés with the English taxpayers' money! Another aspect is the attitude of the bureaucracy towards the world outside it—where its morality undergoes a sea-change. Mr. Oliver Baldwin, for example, has set on record the case of Agha Petros, a representative of the Assyro-Chaldeans, who was induced by the Colonial Office to submit to them a document proving his position which later it refused to return to him, and only through the accident of a change in Government and the coming of a Minister to whom Mr. Baldwin had personal access, was the document returned to its rightful owner.* Another, though rather different case, has been recorded recently from West Africa concerning the coal purchases of the Gold Coast Government.† This is due not to corruption but to the natural tendency of such institutions to harden their professional solidarity into a vested interest.

Some Cabinet Ministers, either with a personal force or with a sincerity of purpose above the average of the politician, have improvised measures for imposing their will on the Civil Service. Thus in the later years of and after the war Mr. Lloyd George surrounded himself with a secretariat which was superimposed on the ordinary bureaucracy; and Mr. Arthur Henderson, when Secretary of State for Foreign Affairs, between 1929 and 1931, surrounded himself with non-official men whom he could rely upon and who were equal to the armour of the official world. Unless the spirit and the efficiency of bureaucracies are changed, and unless permanent devices for making ministerial control a reality are worked out, some *ad hoc* development of this kind will no doubt be repeated, but this is a regrettable second-best and would lead to reduplication.

As for the sufficiency or insufficiency with which the bureaucracy exercises its quasi-sovereignty, one example has been provided in

* Oliver Baldwin, *The Questing Beast*, p. 216.
† *West Africa*, June 2, 1934.

the preceding pages, on the management of our colonial responsibilities. Another is suggested in the way the Treasury has controlled financial policy since the end of the war. Mr. Churchill, Chancellor of the Exchequer at the time, has made no secret as to why and how we returned prematurely to the gold standard with all its disastrous effects of deflation. And Sir Arthur Salter has placed on record what amounts to a severe indictment from the international point of view.*

It is not possible in this compass to seek the reasons for the insufficiencies of the public services, but, as they have already been traversed, certain characteristic weaknesses may be reaffirmed.† One is the lack of thought and long reflection due to excess of business, which again is due to non-delegation and non-devolution. Another is the attitude to "Rules and Regulations." There are far too many of these, and they tend to be treated as ends in themselves instead of as means, and so produce a notorious timidity. "Rien n'est permis mais il y a des choses qui sont tolerées si vous vous montrez raisonnables." That wise remark of a French war-prison governor should be taken to heart by all bureaucrats. Rules may not be made to be broken, but they must often be broken in any vital living organization. Men in power should realize that every time they issue a rule—and how often and how lightheartedly the senior official issues them!—they limit initiative and add delays to the administrative process. One Viceroy of India was told that he should not shake hands when on tour with men drawing less than £300 a year.‡ There goes the fatal habit to regiment and institutionalize. But more serious is the cumulative effect of the poison entering into the life of any public service from the struggle for promotion, which breeds a preoccupation with ulterior interests and which tends to put the wrong men on the wrong rungs, an evil that could at once be mitigated by reducing the disparity between the salary of the promoted man and the man passed over.

The man in the street often comforts himself with the thought that the men in power—in business, in the bureaucracy, or in politics—do not get to their positions without abilities and on the whole they are where they are because they deserve to be there. Nothing could be wider of the mark. Mr. Belloc has said the final

* *International Affairs*, March 1933.
† The present author is now engaged on a study of public administration which will be published subsequently.
‡ Bampfylde Fuller, op. cit., p. 92.

word on this point: "A few are first-rate, many ordinary second-rate, and quite a large proportion are Plumb Stuffed Fools, true Fools, Absolute and of the Nadir: Rooted Fools."

The tolerant man no doubt will continue to argue that although Governments have their faults and Departments of State are not galaxies of genius, and politicians are often egoists, and the people gullible, and ambitious careerists sometimes get more power than they merit, these are all just so many elements in our fallible human nature, just so many incidents of human mortality. He might go further and argue that the whole technique and organization of government has improved enormously in the last hundred years; as also, indeed, has the general level of considerateness. He can go further still: he can argue for and illustrate the extraordinary vitality of modern society in spite of everything—*e pur si muove*. All this is true; but it is the sort of one-sided truth with which the inhabitant of a fool's paradise can delude himself. The point is that although the technique and organization of government have improved enormously the calls made upon the technique and organization by the institutions and the processes of modern society have grown still more enormously. The gap between the improvement and the increasing calls upon it is the problem; it must be narrowed. The ordeal of this generation is to reconstruct our governance in such a way as to fit it for the needs of modern society; to fail is to perish. We cannot afford to-day to be the blind led by the blind, and especially can we not afford to be the blind led by blind crooks.